KU-516-683

Two Men in a Trench II

By the Same Authors

Two Men in a Trench: Battlefield Archaeology –
The Key to Unlocking the Past

Two Men in a Trench II

UNCOVERING THE SECRETS OF BRITISH BATTLEFIELDS

Tony Pollard and Neil Oliver

Photography by Mark Read

MICHAEL JOSEPH
an imprint of
PENGUIN BOOKS

To Trudi and Evie, all my love always - Neil xx

To my Gran, Molly Foy (1915–2002), for giving room to my imagination - Tony

MICHAEL JOSEPH

Published by the Penguin Group
Penguin Books Ltd, 80 Strand, London WC2R 0RL, England
Penguin Putnam Inc., 375 Hudson Street, New York, New York 10014, USA
Penguin Books Australia Ltd, 250 Camberwell Road, Camberwell, Victoria 3124, Australia
Penguin Books Canada Ltd, 10 Alcorn Avenue, Toronto, Ontario, Canada M4V 3B2
Penguin Books India (P) Ltd, 11 Community Centre,
Panchsheel Park, New Delhi – 110 017, India
Penguin Books (NZ) Ltd, Cnr Rosedale and Airborne Roads,
Albany, Auckland, New Zealand
Penguin Books (South Africa) (Pty) Ltd, 24 Sturdee Avenue,
Rosebank 2196, South Africa

Penguin Books Ltd, Registered Offices: 80 Strand, London WC2R 0RL, England

www.penguin.com

First published 2003
1

Copyright © Optomen Television Ltd, Tony Pollard and Neil Oliver, 2003
Contemporary photographs copyright © Mark Read, 2003
Contemporary photographs of Calais, France copyright © Rosie Allsop, 2003
Battle movement maps copyright © Jeremy Ashcroft, 2003
Topographic surveys copyright © John Arthur and Olivia Lelong, 2003
Geophysical surveys, © Iain Banks, 2003
The picture credits on page 382 constitute an extension of this copyright page

The moral right of the authors has been asserted

All rights reserved.
Without limiting the rights under copyright
reserved above, no part of this publication may be
reproduced, stored in or introduced into a retrieval system,
or transmitted, in any form or by any means (electronic, mechanical,
photocopying, recording or otherwise), without the prior
written permission of both the copyright owner and
the above publisher of this book

Set in 10/14pt Rotis Serif
Typeset by Rowland Phototypesetting Ltd, Bury St Edmunds, Suffolk
Colour Reproduction by Dot Gradations Ltd, Wickford, Essex
Printed and bound in Great Britain by Butler & Tanner, Frome and London

A CIP catalogue record for this book is available from the British Library

ISBN 0-718-14594-1

CONTENTS

INTRODUCTION

There's always something very special about revealing an artefact with our trowels or prising a find free from a hunk of dirt in which it might have been imprisoned for centuries. Perhaps it's a spent musket-ball, a button from a soldier's uniform or even a coin from his purse. As we hold the cold metal in our open palms there's a quickening of the pulse and for an instant we become the conduit through which the object, the place and a person long dead are reunited. At least that's the way it seems. In our imaginations a long-lost moment is remade; a doorway to the past is opened and we step through it. During such moments it's almost as though we change from being battlefield archaeologists to something more like time-travelling observers, or even war reporters. This may seem a slightly melodramatic way of describing what it feels like to be a battlefield archaeologist at the moment of discovery, but it is hard to try to put across that unique feeling without getting a little over-excited.

The experience combines a number of emotions: there is triumph and relief at coming across an object, perhaps after hours of finding nothing, but more importantly there is a very strong sense of connection with the past. That feeling is strengthened by the sure knowledge that we're the first people to touch the object since the dreadful noise of battle subsided. This heightened awareness is at no time stronger than when the object is something like a musket-ball that might have taken the life of a fellow human being several hundred years previously.

There must have been quite a few such moments for the archaeologists who excavated at Crickley Hill in Gloucestershire when leaf-shaped points, skilfully knapped from flint, started to appear – first in their tens then in hundreds. Each deadly sharp piece of stone marked the spot where an arrow had fallen 4,500 years ago. The place was a Neolithic fortified enclosure and, as the archaeologists were discovering, the site of the first battle known to have been fought on British soil. These islands have seen a lot of battles since then, and a veritable sea of blood soaked up by field, forest and hill. It could be said that the British people have taken to warfare like ducks to water – at least that's the impression you might get from reading history books. It seems that until relatively recently every dynastic issue or political sore point was settled by force of arms. You need only look at any half-decent map and see the dozens of crossed swords dotted across the land in towns and countryside to get an idea of the huge number of battles fought up and down the country.

We could tell that battlefield archaeology had struck a chord with a wide audience when during our first book tour nine-year-old James turned up dressed in a fantastic suit of home-made armour. A member of the Young Archaeologists' Club in York, he'd come along with his mum, dad and wee sister to ask us a list of thoughtful questions about what we'd found, what we'd liked most and what it had been like to dress up in real armour.

Sometimes we wonder if it's just us who get so worked up about hunting for clues left behind by battles fought long ago – if maybe the pair of us share some kind of rare insanity that prompts us to roam this and other countries looking for the aftermath of war. But then we meet someone like James – and a whole host of others who've attended our talks, seen *Two Men in a Trench* on television or read our first book – and we're reassured to find that what fascinates us fascinates thousands of people of all ages.

History is apparently a subject in decline in schools, steadily being overlooked in favour of the sciences, modern studies and the ubiquitous information technology. Wars of the Roses are out and Word for Windows is in, or so they say. Yet judging by the number of eight-, nine-, ten- and eleven-year-olds who choose to sit through our talks rather than be at home playing computer games, the appetite for finding out about the past is still there. We were both about that age when the bug bit us – and if it gets you when you're young, the excitement of finding lost and hidden stuff is the same at thirty-odd as it is at thirteen. Archaeology too is a growth subject. Our alma mater, Glasgow University, welcomes an ever-increasing number of students into its archaeology department every year.

At every battlefield we investigate, folk living nearby make a point of saying how glad they are to see our work going ahead. It is almost as though they feel that 'their' battlefield has been neglected over the years and that it is high time someone showed it the attention it deserves. We are only too happy to oblige. We went in search of the remains of old Radway church, in the village of Radway in Warwickshire, as part of our examination of the battle of Edgehill. As we painstakingly revealed the lowest courses of the long-lost building's plastered walls, the locals were fascinated to see the brief 'return' of a missing part of their village. Most of them seemed disappointed that we couldn't leave the trenches open at the end of the dig so that they could continue to see the old church. Every day we were visited by small groups keen to see the latest discoveries. By the end of it all, one person told us that our project had really brought the village together. We also get appeals from people keen to have work carried out on their own, local battlefield. We make a careful note of every one and promise ourselves that eventually we'll have the chance to visit it.

What a relief, then: we're not alone and we're not mad – this stuff must actually be fascinating!

We've spent the last twelve months or so investigating another six British battles, all of which played a part in defining the nature and shape of the country we live in. We begin in 1314 with the battle of Bannockburn, near Stirling in Scotland, where Robert the Bruce used guile and the landscape to deliver a catastrophic defeat on the invading English army led by Edward II. The English Civil War of the mid-seventeenth century was the bloodiest conflict ever fought in Britain, and we chose to investigate the first of its many battles, which took place in Warwickshire at Edgehill in 1642. Then we move further south, almost as far as we can go before getting our feet wet, to Sedgemoor in Somerset, where in 1685 the Duke of Monmouth took on the might of the king's army in the last pitched battle to be fought on English soil. Travelling forward four years in time we come back home to Scotland, where at Killiecrankie near Pitlochry in 1689 'Bonnie Dundee' led an almost perfect Highland charge against government troops in the climactic battle of the first Jacobite Rebellion. Our last two sites bring us much closer to modern times: RAF Hornchurch in Essex, which played a crucial role during the battle of Britain in 1940, and the huge guns near Dover in Kent, which spent the years between 1940 and 1944 duelling with their equally massive German counterparts on the French side of the Channel.

As well as the archaeological and historical elements of each project, we've been amazed by how much we can learn about the past by other means. At Edgehill, novice horsemen though we were, we got the chance to view the landscape as the cavalrymen of 1642 must have done. When our mounts unexpectedly bolted under our inept handling, we had a short but unnerving idea of what it might have been like to charge while clad in armour or buff coat and floppy cavalier hat. While preparing for our investigation at Bannockburn, we stood in the face of a charge by heavy horses of the mounted police in Glasgow. As we felt the ground shake beneath their mighty hooves, we caught the vaguest sense of what it would have been like to face down the English horse. Flying over Hornchurch airfield in a helicopter we were able to imagine how the view would have looked to a Spitfire pilot returning home after jousting with Me 109s in the skies over southern England. We sat in the cockpit of the last surviving Spitfire that saw action in the battle of Britain – and still flies today – and peered through a windshield that had once framed attacking German fighters. True, we were on the ground at the time, but what the eye can't see, the imagination can sense. At Killiecrankie we fired a musket at targets composed of tartan and wood – and flesh and bone – and witnessed at first hand the devastating power of lead ball and black powder.

None of our investigations would be possible without the weeks and months of careful preparation and research that precedes every one of our projects. Before we turn up on a site in our van, pitch our tent and get down to work, we've worked out what we're going to do, and exactly where. Selecting the six sites included in this book was not simply a question of sticking pins in a map (though even if we did, the chances are we'd hit at least one battlefield, even if we wore blindfolds!). For one thing, not every battlefield site lends itself to archaeological investigation. Many battlefields have been lost under towns, roads or industrial estates, although we hope that our work will help to make sure that happens less often in the future. Other battles may not have left the sort of traces that make for the multi-disciplined type of project we like to carry out; some battles have left little other than a few metal objects in the ground. Not wanting to limit ourselves to metal-detecting, we tend to prefer battles which involved buildings, fortifications, grave sites or other landscape elements that can be surveyed and sometimes excavated. We also like to use archaeology to question contemporary accounts of battles, and so battles for which there are eyewitness accounts or other documentary sources tend to be on our list of possibilities. Then there is geographic location – we are always keen to look at battles in different types of landscapes, so that we can compare and contrast the impact of terrain on strategy and tactics. This book includes two Scottish sites not just because they are close to home but because as a result of the age-old struggle between Scotland and England a relatively large proportion of Britain's battlefields are to be found north of the border.

As with any other type of archaeological investigation, each of our field projects is preceded by the preparation of a project design, which carefully sets out the aims and objectives of the

investigation. This document is the result of many hours of library research during which we study old documents, maps and historical accounts of the battle. We also consult reports of any previous archaeological work on sites near by – local sites and monuments records and their national equivalents are useful here. We consult national bodies such as English Heritage and Historic Scotland as well as local curatorial services such as the council-based county and regional archaeologists. Most important are site visits, during which we get our first real feel for the battlefield and the intricacies of the landscape. Very often we discover things during a reconnaissance that we had not come across in any of our desk-based work – suspicious lumps and bumps in a field, for instance, or the presence of a recently built house over an area we were hoping to investigate. During these visits we talk to landowners and local residents, who can sometimes provide invaluable nuggets of information about ground that has been farmed by their family for generations or things they have found in their back garden. Permission to carry out work on private land is obviously fundamental and so we are always keen to explain as clearly as possible to landowners what it is we want to do and where we want to do it. Only once all this preparatory work has been done can we even think of loading the tools into the van and packing the tent.

Each project takes approximately three weeks to execute in the field. The first week is devoted to survey, which usually includes geophysical and topographic survey. After spending days walking across the site taking measurements and readings, the team return to the office, where using the wonders of modern technology they process the geophysical results and the collected data to create meaningful plots and detailed site maps. Once all this information has been assembled we make the final decisions – based on the results of both the geophysical and topographic surveys – on where to place our excavation trenches. Only then do we start digging holes. This is the part of the operation filmed as *Two Men in a Trench* and this element, the real meat and potatoes of the fieldwork, lasts a couple of weeks. Once the fieldwork is complete, the trenches backfilled and the tent packed away, we return to the office and lab to begin the long, painstaking process of drawing all our strands of evidence together into a full report.

One of the things we love about archaeology is the way it brings us together with old friends we've worked with many times over the years. Our right-hand man is Dr Iain Banks – usually 'Banksie' in these pages. Iain is our geophysicist and director of excavations, and he spends a lot of time discussing sites with us before we ever get near a battlefield. Paul Duffy, Helen MacQuarrie and Dave Sneddon are our field archaeologists, and it is largely thanks to them that we are able to achieve an amazing amount of work in a relatively short space of time. None of this work would make much sense at all without John Arthur and Dr Olivia Lelong, our dynamic duo of topographic surveyors. Using their high-tech instruments they plot and map the exact location of all our excavation trenches and each and every find made by the metal detectorists. While we are in the field Andy Robertshaw from the National Army Museum is on hand to share his expertise in military

matters, and his knowledge has proved invaluable when it comes to identifying the rusting lumps of metal we pull out of the ground.

Unlike most archaeological teams, our family extends just that bit further to include a bunch of professionals of an entirely different sort – the production team from Optomen Television that follow our every move and turn our archaeological endeavours into the visceral televisual experience that is *Two Men in a Trench*. Our series producer, director and muse was Paul Ratcliffe who, with his assistant producer Jennie Macdiarmid and researcher Sasha Mantel, spent a lot of time working with us in preparing every project (we now regard this trio as honorary archaeologists!). While the fieldwork and filming were under way we spent most of our time in the very good company of cameraman Richard Hill, sound recordist Rex Phillips, and assistant cameramen Patrick Acum and Joe Cooper. While in the field we all relied on the very capable support of location manager Richard Herd and his hard-working team, Carolyn Stopp and Jeremy Cracknell, while our production manager Rosie Allsop kept things running from the office. We also had the pleasure of working with Dominic Ozanne, who directed the Killiecrankie programme.

Just a quick note about the battle progression maps, which were created by Jeremy Ashcroft. The key below explains what the map symbols mean in terms of troop formations.

A map of Britain showing the location of the six battlefields

Killiecrankie ✛

□ Perth

Bannockburn ✛ □ Stirling

Glasgow □   □ Edinburgh

Carlisle □   □ Newcastle

N

□ York
□ Leeds

Liverpool □   □ Manchester

□ Chester

□ Norwich

Birmingham □

✛ Edgehill

Swansea □   □ Cardiff   □ Oxford

□ Bristol   ✛ Hornchurch
London

Sedgemoor ✛

St Margaret's at Cliffe ✛
✛
Cap Gris-Nez

Exeter □

BANNOCKBURN 131/

BANNOCKBURN

NOT A SINGLE SCOTLAND VERSUS ENGLAND RUGBY OR FOOTBALL MATCH GOES BY WITHOUT THE WORDS OF 'FLOWER OF SCOTLAND' ECHOING AROUND THE STANDS AS SCOTTISH SUPPORTERS EXPRESS PRIDE IN THEIR COUNTRY AND DISDAIN FOR THEIR SOUTHERN NEIGHBOURS, THE 'AULD ENEMY'. THESE GAMES ARE ALMOST A RITUALIZED FORM OF WARFARE, FOR THE SONG, WRITTEN IN THE 1960S BY THE CORRIES, PLAYS ON NATIONALIST SENTIMENT AND MAKES MUCH OF THE VICTORY OF THE SCOTS OVER THE ENGLISH AT THE BATTLE OF BANNOCKBURN.

1314

By singing this unofficial anthem, the crowds are sharing in what is almost a collective folk memory.

Most people's impressions of what have become known as the Scottish Wars of Independence have probably been coloured by Mel Gibson's entertaining film *Braveheart*, which, although largely concerned with the life of William Wallace, climaxes with Robert the Bruce leading his men into battle against Edward II's army. In the closing scene Mel Gibson's disembodied voice of Wallace speaks stirringly of the Scots winning their freedom at the great victory of Bannockburn.

When the film was shown, as the credits rolled, cinema audiences across Scotland broke into spontaneous applause. What matter that more than a fair share of the film's historical content was Hollywood make-believe? The film showed the English taking a good beating at the hands of the Scots.

Fact and fiction were intertwined further when at the foot of the Victorian Wallace monument, a highly ornate tower overlooking the Carse of Stirling, a statue of William Wallace was raised. Who was the model for this new likeness of the great man? None other than Mel Gibson himself. In his cinematic *Braveheart* guise, complete with two-handed sword, he is now immortalized in stone. Local youth, however, did not appear to take the statue to its heart and the monument suffered a number of vandal attacks. In order to protect the statue from further damage the local council erected a metal cage around it – a rather ironic development given that the plinth of the statue is adorned with the inscription 'FREEDOM'.

More recently, Donald Dewar, a tireless campaigner for a devolved Scottish parliament, leader of the Scottish Labour Party and latterly the first First Minister of Scotland in almost 300 years until his untimely death in 2000, was regarded by many as another Scottish hero. In honour of his contribution to modern Scottish political life a bronze statue of him was erected in the centre of Glasgow. Unfortunately, though, the statue has fallen victim to mindless iconoclasts. And the target for these attacks? His spectacles. It has become a regular Saturday night pastime for some miscreant to swing on Donald's bronze specs, until they almost twist off his face. Every time they are repaired, at great cost, it happens again, and now Donald is cursed to gaze for ever through a pair of broken glasses. As people interested in history, we are forced to see the past in much the same way that the statue of Donald Dewar sees the future: a distorted and blurred image viewed through a set of imperfect lenses. Can archaeology help us to see more clearly?

We are forced to see the past as a distorted and blurred image ... can archaeology help us to see more clearly?

BACKGROUND

THERE'S MORE THAN A BATTLE WILL KILL A MAN. WHAT DID FOR ALEXANDER III OF SCOTLAND WAS PLAIN BAD LUCK. ONE DARK NIGHT IN MARCH 1286 THE 46-YEAR-OLD KING WAS RIDING TO KINGHORN, EAGER TO BE REUNITED WITH HIS FRESH YOUNG WIFE. THE HORSE STUMBLED, PITCHING HIM FROM HIS SADDLE, BREAKING HIS NECK AND KILLING HIM STONE DEAD. THE FACT THAT DEATH, NOTABLY IN THE FORM OF DISEASE, HAD ALREADY CARRIED AWAY NOT ONLY HIS FIRST WIFE BUT ALL HIS IMMEDIATE HEIRS CAST SCOTLAND INTO A DYNASTIC CRISIS THAT WOULD STILL BE REVERBERATING IN 1314 ACROSS THE BATTLEFIELD OF BANNOCKBURN.

The succession problem created by the king's nocturnal demise was, after some debate, decided by a group of the country's great men in favour of Alexander's three-year-old granddaughter, the 'Maid of Norway'. Obviously, a child was incapable of ruling the country and so a formal committee of guardians was set up on behalf of Margaret, who in any case was still in Norway. The committee consisted of two bishops, two earls and two barons; one of the earls and one of the barons were members of the Comyn family, who were distantly related to the royal house. But not everyone was happy with this arrangement, and at least two individuals thought they had better claims to the throne than the child Margaret. One of these was John Balliol; the other Robert Bruce of Annandale. Robert in particular was keen to rock the boat, and his ambitions were to earn him the nickname 'The Contender'. When he started seizing castles that didn't belong to him, civil war began to look like a real possibility. The committee felt it had little choice but to call for the assistance of Edward I of England, who at least had some real royal authority.

Edward's solution was embodied in a treaty with the Scots signed at Birgham, near Berwick, in 1290, whereby it was decided that Margaret would marry Edward's son, also named Edward. The couple would rule their own independent countries, but from the same household. So in late summer Margaret began her journey from Norway to Scotland. She never arrived. The young queen and wife-to-be died on Orkney and the country was once again cast into dynastic turmoil.

Returning from France, where he had the small matter of a war to contend with, to find that his intervention in Scottish affairs was required once more, Edward realized he had much to gain from the chaos within Scotland, and he went north to remind the Scots that the King of England actually had overlordship over Scotland. That the king of one country should feel he could pull rank over the king of a neighbouring country may seem strange today, but in feudal Europe this was far from unusual: loyalty at that time was not in the first instance to your own king or country but to the overlord to whom you had paid homage and sworn fealty. In asserting overlordship, Edward was harking back to the dim and distant past, when Malcolm III swore allegiance to William the Conqueror.

Edward insisted that vows of loyalty and fealty had to be renewed, and this the majority were prepared to do, with the notable exception of Balliol, who not only was confident of the strength of his claim to the throne based on the rules of primogeniture but also had the powerful

Edward I

**John Balliol, King of Scotland
offers his allegiance to Edward I**

1314

Comyn family on his side. As he had hoped, his refusal did not hold
Balliol back, and on 17 November 1292 John Balliol was made king, but
not before he finally agreed to swear fealty to Edward, who certainly
wasn't going to allow the regal pecking order to be upset.

John Balliol was to rule Scotland for just three years, but for him that
time must have seemed an eternity. Things did not go well. Those who
had pledged allegiance to Edward, including the Bruces, were prepared
to put up with increasing English interference, but those who had sworn
fealty to King John were set on a course that would make war with
England an inevitability. The final straw came when Edward, who was
fighting wars both in France and Wales, tried to press the Scots into his
military service. Balliol, under pressure from his administration, refused
to do Edward's bidding and ignored this call to arms. When the Scots
made an alliance with Edward's enemies, the French, Edward went to
war.

The Scots were quick off the mark and made some headway into
northern England, but Edward soon retaliated and in March 1296 he

took Berwick. It was here that Edward received a letter from Balliol in which he withdrew the fealty he had earlier promised to the English king. Edward treated the letter with contempt and set about establishing Berwick as his new administrative centre in Scotland. New fortifications were thrown up around the sacked town, with workers brought in from outside areas to replace the largely slaughtered local populace. In a telling gesture, Edward himself moved a barrowful of earth on to the new ramparts.

Berwick was just the beginning. The 'Hammer of the Scots' was to begin to earn his *nom de guerre* at the battle of Dunbar on 27 April. On the slopes of the Lammermuir Hills Edward's battle-hardened army outsmarted and outfought the Scots. Feigning a retreat, the English, under the Earl of Surrey, drew the enemy into dead ground where many thousands were put to the sword. Those who survived were taken prisoner, including many of Balliol's inner circle. Castle after castle fell and the greatest prize of all, the spectacular castle at Stirling, was abandoned by its inhabitants before Edward had even knocked on its door. There seemed little doubt that Scotland was Edward's for the taking.

Balliol did his best to save his own hide, sending letters of submission to Edward in Perth and then in July surrendering himself to total humiliation in Montrose, blaming his councillors and their bad advice. In no mood for leniency Edward had Balliol carried off to the Tower of London, where he was to be kept prisoner until 1299. One of the strongest symbols of Scottish kingship, the sacred 'stone of destiny' upon which all Scottish kings had been crowned, was taken from its ancient home in Scone to London where, despite a foiled attempt to steal it back in 1951, it was to remain until officially returned to Scotland in 1996.

Having reestablished his overlordship and left in place an administration dominated by English nobles, Edward began to exploit his new dominion for all it was worth. He was constantly at war, for which he needed money. He levied new taxes and increased old ones. But he soon overstepped the mark and, like Margaret Thatcher when she introduced the poll tax to Scotland nearly 700 years later, discovered that Scots do not take kindly to unfair taxes being levied from south of the border. The Scots began to resist. Leadership this time came from lower down the social ladder. William Wallace was no commoner: his family had knightly status, but they were pretty small fish as far as the wider political scene was concerned.

Wallace too had refused to bow before Edward at Berwick, an act of defiance which made him an outlaw, and this status was reinforced

William Wallace was no commoner: his family had knightly status

Opposite King Robert I

1314

when he killed one of the king's sheriffs at Lanark. What started out as a local man-hunt soon turned into a national uprising. Wallace chased the king's chief justice from Scone, where he was holding a court. As word spread, support for Wallace grew. He was joined by Sir William Douglas, who before Edward's invasion had been the commander of Berwick Castle, and Bishop Wishart of Glasgow, who brought with him the body and spirit of the Scottish Church. But perhaps the most important alliance was with Andrew Murray, who was leading his own rebellion around Inverness in the north. Wallace found himself in command of an army – and it was soon to be tested.

At the battle of Stirling Bridge on 11 September 1297 Wallace demonstrated his flair for tactics. Edward's mounted knights were cut down by Wallace's foot-soldiers as they came across the bridge, where they had no room to deploy. Despite Murray's death, the battle was a great victory for the Scots, who by November were carrying out raids into northern England. Edward had no option but to tear himself away from his war with France to deal with Wallace. Though Edward's nobles had been on the verge of insurrection in the face of the unreasonable financial demands the king's wars were making upon them, this new threat from Scotland united the English again. Edward had no trouble in mustering a fresh force and he marched north once again in June 1298.

The next year Edward delivered a terrible defeat upon the Scots at Falkirk. Wallace used schiltrons, the cruelly effective hedgehogs formed of spearmen clustered together in bodies hundreds strong, a tactic that would be repeated by the Bruce at Bannockburn. Their spear points kept the English cavalry at bay as again and again they tried to break into the press of men. Eventually Edward ordered his archers to loose their arrows and this rain of iron cut fatal holes in the Scottish lines, eventually gaining access for the English horsemen, who did their bloody worst against the now defenceless foot-soldiers. The Scots were cut down in their thousands and Wallace was lucky to escape the field with his life.

With a large proportion of the Scottish army crushed and its leader in hiding, Edward set about subjugating the rest of Scotland. He spared no expense or effort, commissioning one of the most impressive arrays of medieval siege machines ever seen in his determination to batter down the walls of Stirling Castle. During this time the government of Scotland fell to a large extent on the shoulders of Robert Bruce, Earl of Carrick and grandson of Bruce the Contender, and John Comyn of Baddenoch, both of whom had been made guardians in Balliol's absence. Wily Bruce

The death of John Comyn

had sworn fealty to Edward but during the rebellion had come out in favour of the Scottish cause. For a while in 1301 it looked as though John Balliol might return to the Scottish throne, and Bruce realized that his own ambitions for the throne could be thwarted. He also had to contend with the full brunt of the English presence in Scotland, as his lands in the south-west provided an important staging post for Edward as he brought men and supplies across the border and across the sea from Ireland. Bruce was left with little choice but to submit to Edward once more. Others, including John Comyn, were of the same mind, as the seemingly inexhaustible might of England continued to tighten the nut on Scottish resistance.

Edward, no doubt relieved to see an end to the trouble, agreed reasonable terms for all – except Wallace, who was captured and put to death in London in 1305. Scotland was now at peace with England – but still without a king. Bruce's time had come. In February 1306 he did away with his only real rival, John Comyn, stabbing him to death in front of the high altar in Greyfriar's church in Dumfries. Though he had committed both murder and blasphemy, a combination of acts that would surely have turned many Scots against him, Bruce could count on national feeling which, despite the recent peace, was running high as ever. The Scots wanted a king. Supported by his brother Edward, Sir James Douglas (known as the Black Douglas) and Thomas Randolph, Bruce conducted a lightning campaign in which he seized a number of castles and on 25 March 1306 he was crowned King Robert I by the Bishop of Glasgow at Scone.

Edward was understandably livid at Bruce's audacity, and sent north a veteran troubleshooter, Aylmer of Valence, to deal with the upstart. The English scored a swift victory at Methven, where the Scots were caught in the open, and drove Bruce into hiding. Things didn't look too bright for the new king. His wife Elizabeth was taken prisoner and three of his brothers were brutally executed at Edward's orders. As the hunt for Bruce continued, Edward, by now a sick old man, came north one last time, and in July 1307 he died. His successor, Edward II, inherited his father's crippling debts but not his passion for subjugating the troublesome Scots, and so for want of desire and cash called off the hounds. But the English were not Bruce's only problem: the Comyns and their allies had a bloody axe to grind. So Bruce entered a period of sporadic warfare against English garrisons and Scottish enemies alike. With perseverance and by honing a style of fighting based more upon guerrilla tactics than massed battle over open terrain, he accumulated successes and the Comyns were forced into exile south of the border in 1309. It was to be a war of attrition counted in years rather than months but by the end of 1313 the English garrisons and King Robert's Scottish foes had been all but driven out of Scotland.

In the summer of 1313, Bruce's surviving brother Edward laid siege to the key remaining English stronghold, Stirling Castle and persuaded Mowbray, the constable there, to agree to surrender if no English force arrived to relieve him within a year. The following year, Edward II himself came north at the head of a mighty army bent upon just that objective. Robert Bruce was there, determined to stop him.

In February 1306 he did away with his only real rival, John Comyn, stabbing him to death in front of the high altar

THE BATTLE

AS IS OFTEN THE CASE FOR A COMMANDER,
ROBERT BRUCE, OR ROBERT THE BRUCE, AS
HE ALSO BECAME KNOWN, MADE CAREFUL
PLANS FOR ONE SORT OF BATTLE, BUT
ENDED UP FIGHTING ANOTHER. ON 23 JUNE
HE WAS WITH HIS ARMY IN 'THE PARK' –
OPEN WOODLAND STRETCHING A COUPLE
OF MILES SOUTH FROM STIRLING CASTLE.
HERE THE TREES OBSCURED HIS MEN FROM
VIEW AND WOULD MAKE IT IMPOSSIBLE
FOR THE ENGLISH HEAVY HORSE TO RIDE
THEM DOWN. TO THE EAST, THE GROUND
FELL STEEPLY AWAY TOWARDS THE CARSE,
THE SOMETIMES WATERLOGGED AND
ALTOGETHER UNPREPOSSESSING FLOOD
PLAIN OF THE RIVER FORTH.

The Bruce's style was to strike fast, surprising the enemy, and then disappear via a carefully planned escape route. As he waited to face what would undoubtedly prove to be a host far greater than anything he himself could ever hope to put into the field, at least he knew he had the superior ground. The plateau on which the Park stood sat relatively high, overlooking the direction from which the enemy would be likely to advance. Furthermore, were things to go badly for the Scots, they could fall back through the trees and melt away towards the north.

The Scots army had occupied this area for days – practising moving and fighting in schiltrons of massed spearmen, and the crucial movement into tree cover if the enemy attack proved overwhelming. The Bruce had split his army into three main 'battles': Thomas Randolph, Earl of Moray, led the vanguard; Sir Edward Bruce had the centre; and command of the rear was split between Walter, the young Lord Steward, and Sir James Douglas. The king himself commanded a fourth body, essentially a reserve, and Sir Robert Keith, Marshall of Scotland, led a handpicked force of 500 mounted men. That mounted knights are vulnerable to archers and of less use when it comes to handstrokes among trees and broken ground was a lesson that the Bruce had learned well. Every knight and squire was commanded to get down off his mount and stand to with the infantry.

Expecting his foe to come at him along the old Roman road leading to the castle, the Bruce had booby-trapped the ground on either side with a honeycomb pattern of three-foot-deep pits camouflaged with turf. The sequence of events he had envisaged was simple: seeing the Scots step out from the cover of the trees directly in front of them, the English horse would be ordered to charge. Careering towards their foe they would fall horribly foul of the pits and Scots spearmen would advance into the screaming mêlée, in strictly choreographed formation, to butcher the fallen. A heavy blow would be dealt against the invaders, even if Stirling Castle was ultimately relieved. In the less likely event of an English attempt at outflanking, by descending on to the Carse and passing the Scots to the east, his men were still perfectly placed for a safe withdrawal after any skirmishing. This then was how the Bruce saw forthcoming events – a chance to severely bloody Edward's nose without putting his own army at unacceptable risk.

As expected, Edward approached Stirling Castle from the south. The host he led inspired awe in those who saw it: thousands upon thousands of knights, men-at-arms, archers and the rest wound their way northwards, banners snapping, arms and armour buffed to brilliance.

Careering towards their foe they would fall horribly foul of the pits and Scots spearmen would advance into the screaming mêlée

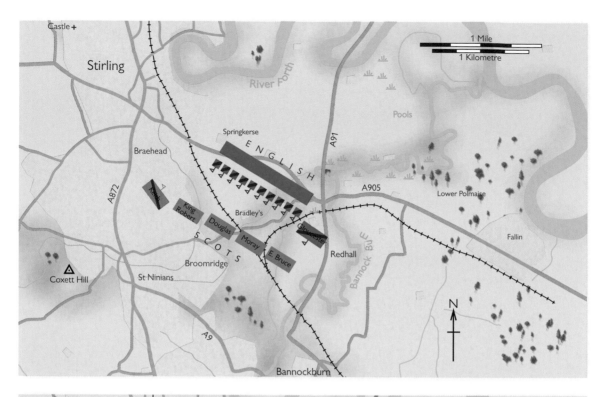

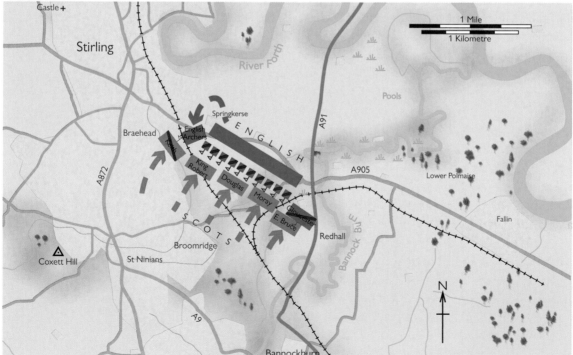

Movement of troops during the battle of Bannockburn superimposed on a modern map

Aylmer of Valence, Earl of Pembroke

Relief of the castle was a matter of national pride and the English king was pulling out all the stops. The Earls of Hereford and Gloucester shared the vanguard while Edward and the Earl of Pembroke had the rear. In terms of deployment, the English king and his military advisers had contrived a complicated arrangement of ten bodies of heavy horse with archers in front and behind, supported by infantry. In the event, though, none of that would matter.

As Edward and his men came within sight of their intended destination, they saw Scots spearmen covering the road from the security of the wooded parkland. Edward lost no time in making it clear that he hadn't come all this way for nothing and fighting began. Here Edward broke slightly from the script written for him by the Scots king, for the fighting involved two separate actions that played out simultaneously. Some 300 mounted men-at-arms under the command of Sir Robert Clifford and Henry de Beaumont rode down on to the fringes of the Carse, presumably looking to get around the Scots. Bruce himself spotted the feint and sent word to Moray – who quickly led a 500-strong schiltron down the slope from the plateau and into the riders' path. Again and again Clifford and de Beaumont led charges against them, but their efforts were in vain. Infuriated, the knights were reduced to hurling their maces and lances against the defenders – but these were just piled up inside the schiltron as spoils of war. The knights were finally forced to stop when they spotted the arrival, on the top of the slope, of a force led by Sir James Douglas. Concluding that if they could not handle this many-legged, many-pointed beast on its own, they surely could not deal with anything more, they withdrew.

But while schiltron and cavalry fought one another to a standstill on the fringes of the Carse, back on the Roman road an English knight was hurtling towards immortality. Henry de Bohun – nephew of the hereditary constable of England Humphrey de Bohun, Earl of Hereford – clattered on to the pages of legend by attempting nothing less than single combat with the Scots king. When de Bohun and the rest of the English vanguard arrived on the ground beyond the pit traps, the Bruce was some distance ahead of his own army and effectively alone, mounted not on a destrier but on a hackney. De Bohun saw that with one successful tilt at the figure sitting upon that lesser mount, he could secure victory for his king. Visor lowered and lance raised, he galloped towards his target – who appeared rooted to the spot. Far from being transfixed, however, the lion was just allowing the prey to come to him. When the young knight was almost upon him, the Bruce pulled his horse out of harm's way, rose up on his stirrups and swung two-handed with his axe, with such force that the shaft split end to end as it split the two sides of de Bohun's helmeted head from each other. When the Bruce's retinue chided him for taking such a personal risk, he observed only that he had broken his favourite battleaxe.

Beaten off by both engagements, the English army now took time to draw breath and consider how best to proceed. They had come here to lift the siege on the castle – and indeed, in terms of the customs of the time had done so simply by bringing an army so close to it. Surely they could expect the Scots to do what they always did – namely melt away into the hills while gloating at the way they had caused their big brother to yelp in indignant pain? However, they would still need to take steps to ensure that this latest clash with the Bruce would go the way of all others. It was late afternoon now and there would be no more fighting today. It would be best to use the long twilight of this Scottish midsummer to set up camp. Clifford and de Beaumont had noticed that while the lowest expanses of the Carse were an unappetizing mire of pools and meandering rivulets, further to the west there was an area of drier, hard ground where an army could camp – and fight too, if need be, for they were ever mindful of the Scots' propensity for surprise attack. To

Far from being transfixed, however, the lion was just allowing the prey to come to him

The Bruce and de Bohun

get to it, however, they would need to cross the Bannock burn which crossed the ground east of the plateau. Teams set about creating hard standing for men and animals on either side of the stream, and thatch and wood were looted from the nearby village of Bannockburn to be thrown upon the soft ground.

It must have been late in the evening at least before the bulk of the force was in position on the relatively dry ground beneath the Scots' plateau. The thousands of men and horses bedded down as best they could, armour and saddles still buckled in place for fear of sudden need of both; pickets were placed between the army's flank and the Scots-infested wood to the west, but since Stirling Castle, to the north-west, was the final destination, the English army deployed themselves with their front towards it.

If the English camp that night was overshadowed by disgruntled

The battle of Bannockburn

chagrin mixed with physical discomfort, the mood among the Bruce's Scots was altogether different. The day had gone well for them: English had fallen to Scots spears and axes with negligible losses on the home side and the glory of the day was all Scots. Whether or not the Bruce was wholly satisfied by events remains a moot point – and just when he decided to gamble his modest winnings of 23 June on a rollover into 24 June is lost to history. In any case, any last doubts he may have had were laid to rest after the arrival of an unexpected visitor.

The Bruce needed at all times the support of the titled great and good who commanded fighting men within his fledgling realm. That night, as usual, he would have summoned his war council so that he could hear the views of those upon whom the success of any campaign depended. And into this gathering walked one Alexander Seton, a turncoat from the English side but a Scottish knight by birth. The English army was demoralized and badly led, he said; having already tasted defeat, they were in no mood for any more. He had switched sides rather than put up with their moaning incompetence. Strike *en masse*, at dawn, said Seton, and shattering victory would go to the Scots.

In the half-light of dawn, at around four in the morning, English soldiers saw a strange and unexpected sight. As they shook off what sleep they had scrounged from the damp dark, shouts from their pickets made them look west towards the wooded plateau. There, stepping out of the shadows and dropping to their knees in their thousands, were the Scots. Far from fleeing, they had camped in the shelter of the wood and were kneeling in front of its trees. It was the feast day of St John the Baptist and every man among the Scots force had already heard mass. Now as they stepped on to the field of battle, they knelt once more, to offer up the Lord's Prayer. Edward, seeing the spectacle, asked incredulously of those around him if it was possible this rabble meant to fight him? Or was his foe kneeling to beg for mercy? That they do, said Sir Ingraham de Umfraville, a dispossessed Scottish knight now fighting against his own king; not from you, though, but from God, for what they are about to do.

That the Bruce had come to Stirling Castle with a view to facing the might of England in open battle seems unlikely. But it seems that as he perceived a set of circumstances he had not perhaps foreseen, he adapted his plans as every truly great commander does when he sees before him a chance not to be missed and he exploited the manoeuvrability he had drilled into his men. Three or perhaps four schiltrons sprang up and ran over the half-mile or so of broken ground separating them from the enemy. It was a move of the utmost audacity – taking foot-soldiers over terrain ideally suited to the heavy horse for which the English host was famed. But crucially, the Scots were on the move while those horsemen were still at their breakfast or asleep.

As the Scots approached the English force on its left flank, there was a great hullabaloo among the English as tens of thousands of men, deployed to the north-west, responded to their commanders' desperate orders to turn *en masse* to their left and regroup for a battle none of them had foreseen.

Down bore the first of the schiltrons into what had been hastily mustered of Gloucester's vanguard. As the spearmen collided with mounted men there was a terrible puncturing and rending of flesh. It was the English horse and men who took the worst of it. Skewered upon iron-tipped shafts, the front rank of horses became an obstacle to those behind them. There was nowhere to go forward – and it was rapidly becoming impossible to go backwards either, as men and horses in their thousands pressed towards the fighting.

All along the English front it was the same. Horses came up against

As the spearmen collided with mounted men there was a terrible puncturing and rending of flesh

schiltron and impaled themselves upon the points. Furthest towards the north-west, where the English front had so recently turned to form its right flank, archers aimed at the oncoming Scots – the schiltron led by Douglas – and briefly the arrows had a galling effect. But the Bruce unleashed his five hundred horses, under Keith, and the English bowmen soon quailed in the face of them and broke towards their own rear. The Scots archers now harried those of the English horse not already impaled upon spears or crushed by the press of numbers.

Proud Edward's army had no room in which to manoeuvre. Hemmed in by the streams (Pelstream and Bannock burn) on both sides and by advancing Scots to the front, the cavalry had no space in which to deploy properly. They were now just chopping blocks for the savage attentions of the spears, swords and axes wielded by the advancing schiltrons. Though the Bruce's army was outnumbered by as much as four to one, in the circumstances in which the English force found itself superior numbers were irrelevant. Whole companies of English soldiers, trapped towards the rear of the hellish crush, never had occasion to draw sword during the entire battle. In some parts of the front line, an obscene bank of slaughtered men and horses that reduced the action to mere shouting of insults separated the two forces. The Bruce's military genius and strength of nerve had given his army the advantage from the start – and the fierce courage of the men of his schiltrons was breaking English hearts.

As the thoughts of the redundant English soldiers were turning inevitably to withdrawal, the Bruce sent his infantry reserve into the heaving crush. The effect was instantaneous. Already hopelessly demoralized by the sounds of their own countrymen dying by the hundreds in front of them, many English decided that their best option was to head for home.

As chunks of the English army turned and fled, a final attack was triggered. Up on top of nearby Gillies Hill, a force of several thousand untrained and ill-equipped Scots men and women stood waiting – the so-called 'small folk', who knew that sooner or later the fighting would cease and they could flood on to the field in search of plunder. Eager not to miss out on the best of the spoils, they fashioned makeshift banners from rags and staffs and, armed with what weapons they had been able to muster, they flooded down the slope in the direction of the fleeing English. The English soldiers mistook the small folk for another infantry reserve and promptly redoubled their efforts to leave. Through the pools and rivulets of the Carse they fled, trying desperately to put distance

Coment le grant pouple bataillerent a côtre le iour de iugemet par orguil x par enuie x par couetise.

Coment le cômoinre gent checou leua a côtre autre z uou dza autre ocire p le aller pur met trise. E ceo est dunt nouf esperouf breu q le iour de dreyt iugemet for met aproche.

The battle of Bannockburn, 1314, when the Scots under Robert the Bruce defeated the English

between themselves and the horror behind them. It was said that countless hundreds of men on foot drowned in those waters or were smothered to death in cloying mud as they were gradually overtaken by their foes, their faster fellows or their own men on horseback.

Edward had no option but to join the rout. Surrounded by his personal bodyguard, he galloped towards the castle in search of sanctuary. Its governor, Mowbray, now in the last hours of his tenure of the place, barred the gates against his king, saying that if he let him in, the place would fall and Edward would become a prisoner of the Scots. Heeding his advice, Edward and his men rode on, eventually finding their way home by a circuitous path.

WHO FOUGHT HERE

SCOTLAND AND ENGLAND IN THE FOURTEENTH CENTURY WERE HARDLY STRANGERS TO WAR – AS 'NEIGHBOURS FROM HELL' THEY SURELY RANK AMONG THE MOST BELLICOSE IN HISTORY. HAVING MADE IT A PERSONAL QUEST TO EXERCISE ANCIENT ENGLISH CLAIMS OF SOVEREIGNTY OVER HIS NORTHERN NEIGHBOUR, EDWARD I HAD BATTLED IN SCOTLAND REPEATEDLY. THE SCOTS HAD FOUGHT HARD IN THE FACE OF THIS AGGRESSION; AND WHEN THERE WAS NO APPETITE FOR RAIDS SOUTH OF THE BORDER, THEY BLED WITH THE SELF-INFLICTED WOUNDS OF INTERNECINE SQUABBLING.

Scotland's greatest weakness was always the duplicitous self-interest of its nobility, and their incessant machinations in pursuit of personal gain led periodically to bloodshed. Edward indulged similar fantasies of domination in Wales – and made war in France too in pursuit of riches greater than anything available at home. Wales he successfully brought to heel and it is fair to say that he lost no ground in France either. When Edward died in 1307, his son, Edward II, took up the cudgels when required, though with markedly less natural ability. And yet despite what looks from the twenty-first-century perspective like constant war, neither Scotland nor England gave any thought to keeping permanent armies. The battle of Bannockburn in 1314 – like those at Stirling Bridge and Falkirk before it – was fought in the main by armies composed of short-term conscripts more at home with ploughshares and ditching spades than spears and swords. The task facing the commanders on both sides, then, was to fashion this raw material into cohesive fighting units.

THE SCOTS

For the Bruce, the most pressing problem was how best to raise and equip sufficient men from a population so much smaller than that of his enemy. The recent bout of warring, since the rebellion by William Wallace, had left the country sorely depleted in terms of both fighting men and resources. Scotland was a poor country. Its nobility were more aware of this than most and spent a lot of their time grovelling on their knees before whichever monarch would grant them land in the more prosperous south. It was always a challenge to find the men and resources at home to create an army for use against England.

However, by operating what were essentially protection rackets in the north of England, by which he accepted a retainer for not destroying property, the Bruce had amassed enough cash by the time of Bannockburn to equip his men with protective gear and weaponry. In the tradition of the canny Scot, he minimized his costs by having his force all gather on the proposed battlefield itself, so avoiding having to keep men in the field for weeks on end.

While the Scots army was famously outnumbered at Bannockburn, in one component at least they were certainly not outclassed: the foot-soldiers. The men the Bruce trusted most were his commanders, and while their English counterparts chose to fight in the cavalry, the Scots nobility loyal to the Bruce fought almost exclusively on foot among the common soldiery. For this reason, the calibre of the Scots infantry was conspicuously higher than that ranged against them. Foot-soldiers also

While the Scots army was famously outnumbered at Bannockburn, in one component at least they were certainly not outclassed

made up the bulk of the army. They had been drawn from all corners of the country: John Barbour, writing fifty years after Bannockburn, notes that the king's own contingent or 'battle' was made up of men from his home patch – men of Carrick, and of Argyll, Kintyre and the Isles – who in the main owed personal allegiance to him. By exploiting such ties, he applied a glue to his army that was absent from the opposing side. Within the Bruce's army Thomas Randolph, Earl of Moray, led his own men too, from Ross and the far north. Like the pals' regiments of the First World War, men who came in together fought together and were held by bonds of loyalty, kinship and friendship that were not so apparent among the English. Crucially, too, the Bruce had had his men together in the vicinity of Stirling Castle just long enough to school them in the ways of the schiltron. At the army's core were men who had served the Bruce for years and who were justly proud of what they had achieved so far. They provided a backbone which supported the rest of the force.

The best armour was worn by the foot-soldiers, each of whom had either a chain-mail shirt or a padded jacket. In addition, each wore leather gloves covered in mail or metal plate and an iron hat. They may have carried swords and axes for close-quarter fighting but the prime weapon for the Bruce's infantrymen was the 4–4.5-metre-long iron pointed spear. This was a heavy and cumbersome weapon and effective use of it required rigorous and repetitive drilling.

A reasonable estimate for the infantry force fielded by the Bruce is between 5,000 and 7,000 men.

The number-one 'must-have' in the mind of every warlord of the fourteenth century was the mounted knight. Some was good, more was better and too many was just right. The war horse of choice was the destrier (the name derives from the Latin '*dexter*', meaning 'right', since the horse was led by a squire on the knight's right-hand side). These beasts had to be imported from France and Spain at a cost of anything from £50 upwards – at a time when the average knight earned four shillings a day when he was on campaign. The most desirable destrier was an aggressive stallion, standing seventeen hands high and with a small head and ears. This was before the time of cavalry of the kind that played a crucial role at English Civil War battles like Marston Moor – when more docile mares were prized for their ability to work together. The fourteenth-century knight hungered for personal glory and an ill-tempered, kicking, biting stallion that would make war all on its own was favoured every time. A luxury commodity among the rich landlords

King Robert the Bruce

Tony as a Scottish spearman

of England, destriers were practically unheard of in Scotland. Instead, the Bruce's knights were mounted upon lighter, high-stepping horses known as hackneys. Typically standing no more than fourteen hands high, they could not so easily bear the weight of a fully armoured man. Contemporary illustrations in which the fully armoured knight appears to have his feet almost dragging along the ground on either side of his mount in the manner of a Thelwell drawing are accurate enough. A knight thus mounted had to choose either to wear heavy armour and chain mail at the expense of movement, or to wear lighter protection so as to have to have superior speed and mobility. Even hackneys were hard to come by in Scotland.

For these reasons of expense and availability the cavalry wing of the Scots army numbered no more than about five hundred. Under the command of Sir Robert Keith, they were light and manoeuvrable, and functioned as a scouting unit, keeping tabs on the enemy, as much as an offensive tool on the battlefield.

The knight's weapon was the 4–4.5-metre-long lance, which was held out over the horse's head, its killing power delivered with all the weight and speed of the heavily armoured man and animal combined.

There is some debate among historians as to whether the Scottish bowman carried the long or the short bow, but the latter seems the most likely. The short bow was the older weapon and in practised hands was reputed to have a rate of shot even greater than that of its longer, more powerful successor. Among the Bruce's archers, the most skilled were the men of Ettrick Forest, who were able to let fly twenty arrows or more in a minute from their bows, compared to the typical maximum of fifteen from the longbowmen. Accounts vary as to the significance, if any, of the role the Scots archers played at Bannockburn. Numbers for archers are especially vague, but there are unlikely to have been more than a few hundred of them.

Opposite **Neil wearing helmet and chainmail**

THE ENGLISH

Every account of the battle of Bannockburn puts huge emphasis upon the English cavalry, but the bulk of the host that travelled north to the rallying point at Wark on Tweed was made up of foot-soldiers. Their numbers were drawn primarily from the north and centre of England, it not being the practice of the time to levy southerners to fight as far afield as Scotland. Others had been pulled in, however, from Wales and from Ireland: 5,000 men were ordered up from Wales, and a similar number from across the Irish Sea. It is difficult, however, to know how many actually answered the call or saw service at Bannockburn.

The English infantry force that marched to Stirling Castle probably numbered between 14,000 and 16,000 men. In appearance, the English foot-soldier would have been essentially identical to his Scottish counterpart – armoured with chain mail or padded jacket and wearing an iron hat.

The English infantry force that marched to Stirling Castle probably numbered between 14,000 and 16,000 men

Heavy horse or cavalry were the tank battalions of their day. Given enough space to reach a gallop, hundreds of mounted men working together with a single objective became, in theory, an unstoppable juggernaut. Edward therefore sought to raise as many as possible, putting out a general call to knights not just in England and Wales but also in Europe. He went to great lengths to secure the presence, for example, of Sir Giles d'Argentan, reputedly the third greatest knight in Christendom. According to Barbour, rich men with a taste for glory and plunder came in great numbers – '. . . apart from his own chivalry, which

was so huge it was fearsome, he [Edward] had with him good men of great spirit from many a far country' – although recently historians questioning Barbour's claims have suggested that while men may have answered Edward's call from Gascony, it may be unrealistic to imagine great numbers or much of a mix of European nationalities.

Unlike Scotland, comparatively rich nations such as England and France had the wherewithal to provide realistic numbers of destriers. The English king had the support of more wealthy noblemen too – who were expected to raise and equip large numbers of mounted men whenever the king's fancy turned to conquest. Every knight was expected to have at least one destrier, two palfreys – light horses prized for striding with both right and left legs in unison, giving a smooth ride – and as many other mounts besides as he could provide men and supplies for.

The English cavalry, once assembled, was split into ten 'battles' and deployed in three lines of three battles each, with the tenth as an advance guard. Like their Scots counterparts, they carried 4–4.5-metre-long lances, as well as swords and axes or maces for close-quarter fighting. Mounted on the larger destriers, they could take advantage of the best and heaviest armour available – both for themselves and for their horses.

Edward's cavalry wing is likely to have amounted to about 2,500 to 3,000 men – considerably less than some of the more fanciful estimates, but still a huge force for the time.

Edward I had noticed the value of archers when they had been used against his men fighting in Wales in the late thirteenth century and taken the idea for his own, using it to great effect. By the time of Bannockburn, and earlier, the English archer with his longbow of red yew – trained from boyhood to give him time to develop the muscle for the draw weight of as much as 150 pounds, and the skill to aim it – was as fearsome a prospect as anything likely to be encountered by a medieval soldier. With a rate of shot of about fifteen arrows a minute and a maximum range well in excess of 200 metres, they rained death down upon the fields of Europe for decades and centuries to come. It had been the English archers who had broken up William Wallace's schiltrons at Falkirk in 1298, enabling the English heavy horse to get in among them and finish them off. The bowman had little protection in close combat – generally preferring to run away than to face oncoming infantry or, God forbid, cavalry – and was lightly armoured. Numbers are again hard to come by, but there were probably 2,000 to 3,000 English archers on the field at Bannockburn.

TACTICS

In the world of football, when squads are pulled together from local teams for an international match, the challenge is to give the players enough time to train together so that they can become a tight team rather than just a disparate collection of solo stars. So it was too, for the Scottish and English leaders before Bannockburn. One of the most telling facts about Edward's approach to this Scottish campaign was how late he left his preparations. Though he had had a year's warning of the fight to come, he did little by way of summoning a credible force until December 1313. The final writs calling men to the rallying point did not go out until the following May and the army was not in place north of the Tweed until 17 June, just six days before the first fighting took place. By the time he had his northerners, midlanders, Irishmen and Welshmen gathered together, never mind whatever Continental players he had successfully recruited, there was no time for any team building. Sure, he had glamour boys like d'Argentan, third best player in the world – not to mention controversial signings like de Umfraville, who had played for Scotland in his time – but his players were lacking in team spirit.

The Scots, by contrast, were fielding a team who had played together long enough to be ready to take commands and to operate together for the common good. The Bruce had been on the comeback trail for years.

Andy Robertshaw faces a Scottish schiltron

For a while there, in fact, it had looked like relegation for the big man from Carrick, but he had established a winning combination in recent years and the younger, more recent additions to the team preparing for Bannockburn had the presence of seasoned pros – James 'the Black' Douglas and Sir Robert Keith, to name but two – to help steady their nerves on the big day.

The Bruce knew that the English army would turn up at Stirling Castle on or before midsummer 1314. This meant he could prepare well in advance of any fight. If there was a word he lived by as a commander, it was 'caution' – and he did not forget the need to be wary in the face of superior forces when he readied his men. For these reasons, he positioned them close to and within the woodland of the Park to protect them from the English cavalry; he booby-trapped the ground on either side of the Roman road – the most obvious line of advance for the enemy; and he was prepared primarily to protect his army's position. Ever the opportunist, he had also schooled his men in the use of a tactical formation that would ensure their safety while allowing an offensive strategy if the chance allowed.

Key to the Bruce's plans for tackling the English was the hedgehog of spearmen that had been used with some success, initially at least, by William Wallace at Falkirk in 1298. To be effective against massed cavalry, schiltrons had to be on a scale large enough for any holes made in the line to be filled without the main body suffering. Two concentric lines of men, each hundreds strong, were placed one inside the other. All the men faced outwards, the outer line planting their spears in the ground and pointing them out at forty-five degrees or so and the inner line holding their spears over the shoulders of the men in front. Inside this double ring were hundreds more men, controlled by experienced commanders and ready to step into any breaches in the lines.

At Falkirk, Wallace's static schiltrons, kept in place around circles of stakes and rope, had been sitting ducks for Longshanks' longbowmen, who were able to break the lines, allowing the heavy horse to run them down. With that in mind, the Bruce prepared his own schiltrons to be highly mobile when necessary. These preparations paid off on the first day, when Moray's men were able to intercept Clifford's cavalry force and rebuff successive charges from them. According to Barbour, Moray was heard to shout: 'Don't be afraid of their menace, but set spears before you, and form yourselves up back to back, with all the spears' points out. In that way we can best defend ourselves if we are surrounded by them.'

All this required practice and the Bruce took the time to ensure that his schiltrons were well drilled in the discipline needed both to stay together on the move and to hold the line when stationary and under attack. On the second day of the battle, three or four great schiltrons advanced in quick time to hem in the English army before it even had a chance to deploy – and, once in position, they either held their ground against charges from the English horse or advanced steadily, giving the opposition no room in which to move.

In the English camp it seems that strategy was hopelessly lacking. Edward had amassed a huge host and got it into position, but it would appear that he had given no real thought to the question of how to tackle the enemy. He had a complex plan for the deployment of his archers, infantry and cavalry – but having been prepared without knowledge of the circumstances under which the battle would be fought, it proved inflexible and ultimately useless.

Experienced leaders of men were there with Edward as well, but his command structure was sorely lacking too. The Earls of Gloucester and Hereford, seasoned campaigners both, were men used to command – but they vied with one another for dominance rather than keeping their minds on the job. By giving them joint command of the vanguard, Edward displayed a telling ignorance of the forces at play within his top brass that was to cost him dear. Personal rivalries were therefore allowed to get in the way of a clear vision and having had his nose blooded on the first day, Edward seems to have allowed any vague plans he may have had to fly out of the window. Sir Ingraham de Umfraville, the Bruce's own cousin, should have been invaluable to Edward as a source of intelligence. He was driven more by a desire to win back his own lands in Scotland – lands taken from him by the Bruce – than any real loyalty to Edward, however, and this lack of commitment to the cause was common to many individuals commanding the English host. By the time the English army was encamped on the Carse, the initiative was firmly with the Scots.

In the English camp it seems that strategy was hopelessly lacking

THE AFTERMATH

'AS LONG AS BUT A HUNDRED OF US
REMAIN ALIVE, NEVER WILL WE ON ANY
CONDITIONS BE BROUGHT UNDER ENGLISH
RULE.'

The Declaration of Arbroath, 1320

ALTHOUGH THE BRUCE SENT EDWARD
'HOMEWARD, TAE THINK AGAIN', HOME WAS
NOT REALLY WHERE THE SCOTS WANTED
HIM. VICTORY AT BANNOCKBURN
NOTWITHSTANDING, IT WOULD HAVE BEEN
MORE SATISFACTORY FOR THE SCOTS — AND
THE BRUCE IN PARTICULAR — IF EDWARD
HAD BEEN CAPTURED OR KILLED ON THE
FIELD.

As Fiona Watson has pointed out, Bruce required two outcomes of the battle: an end to the war and English recognition of Scottish independence, with acknowledgement of his royal legitimacy. But even if Edward II was no hammer of the Scots, he was not going to be given a bloody nose and then come out shaking hands: it suited him very well to continue the war and have the Bruce constantly looking to his laurels. The Bruce may have won the battle but he certainly hadn't won the war.

Fighting continued in the border lands in a series of raids and counter raids that were to set the pattern of the Anglo-Scots relationship until the sixteenth century, when full revenge for Bannockburn was exacted at the battles of Flodden and Solway Moss. The Bruce's inability or unwillingness to bring an end to the war did him few favours in Scotland and an abortive campaign in Ireland can only have added to a growing feeling that the hero was more concerned with his own glorification than with the needs of his country. The catalogue of woes continued. The Scots recapture in 1318 of Berwick, which had since 1296 been a symbol of English domination, was not the success it seemed, for it prompted the Pope, who had been trying to stop the constant warring between the two sides, to excommunicate the entire population of Scotland.

The Declaration of Arbroath

Edward stirred the pot of unrest by inviting Edward Balliol, son of the exiled King John, to come over from France. Balliol's presence in London helped to remind everyone that there were more legitimate claims to the Scottish throne than the Bruce's. The ghost of Comyn came to haunt King Robert in the form of a plot hatched by Balliol supporters and Comyn sympathizers and distant relatives. The Bruce got wind of the planned coup and rounded up the suspected ring-leaders; those found guilty were either imprisoned for life or executed.

Despite all this, support for King Robert among his people was strong. A number of leading Scottish nobles expressed their loyalty when, in an effort to release Robert from excommunication, they wrote of the Bruce in a letter to the Pope in 1320, 'We are bound both by law and by his merits that our freedom may be still maintained, and by him, come what may, we mean to stand.' The letter, which has since become known as the Declaration of Arbroath, expressed the determination of the Scots to remain an independent nation in the face of English aggression, and did more than its job, for the Pope not only allowed Robert back into the Church's fold, but also recognized Robert's authority as King of Scotland.

Perhaps motivated by a new feeling of security and self-assurance,

**King Edward II and
Queen Isabella**

and by the realization that all the fighting was achieving very little, in 1323 Robert signed a thirteen-year truce with England. His wife Elizabeth was released from imprisonment by the English and the following year Robert was blessed with a son, David – surprisingly, perhaps, as Robert was not a healthy man: modern reconstructions of his face based on his skull show not just serious war wounds but also the scars of syphilis. In 1327 Edward II was brutally assassinated by his own nobles, and, his own health notwithstanding, Bruce wasted no time in taking advantage of the ensuing chaos by breaking the truce and invading England once more. By taking control of large swathes of northern England he finally got what he was after, a treaty in which his status as king of an independent Scotland was acknowledge by Edward III's regents.

In June 1329 the warrior king Robert I died in Cardross and was buried in Dunfermline. Before burial the king's heart was removed from his body and taken on crusade by his old friend and ally, Sir James Douglas. While on crusade Sir James was killed fighting the Moors in Spain. Just before he died he is said to have hurled the Bruce's heart at the enemy as a final act of defiance. The heart was somehow recovered and brought back to Scotland, where it was buried in Melrose Abbey. In 1921 workmen carrying out repairs unearthed the heart, enclosed within a small, conical casket of lead, from its resting place beneath the Chapter House floor. The heart was thereafter reburied in a fresh casket. It was then 'rediscovered' in 1996 during archaeological excavations, after which some scientific analysis was carried out, but the casket was not opened. The heart was reburied again in June 1998 and two days later, on the anniversary of the battle of Bannockburn, the Secretary of State for Scotland, Donald Dewar, unveiled a plinth commemorating the burial site.

By the time of his death Robert the Bruce had achieved all he could possibly have hoped for. Scotland was recognized as a sovereign nation by its southern neighbour and the Bruce's acknowledged royal lineage would continue through his young son David, who became the new King of Scotland, David II. As always it was only a matter of time before hostilities between Scotland and England were rekindled, but these were chapters to be written around other battles. Bannockburn passed into memory, where it resides, for the Scots at least, in a place of honour.

Just before he died he is said to have hurled the Bruce's heart at the enemy as a final act of defiance

the **Dig**

It takes necks of purest brass to turn up in the vicinity of Stirling Castle intending to locate Bannockburn battlefield. There has been considerable disagreement among historians over the exact location and more so than with any other battle we've investigated, the location is a topic of conversation that seems as relevant to the people there as the news headlines. Every person we talked to, whether in the offices of Stirling Council, the galleries of the town museum, in the cafés or in the pub next door to the visitors' centre, had an opinion about where the fighting had taken place – and they were prepared to defend that opinion against all comers.

Few contemporary eyewitness accounts of the battle survive; those that do were generally written some time after the battle and either lack detail about the location or are highly ambiguous. There is general agreement that the battle was fought close to the place known today as Bannockburn, but at least two separate locations have been proposed as the battle site. The picture is further confused by the fact that the battle took place over two days, with the initial contacts on the first day taking place in different locations from the main encounter on the second.

Traditionally, the first day's fighting is believed to have been at a crossing of the Bannock burn on the Roman road into Stirling. Today the route of the Roman road is largely obscured by modern roads, although there are areas in open fields where its route can be found. The location of the pits the Scots dug across the route in preparation for the arrival of the English is at present uncertain, but is traditionally thought to be on the ground to the south of Bannockburn. It is in this area that the English vanguard is thought to have made contact with the Scots, who were at the time occupying the higher ground, protected by woodland.

There is little sign of any woodland today, apart from

Balquhidderock Wood, which occupies the slope where the higher terrace drops down on to the Carse and is preserved as parkland. It has been suggested that this is a remnant of the woodland that was here at the time of the battle – an idea extrapolated from the presence of woodland here on an eighteenth-century map. However, the presence of woodland in the eighteenth century does not necessarily mean that it was there several centuries before.

It is about the location of the main battle that began early in the morning of 24 June that controversy still rages. One school of thought has the battle on the Carse itself, with the Scots coming off the high ground to advance on the English. This is probably the most widely held opinion, with most maps showing the battle site in a large meander of the Bannock burn. A recent reassessment of available sources by Fiona Watson and Maggie Anderson has come down in favour of an intermediate terrace known as Dryfield of Balquhidderock, some fifteen metres above and to the west of the Carse and the area where the English camped. In his book *Bannockburn Revealed*, William Scott has argued against this location as he believes that the terrace was covered with woodland at the time, which would have made the deployment of the English cavalry impossible. Unfortunately, this second location has suffered from modern development and is today occupied by housing and schools, and the last twenty years have seen housing also impinging upon the lower ground at the base of the terrace, along with the A91 dual carriageway.

Another location that appears to have played an important role on the second day is a portion of the Bannock burn itself. Sources refer to a 'Great Ditch' or chasm in which many of the English appear to have perished in their attempt to flee the field. Those in favour of the Carse location for the battle claim that this portion of the Bannock burn is on the Carse itself, but others point to a very obvious defile that cuts through the higher ground to the south-east of the terrace location.

Knowing how deeply passions run on the subject of

Statue of King Robert the Bruce by Pilkington Jackson

Bannockburn, it was with collars turned up high and hats pulled low that we arrived at the National Trust for Scotland's visitors' centre across the road from the modern village of Bannockburn. Before getting down to work, we strolled up to Pilkington Jackson's famous statue of King Robert the Bruce. Behind it in the middle distance is the castle that provoked the fight in the first place, looming over the town from a crest of rock. The statue stands on the ground where, tradition has it, the Scots king located his headquarters in advance of the battle – and given the views it commands of the surrounding area, it's easy to see why it would appeal to a commander. As we surveyed the scene, we imagined how the Bruce must have felt as he looked out from here, southwards in the direction from which Edward's army was likely to appear.

Today Bannockburn is a suburb of Stirling. Buildings cover much of a series of natural terraces that give way in the west to farmland and then to higher ground planted with trees. To the east the housing eventually peters out in the face of another landscape feature crucial to the events of 23 and 24 June 1314: the Carse. The westernmost extreme of this level expanse, stretching towards the Ochil Hills, is skirted by a railway and major roads. Today this flood plain of the river Forth is carefully drained farmland, but it is still broken up by the meanders of streams making their lazy ways towards the river. Of special note are two burns that were encountered by English troops at various times during those two days. One is the Pelstream; the other, of course, is the Bannock.

There has been much discussion about changes in the landscape that may have taken place in the years – nearly 700 – since the battle. Apart from the obvious transformations of modern development – houses, roads, power lines, the railway – there are other invisible changes that we had to take into account if we were to try to understand the topography. An important one was the suggestion that the level of the Carse has been lowered in some places by the removal of peat and as a result of modern drainage. Without detailed environmental surveys it is difficult to establish the extent, if any, of such a change. It is likely, however, given the presence of arable fields there, that the area has been well drained in recent centuries and it seems reasonable to suggest that the area we were looking out at was generally much drier now than it had been at the time of the battle, although we should not overlook the fact that the battle was fought in midsummer.

The Roman road

Traditionally, part of the first day's fighting – when the Bruce clashed with the English knight de Bohun – was located at a crossing of the Bannock burn on the line of the Roman road that had for centuries provided the main thoroughfare into Stirling. Though today modern roads largely obscure it, we were convinced that isolated patches of that ancient road would have survived in the open fields. Modern Ordnance Survey maps depict its route with a dotted line, but we suspected this was a line of faith as much as anything else. We had to get on the ground if we were going to get any answers. Find the line of the Roman road that the English army had marched along, we thought, and we would begin to close in on the area where the two opposing forces first beheld one another.

We knew that some work had already been done on patches of the Roman road in private gardens within the town. One of these earlier excavations had found a compacted surface around seven metres wide. Outside the town, and closer to our area of operations, there had been two digs in the 1970s and the 1990s. The first excavation, in advance of road building, had found a tantalizing layer of hard-packed stones but the second had found nothing at all.

A few weeks before we turned up to start our excavation, we had sent out our geophysics expert Dr Iain Banks to see if his boxes of tricks could reveal any signs of a buried road. Geophysics is a time-consuming process but Banksie steadily worked his way with his equipment over the locations we were interested in – three on farmland on the southern outskirts of Bannockburn, one next to a garden centre on the busy road leading to the visitors' centre and a third on ground close by the Bruce's statue.

The results from the farmland and the visitors' centre were inconclusive, but Banksie was suspicious about an anomaly in the field by the garden centre. We had been drawn to this location because the A872 road was roughly on the line of the Roman road as depicted on the OS map. It seemed reasonable to suppose that the two roads might be close together and following the same line. Banksie's machines were telling him that an approximately 6.5–7-metres-wide buried feature appeared to be running across the field beneath the grass. This was surely worth a look.

When we arrived on site, we lost no time in getting a mechanical digger to check out Banksie's 'linear anomaly' and it was with great expectations that we opened a trench orientated, we hoped, so that it would cut right across the buried feature. But a few hours' work revealed no more than a uniform spread of small rounded stones; frustratingly, there were none of the features we would expect of a Roman road. Such roads were designed and built by skilled engineers and tend to

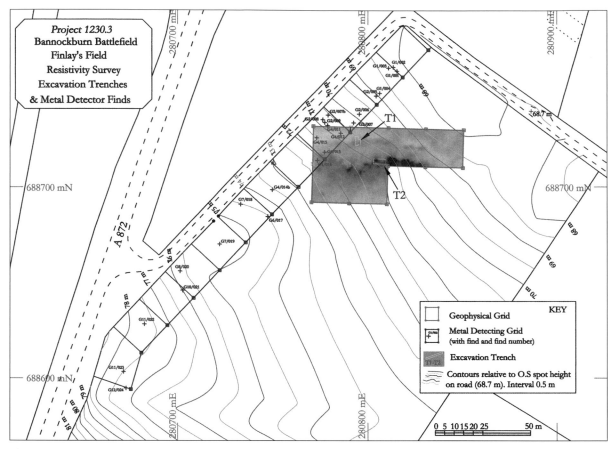

Geophysical survey of possible booby-trap pit

display a certain uniformity, normally having a drainage ditch on either side to keep the surface dry, and a slightly cambered surface, again to encourage water to run off it. We might even have expected large stones along either side, acting as a kerb and preventing the smaller stones of the compacted 'road-metal' from slipping into the parallel ditches. But we found none of that – all we were seeing was what looked like the stones of a river bed. It seemed that the geophysics equipment had been picking up what is called 'fluvio-glacial' material – the remains of ancient rivers created by glacial melt water that have long since dried up, leaving behind just the river-worn pebbles that the water once ran over. Banksie was at a loss to explain why his machines had indicated a band running in a

straight line. It was just one of those moments when people working with sophisticated equipment have to shrug their shoulders and move on.

Our fortunes were to change, ironically, when we turned our attentions to a field that Banksie and his crew had not been able to 'geophysic' because there had been a crop of wheat there, although Banksie had been able to consider the contours of the field from the road running alongside. He was keen to look at what lay beneath a couple of clearly visible terraces. Now that the crop had been harvested, rather than use up precious time with yet more geophysical survey we decided to bring in the mechanical digger. It's hard to imagine how archaeologists coped in the days before Mr Bamford invented his JCBs. Here we watched the machine open up some of the longest trenches we had ever used on any of our battlefield projects.

The first trench ran down the fairly steep slope of the field, cutting across the line of the level terraces that, we suspected, would have looked to any sensible Roman engineer like good surfaces on which to build a road. The first thing that caught our eyes, as we followed the machine's path and scrutinized every inch of the surface being revealed, was a spread of crushed coal that began about halfway along the trench and continued for some metres down the hill. We knew from our research that this whole area around Stirling had been subject to coal extraction in the eighteenth and nineteenth centuries, and our hunch was that our field had been part of that industry. As the machine progressed downhill, it began to reveal the topmost courses of masonry too, increasing our suspicions that we had indeed uncovered a site related to a long-deceased coal industry. When we began investigating these traces, however, we finally hit our equivalent of gold.

To ensure that we were exposing enough of the subsoil across the field to make our investigation thorough, we opened up a second trench a hundred metres or so across the field and a third down slope from the first – separated from it by a twenty-metre-long break. We also excavated test pits across the field with a view to assessing the presence or absence of archaeological remains. The second trench contained no trace of surviving archaeology, Roman or otherwise. The test pits revealed nothing of interest either and the third trench contained yet more traces of crushed coal. Where was the road?

The industrial remains were proving fascinating in their own right. As we exposed more and more of

Helen recording trenches near Bruce's monument

the masonry – by extending the trench using picks and shovels – a neat square platform appeared, approximately two metres on a side and surrounded by crushed coal. Content to leave these intriguing remains intact for future research by industrial archaeologists, we pressed on with our search for something rather older than buildings and structure related to an eighteenth- or nineteenth-century coalmine.

Eventually, our attention turned to the twenty-metre strip we had left unexcavated between trenches one and three. Having failed to find our road in any of the giant trenches we had already opened, we decided there was no way we were going to miss out on it for want of twenty metres' worth left undug. Having removed the plough soil on the last piece of the jigsaw, we began to see something that lifted our spirits: a rough line of large boulders. Further excavation revealed a spread of compacted stones. And we dared to allow ourselves to get truly excited when we spotted the dark, damp fill of ditches on either side of the hard stone surface. Now we had all the components we were looking for: the compacted stones were the 'road-metal', the line of large boulders was the remains of one supporting kerb (on the downhill side of the road) and the ditches on either outside edge were gutters for drainage. We had our road! It was wide enough, in the Roman tradition, to allow two wagons to pass in opposite directions and must have been the work of skilled builders for it to have survived so well. Further investigation of the compact surface revealed a third ditch, running up the centre of the road, which confused us until we realized that we were looking at evidence of a later remodelling of the road. It seemed that in a later period of the Roman occupation, engineers had decided that the traffic using the route was no longer heavy enough to justify a two-lane carriageway. The ditch had been dug to halve the width of the road and allow its continued use and maintenance as a single-lane route.

These road remains had been protected beneath the crushed coal. It seemed that, luckily for us, the development of the industry had preserved what we were looking for, while in every other part of the field we had looked at – and where there was no trace of coal working – centuries of ploughing had destroyed all sign of it. Sealed beneath the coal dust and the masonry rubble, a little island of the road used by Edward II and his army had survived. The surface we were standing on now was the same surface marched upon by an English army intent on driving away a rebellious Scottish host and relieving a castle.

The booby-trap pits

Every account of the battle you'll ever read describes the Scots' cunning creation of a medieval minefield to welcome their English guests. Barbour notes: 'And in an open field beside the road, where he thought the Englishmen would have to go if they wanted to move through the Park to the castle, he had many holes dug, a foot in diameter and all as deep as a man's knee, so thickly that they could be compared to a wax-comb that bees make. All that night he was working, so that before day he had made those holes, and had concealed them with sticks and with green grass, so that they could not really be seen.'

While much has been written about the pit traps, no one has ever managed to find them on the ground – and so it was to this challenge that we next turned our attentions. Discovery of the pits would give us the best evidence yet for the location of that first clash on the first day of the battle. In early February 2001 the *Mail on Sunday* published a fascinating aerial photograph, one of a series taken in 1984, which showed a cluster of dark, pit-shaped features in fields close by Pirnhall Farm. The accompanying story suggested that these were the pits created by the Bruce. The dark splodges in the picture seemed to us to be rather larger than the pits described by Barbour – in fact some looked big enough to bury a small car in – but we knew that only excavation would say one way or the other.

Banksie's geophysical survey in search of the Roman road had been partly on land belonging to Pirnhall Farm, and while his machines had drawn a blank there in search of the road, he had had more luck in hunting for booby traps. So noticeable on the ground were the depressions that had created the splodges in the photograph that, knowing of the coal mining in the area, he realized that he was looking at the tops of mine shafts. Knowing better than to risk life and limb by poking about in such features, perhaps causing subsidence, Banksie wisely decided to examine the features visible in one of the other aerial photographs in the 1984 series. This time, geophysical survey seemed to suggest the presence of two buried pits.

So we brought along our trusty mechanical excavator to see what was waiting to be seen. Sure enough, removal of the plough soil in the first trench we dug, followed by a careful clean-up with trowels, revealed a roughly circular, pit-like feature. It was well over one metre across, however, and therefore surely too large to be one of the Bruce's pits. In the second trench, it was a slightly different story, but no more encouraging: removal of the plough soil here exposed crumbly, sandstone bedrock just a few centimetres beneath the surface. Punched through this thin, gently sloping shelf of friable stone was a pit of a similar size to that in our first trench. Further excavation of both features did nothing to dissuade us of the conclusion that the pits were far too large to be part of the Bruce's defensive system – and too far apart to fit Barbour's

description of them being like a honeycomb. Grudgingly, we realized that we were looking at test holes dug by coal miners in search of workable seams. It wasn't the result we'd hoped for – but we had nonetheless proved that the tantalizing images on the aerial photographs were not the pits dug by the Scots.

The Bruce's headquarters

With the permission of the National Trust for Scotland to carry out a small-scale excavation, back at the visitors' centre Banksie and his team completed a geophysical survey on the open parkland to the south of the Pilkington Jackson statue of the Bruce – and produced some intriguing results. If the traditional story – that this had been the headquarters for the Scots – was accurate, we would expect the army to have left behind traces of their presence. We opened two separate trenches over anomalies that Banksie thought might prove to be the remains of temporary structures, camp fires and other evidence of the traces of hundreds or even thousands of men having camped out for several days.

It's impossible to carry out excavation on such a famous location, visited every day by hundreds of people, without attracting spectators. Human curiosity about holes in the ground never ceases to amaze us and every time we looked up from our labours, we would find a small audience politely and quietly looking on.

'Found any gold?' is a popular, good-natured inquiry, together with numerous invitations to dig sundry back gardens. But the interest is always encouraging – and can often enliven days that would otherwise be spent silently working on through the rain and the wind of a typical British summer. Paul Duffy, our dreadlocked

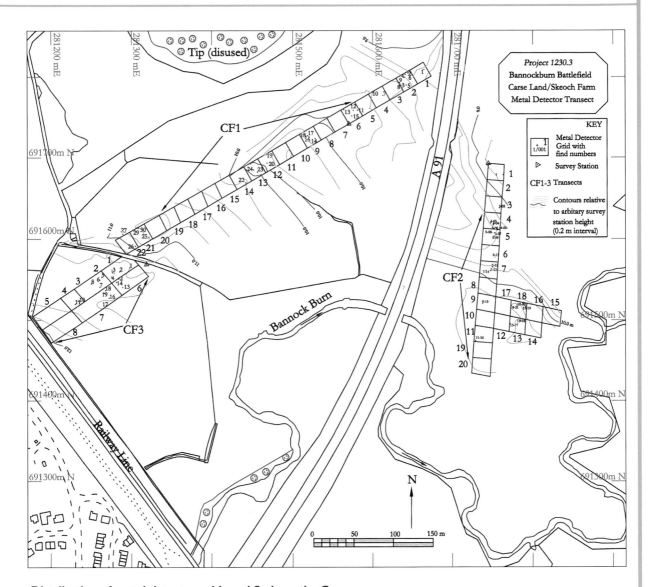

Distribution of metal-detector grids and finds on the Carse

colleague, was delighted on one occasion when an American couple recognized him from the television series. He was hard at work in one of the trenches at the visitors' centre when the pair rushed over to him – with a copy of our book in hand – and asked him to sign it for them. This almost never happens in the day-to-day life of a jobbing field archaeologist and it fairly gave him something to talk about in the pub that evening.

What we found was rather less conclusive than we

might have hoped. In one trench we recovered a single sherd of pottery with a distinctive green glaze on its surface. This was almost certainly medieval, but since it was not associated with any other telltale remains, it was impossible to say if it related to the events of June 1314. In the second trench, careful cleaning of the revealed subsoil with trowel and brush uncovered a shallow pit packed with small stones. This was a man-made feature, but it was too ephemeral for us to attribute it confidently to the Scottish camp. That there had been some kind of human activity up on this plateau at some time in the past was clear, but more intensive excavation than we had time for would be required to tell the full story of what had gone on.

Metal-detecting

In our bid to find the most likely location for the battlefield itself, in particular the site of the clash on day two, we had investigated the available evidence – the documents, maps and aerial photographs – and we'd decided to conduct fieldwork in four locations. Given the extremely large areas of ground, we called in a local metal-detecting society to help us search for the detritus of war. The location of fierce fighting would be determined by concentrations of weapon and armour fragments, together with personal items such as buttons and buckles ripped from clothes in hand-to-hand fighting, and coins spilled from purses.

When we began our investigation, there had not been a single documented find of metalwork related to the battle of Bannockburn, other than a battleaxe which regularly appears as a drawing in books on the battle. That in itself was odd, as every other battlefield we've investigated has been subject to years of ploughing and metal-detecting that have thrown up the occasional relevant find. And so it was with some trepidation that we began metal-detecting here.

The Carse of Stirling

On the flood plain of the river Forth, where several of the different locations for the climactic fight on 24 June have been suggested, our topographic surveyor John Arthur laid out two corridors of twenty-metre-square

A stirrup

grids stretching in long lines on either side of the modern road (the A91) that bisects the Carse. The ground here was horribly wet and sticky, and we sympathized with anyone on horseback or on foot who had to get across it with any kind of speed. The familiar 'bleeps' from the metal detectors were plentiful and soon there were the usual long lines of little brightly coloured pin-flags marking the signals stretching off as far as the eye could see. Once the metal-detector sweep was completed, we began to excavate carefully each of the many hundreds of signals. Given that we were on farmland, we expected to find a fair few tractor parts, bits of barbed wire and the like, but we could hardly have predicted the haul of junk we unearthed. Signal after signal revealed bottle caps, ring pulls, drinks cans, broken tools, batteries and every other kind of unhelpful rubbish you can imagine. We're used to this kind of material, of course – it's an inevitable component of every battlefield survey we undertake – but usually

A possible sword hilt

there's some cheering grain among the chaff. On the southern side of the road, however, there was not a single find relevant to the battle of Bannockburn.

The northern side told a depressingly similar story. The only finds that even briefly alleviated our increasing gloom were a few lead musket-balls. We knew that the area had seen many battles and skirmishes over the centuries, and it was likely that these bits of shot could be attributed to one of those. They certainly did not belong to any fighting between Scots and English troops in 1314.

Perhaps our experience diminished the likelihood of the second day of the battle of Bannockburn having taken place on this part of the Carse. A more likely conclusion, though, given the severely corroded nature of the modern ironwork we uncovered, was that any material that had been in this often sodden ground for the best part of seven centuries would have had very poor chances of survival. We suspected that we were in the right place, but that the relevant material had simply succumbed to the elements.

The Dryfield of Balquhidderock

The alternative site recently suggested as the location of the second day's fighting, known as the Dryfield of Balquhidderock, is an expanse of high ground some fifteen metres above the flood plain. It is separated from it visually by a strip of woodland hugging the steep slope. Although buildings have now obliterated the majority of the level ground, we were attracted by the self-contained, apparently undisturbed patches that served as an extension of the nearby school playing fields. This time, our metal-detector survey corridor was laid out by Paul Duffy.

As with the Carse, the ground here generated signals aplenty from our metal detectors. But when we started excavating them, a sadly familiar story began to unfold. With the ground being close to a school, we should have expected it, but nevertheless the sheer quantity of rubbish was truly depressing: ring pulls, foil wrappers and the rest of the kind of litter generally discarded by children was soon filling our collection bags.

On a lighter note, there was a surprising amount of loose change around, presumably pocket money dropped from trouser pockets. On one occasion, on turning up to check on progress, we asked a member of the metal-detecting team what had been found. 'Two pound seventy-five,' he replied.

But just when all hope was waning, one of the metal detectorists gave an excited shout. Running over to investigate, we found him holding up a rectangular block of rusted iron, about 10 centimetres long, 6 centimetres high and 3.5 centimetres deep. It was heavy – solid all the way through and seemingly undiminished by the corrosion showing on its outside surfaces. And something about the shape began to ring bells in our heads. With the suggestion of knobs at either end of the main rectangular body, and the worn stump of a possible point on its top, it had the look of the business end of a war hammer – or perhaps even the core of a battleaxe head. Men who have spent soul-destroying days in the rain putting scrap metal into bin bags can fall victim to the occasional flight of fancy, but we've had enough experience of this stuff to know a possible find when see it. It was carefully bagged and numbered, ready to be taken back to the laboratory for further investigation.

Broomridge

Still determined to find evidence of medieval fighting, we moved our metal-detecting squad on to a suspicious-looking gorse- and grass-covered knoll called

Broomridge. Not far from the Dryfield, it rose up beyond a development of modern houses facing east towards the Carse and the Ochil Hills, a patch of rough ground suitable for dog-walkers and courting couples.

John Arthur laid out a short corridor of grids to survey and we spent an afternoon investigating the

Broomridge in the teeth of a furious downpour of rain – and it is to our metal detectorists' eternal credit that they toughed it out with us without a word of complaint. The results here, however, were like those on the Carse and at the Dryfield. There was modern junk by the bagful, but not a single find that we could even tentatively attribute to the battle.

The 'Great Ditch'

There has been great speculation and debate by historians over the years concerning the location of the 'Great Ditch', the portion of the Bannock burn in which so many fleeing English soldiers were said to have met their deaths. The Bannock burn is, in the main, a gently flowing stream that meanders across the Carse to the river Forth, but there are places where the watercourse has cut deep into its bed and in effect created a 'great ditch'. These places are certainly much wider and deeper than the ditch you would expect to find running alongside the edge of a field, for instance. The most dramatic location, however, is the steeply sided ravine which cuts through the high ground away from the Carse for the best part of a mile between Beaton's Mill and Skeoch Mill.

We imagined that English troops fleeing down the precipitous slopes along this stretch of the burn – desperately trying to make it back towards the Roman road while fending off pursuing Scots – would have inevitably lost belongings here. We felt that it was worth deploying our metal-detector squads here to search for evidence.

Our grids in place, we sent the team out over the ground – and before long the area was strewn with pin-flags. All the signals proved to be rubbish, probably thrown down the slope from the private gardens at the top. The best our doughty squad could come up with was a couple of musket-balls and some possible grapeshot. On any other site we would have been delighted with these but here we were disappointed, for, like those on the Carse, they could probably be safely attributed to one of the later skirmishes in the Stirling area.

The stakes

Most of the artefacts we come across on battlefields are made of metal, which, like pottery and stone, tends to survive quite well under most conditions. It is much rarer to find organic artefacts, such as those made of wood, which tend to decay. Imagine our excitement, then, when we learned that the Bannockburn area appeared to be an exception to this rule, as wooden objects apparently related to the battle had been found there. An article in an archaeological journal reported the discovery in 1924 of wooden stakes by workmen while cutting a drain in Milton Bog. The wood had been preserved because it was in wet ground, in the bog, and damp conditions help to preserve wood from decay. The article suggested that the lengths of wood, which had sharpened tips, were stakes that had been set in the bottom of the pits dug by the Bruce's men along the edge of the Roman road. If this was so, it was great news, as it meant that if we excavated near the find spot we stood a good chance of finding more stakes and the pits in which they had been placed.

To our delight we learned that the stakes were still to be seen in the Smith Museum, in Stirling – so often finds made in the nineteenth and early twentieth centuries go missing over the years or never find their way into museums. We dashed off to see these tantalizing objects. The stakes occupy pride of place in the museum, laid out in a glass case in a section that displays all sorts of local archaeological finds. It was amazing to see the wood so well preserved, with the grain still visible, and each of the four pieces displayed a convincing point at the end. We couldn't help but wince at the thought of a horse and rider stumbling into a pit to be impaled on these frightening-looking spikes. And we became keener than ever to start excavating on Milton Bog.

First, though, we needed to find out more about the stakes in the museum. We asked our friend Dr Jennifer Miller, who is a palaeo-botanist – a specialist in the remains of ancient plants – to tell us what sort of wood the stakes were made from and identify any marks left by the tools used to sharpen them. The museum's curator, Elspeth King, kindly provided permission for her to remove a small sample from one stake so that we could send it off and get a radiocarbon date, which we hoped would prove that these were indeed the stakes used by the Bruce and his army to trap Edward's horsemen. We waited with high hopes while Jennifer carried out her examination. When she came to report her initial findings, we had a bit of a shock.

'They're not stakes,' she said.

'What?' we replied in unison.

Jennifer explained that the ends of the pieces of wood had not been sharpened at all: they were simply the pointed ends of tree roots, from the Scots pine.

'Fine', we said; at least they were wood, we thought.

Then came the sucker punch: 'They may be thousands of years old.' Obviously pleased with her announcement, she explained that the well-preserved remains of ancient Scots pine trees had been found in other parts of central Scotland, usually buried in peat.

We weren't going to take this sitting down. 'But the report clearly says that the pieces of wood were pointing upwards. Roots don't do that, surely?'

'Yes they do,' she replied. 'These trees have horizontal roots but also vertical anchorage roots.'

Our last hope rested with the dating sample, which had been sent to Florida. A couple of weeks later we got a reply from the lab. The roots were almost 7,000 years old! Jennifer had been bang on the money. This news meant that they were part of the great ancient forest that covered much of Scotland during the Mesolithic period after the melting of the glaciers about 10,000 years ago. To Jennifer's delight, the roots were the oldest known Scots pine roots in central Scotland. She dashed back to her office to begin work on a scientific paper on her discovery and we were left to ponder how we were going to break the news to Elspeth King. After all these years of the pieces of wood being displayed as the Bruce's stakes we had proved that they were nothing more than ancient tree roots.

As it happened, Elspeth took the news philosophically and was really interested in the results. She argued that the old date didn't discount the possibility that old wood may have been used as stakes by the Scottish soldiers at Bannockburn, although this seemed highly unlikely to us. We left Elspeth composing a new display panel. As for us – well, we never did dig holes in Milton Bog.

Conclusion

It is hard to admit defeat, but for us Bannockburn seemed to be a battle lost. Despite all our efforts, in some of the most terrible Scottish weather, we failed to recover a single artefact that we could attribute without doubt to the battle fought there in 1314. We found only a couple of heavily rusted pieces of metal, which we hope to have scientifically analysed, one of which we thought may have been a war hammer. On the basis of this disappointing result there are undoubtedly those who will claim that we were looking in the wrong place. In many cases we too would say that a total absence of finds indicates that we were looking in the wrong place. But at Bannockburn there are a number of factors to take into consideration before we use these results to start making claims about where the battlefield is or isn't.

First, even though we covered as much ground as we could, we managed to survey only a relatively small area within our overall target zones (on the Carse and up on the Dryfield). We may have just missed concentrations of finds quite close by to where we were searching – and there is certainly scope for more work here in the future. A slightly more depressing possibility is that the physical remains of the battle, in the form of metal objects, haven't survived. Having taken place almost 700 years ago, Bannockburn is by far the oldest battle we have ever investigated and it is possible that all those years have seen off any battlefield artefacts. Although metal usually survives well, it is not immune to decay. This is especially true of iron, from which most of the weapons would have been made. In the damp soils of the area – particularly on the Carse which is constantly being soaked by rain and then drying out – iron would rust and may decay to nothing relatively quickly, as evidenced by some of the more obviously modern finds we located. This doesn't of course explain the total absence of any non-iron objects, made from more decay-resistant metals such as copper alloys. Also, it has been argued by some that the soils of the Carse have been reduced through peat cutting – a process which, they contend, has removed the land surface that was there in 1314. This is possible, although the fact that we found musket-balls from the mid sixteenth century on the Carse suggests that any peat clearance took place in the relatively distant past.

The musket-balls were undoubtedly a highlight of our rain-sodden searches. It is certainly the first time we have ever found a battle that we didn't know had been fought! We have since learned that several skirmishes took place in and around Stirling during the final phases of the English Civil War. Stirling Castle was held by the Royalists for most of the period and the so-called battle of Stirling, which was really no more than a heavy skirmish, took place on 12 September 1648. That may well have been the fight that produced our musket-balls and grapeshot.

Another high point was the discovery of the Roman road beneath the remains of the old coal dump. It is perhaps ironic that the process of industrialization, along with the associated process of urbanization, which has destroyed so much, had in this case protected the road, which in all the other areas we searched had been destroyed by the farmer's plough.

Just, though, as this chapter was about to go to press and we had come to terms with not having found the battlefield, we enjoyed a pleasant surprise. In the pouring rain and at the very last minute our detectorists had bagged a couple of unpromising-looking pieces of rusted iron from the Carse. When these were cleaned up we beheld what we now believe to be a pair of medieval stirrups! (see page 48). Could these have belonged to the mounted men of the English heavy cavalry? Obviously two stirrups don't tell us any more than the fact that mounted men were here, and we are pretty sure that the English camped on the Carse, before perhaps fighting on the higher ground. But what is interesting is that the stirrups are broken and had been torn from their straps – which suggests violence. In addition, the grids from which this very exciting pair of finds originated were within a distinct bend in the course of the Bannock burn as it flows over the Carse, close to the spot where many maps mark the site of the battle. Here the stream sits at the bottom of a wide hollow and is itself several feet deep. It certainly wouldn't have been an easy obstacle for fleeing troops to negotiate, especially if they were weighted down with armour. Could these stirrups have been torn loose from the English cavalry in the mêlée as they made their desperate flight across the burn at the place known as the Great Ditch? The stirrups have since been added to by a possible broken sword hilt found close by (see page 49). This again did not come to light until we began working on our finds in the lab. The case for the site of the battlefield may still be open, but the evidence has definitely tipped in favour of the Carse. The scales tipped even further when we learned from an X-ray that the object from the higher ground, which we thought might have been a war hammer, was in fact nothing more than a plumber's clamp.

EDGEHILL 1642

EDGEHILL

ALL WARS ARE TRAGIC, BUT THERE IS
SOMETHING ESPECIALLY CRUEL ABOUT A
CIVIL WAR, WHERE LOYALTY AND
ALLEGIANCE TO ONE SIDE OR ANOTHER CAN
DIVIDE FAMILIES AND FRIENDSHIPS:
BROTHER FIGHTING BROTHER, OR FATHER
AGAINST SON, OR FORMER COMRADES
RANGED ON OPPOSING SIDES.

1642

Before the English Civil War broke out in 1642, Sir William Waller, who fought on the Parliamentarian side at the battle of Edgehill, was close friends with the renowned Royalist leader Sir Ralph Hopton. Although Hopton wasn't present at Edgehill, both men would later meet on several occasions as the commanders of opposing forces. Before the outbreak of war they had served together as soldiers at home and abroad. Indeed, as Members of Parliament they had supported the same side in the lead-up to the war; it was only when Parliament took control of the army that Hopton felt it had gone too far and thereafter he became a firm supporter of the king's cause.

We can gauge the strength of the two men's relationship, even after they had taken opposing sides, from a letter written by Waller to Hopton not long before the battle of Lansdown in July 1643. The letter is written in the rather difficult English of the time, but it is still a moving testimony to the power of friendship.

To my Noble friend Sir Ralphe Hopton at Wells
Sr
The experience I have of your worth, and the happinesse I have enjoyed in your friendship, are woundinge considerations when I look up this present distance between us. Certainely my affections to you are so unchangeable, that hostility itselfe cannot violate my friendship in your person, but I must be true to the cause wherein I serve; The ould limitation usque ad aras holds still, and where my conscience is interested, all other obligations are swalowed up. I should most gladly waite on you according to your desire, but that I looke upon you as you are ingaged in that partie, beyond a possibilitie of retraite and consequentlie uncapable of being wrought upon with any persuasion. And I know the conference could never be so close betweene us, but that it would take wind and receive a construction to my dishonour; That great God, which is the searcher of my heart, knows with what a sad sence I goe upon this service, and with what a perfect hatred I detest this warr without an

'I detest this warr without an Enemie'

Enemie, but I looke upon it as Opus Domini, which is enough to silence all passion in mee. The God of peace in his good time send us peace, and in the meane time fitt us to receive it: Wee are both upon the stage and must act those parts that are assigned us in this Tragedy: Lett us do it in a way of honor, and without personall animosities, Whatsoever the issue be, I shall never willingly relinquish the dear title of

Your most affectionate friend and faithfull servant
Wm Waller

After Lansdown, where Hopton's side gained the upper hand, the two generals were to meet in battle again, most notably at Cheriton, when it was Waller's turn to be the victor. Both men survived the war: Waller returned to his life as MP for Andover, while Hopton, being on the losing side, was less fortunate and spent the rest of his life in exile. Such are the fortunes of war.

How terrible it must be not only to go to war, but to fight against your friend. As two good friends it made our blood run cold even to imagine such a situation as we walked the hallowed ground of Edgehill.

1642

Sir William Waller

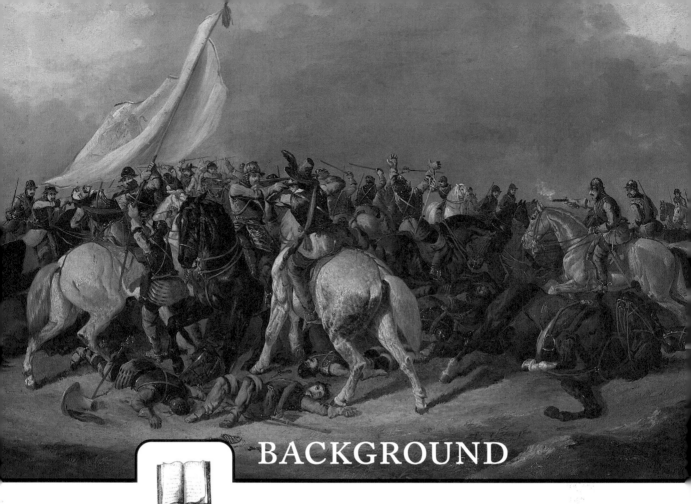

BACKGROUND

'A SUBJECT AND A SOVEREIGN ARE CLEAR
DIFFERENT THINGS.'

Charles I

KING CHARLES'S UNREPENTANT
DECLARATION – SPOKEN FROM THE
SCAFFOLD WHEN ALL WAS LOST – GOES
SOME SMALL WAY TOWARDS EXPLAINING
WHY ENGLAND ERUPTED IN CIVIL WAR. IT
WOULD BE WRONG, HOWEVER, TO SAY THAT
HE ALONE WAS TO BLAME. HISTORIANS
HAVE SPENT THE LAST 350-ODD YEARS
DISCUSSING THE CAUSES OF THE WAR –
WITH LITTLE AGREEMENT.

It can safely be said that religion, politics, economics, constitutional issues and clashes of personality all conspired to take the country over the brink. But even for a people as bloodied and scarred by centuries of intermittent fighting as this one, there was something unique about what happened when Crown and Parliament took up arms against one another – and herein lies the fascination that has obsessed so many writers.

For until the outbreak of the English Civil War, in 1642, the ethos behind the fighting had always been different. When for example the hopelessly outnumbered Scottish army took the field at Bannockburn in 1314, every man standing – from King Robert himself on the Scots side to the lowliest serf among the English – understood that the day would end with one or other king victorious. At the finish, it was all about the rights of one king over another. It was a battle fought along national lines with an agenda easily understood by its protagonists.

It is important to note, though, that the notion of 'civil' war was nevertheless not a new one. The Wars of the Roses in the fifteenth century were a civil war in all but name. And civil war would come again in the eighteenth century: the two Jacobite rebellions of 1715 and 1745–6 have been hijacked by those with an agenda rooted in Scottish nationalism – as though they were about Scots asserting their rights over English foes – but in truth they were more complicated affairs, with the armies on both sides counting Scots and English, Catholics and Protestants, among their ranks. They were never a straight fight between Scotland and England but, significantly, the right of the victorious leader to rule as king was taken for granted by the men on both sides.

Here then is the crux of the matter: what made the English Civil War so unusual was that it was not about two sides vying for the throne and the kingdom; as matters drew to their conclusion, it became a fight to decide whether the monarchy – and one particular monarch – should exist at all.

In 1640 a welter of political, economic, religious and constitutional troubles brought to an end an eleven-year period during which Charles I had ruled without a parliament. Nothing unusual there, unthinkable though this sounds to us today when the democratic process is taken for granted. Kings and queens had summoned parliaments only when they wanted money for a war or for some other extravagant expense. Indeed it was commonplace for years to go by without the monarch feeling the need – let alone the obligation – to consult the rich and powerful lords and landowners who comprised the members of the two Houses. When Charles had dissolved his last parliament in 1629, he was so unimpressed

What made the English Civil War so unusual was that it was not about two sides vying for the throne; it became a fight to decide whether the monarchy should exist at all

with proceedings that he had specifically forbidden anyone even to think about calling for another one to sit at any time in the foreseeable future.

Charles would not have ascended the throne in 1625 after the death of his father, James I of England and VI of Scotland, had it not been for the untimely death of his elder brother Henry, Prince of Wales, in 1612. Charles was said to lack the charisma of his sibling. Weak of mouth and chin, slight of figure, delicate in his movements and unusually fastidious in his personal habits, he lacked physical presence. He also had an unfortunate talent for intrigue and double-dealing that made him hard to believe and even harder to trust.

Opposite **Charles I**

But the character trait that was to cause him most trouble was his stubborn refusal to heed the opinions of others on how he should rule his kingdom. Charles had been taught by his father that he owed a double debt to God: first, that he had made him a man; and second, that he had made him 'a little God' to sit on a throne and rule over other men. Above all, he was utterly and implacably opposed to any suggestion that Parliament – a collection of often self-interested gentry rather than the elected representatives of today – should have any real say in how he should govern.

Another spoon stirring the pot was that of religion. Charles was accused by many of favouring Catholics, but except for the undoubted affection he had for his devout Catholic wife, Henrietta Maria, he was resolutely faithful to the Church of England. In a country with a strong Puritan element, however, his fondness for ritual and ceremonial was enough to raise the spectre of Rome in the hearts of many influential observers. James I had reintroduced bishops to Scotland – potentially troublesome enough – and Charles inflamed matters further when, in 1637, he and Archbishop Laud sought to introduce a new Prayer Book north of the border as well.

The National Covenant was signed in Scotland in 1638, bringing the rule of the Church there by bishops to an end. Charles attempted to force the issue and the Scots duly raised an army under Sandy Leslie, a tough professional soldier who had learned his skills fighting on the Continent. Although Charles proposed an invasion to quell the rebellious Scots, it never happened. Still smarting from the pain of not getting his own way, he enlisted as his new commander Thomas Wentworth, Earl of Strafford, who had been running the show in Ireland as Charles's Lord Lieutenant. Earlier in his career, Strafford had been an opponent of the king, but he had enraged his former allies by changing allegiance and siding with the throne for, at least as they saw it, personal gain. He ruffled yet more

feathers on his return to England: by taking the title of Earl of Raby, he mortally offended Sir Henry Vane, owner of Raby Castle. And so it was said that Sir Henry and his son began – or at least perpetuated – a whispering campaign that suggested Strafford's Irish army was to be used not for the purposes of whipping the Scots back into line but for showing the English Puritans who was boss. So when Charles summoned a parliament in 1640 to raise money to prosecute his war in Scotland, he got short shrift. In an atmosphere of mutual distrust, Parliament refused point-blank to meet the king's demands for cash without his agreement to long-term reform of the monarchy. The temperature rose by a few more degrees yet.

Despite lacking the necessary financial backing for a realistic campaign in the north, Charles pressed on bloody-mindedly and assembled what force he could. Charles's commander-in-chief was the Earl of Arundel, but his rather more able lieutenant-general was Robert Devereux, Earl of Essex, who would in time command Parliament's army against the king at Edgehill. The royal army faced the Scots in a disastrous clash at Newburn, near Newcastle upon Tyne, and was quickly sent packing. Not content with bloodying the king's nose, the Scots demanded that Charles pay for the day-to-day costs of keeping the army in the field until an agreement had been reached over Church affairs. Already cash-strapped, the king had no option but to go cap in hand to Parliament once more. This was the so-called Long Parliament – in contrast to the Short Parliament that had preceded it – which would not be formally dissolved for twenty years. Its dominant figures saw that they now had a strong hand of cards with which to play.

Those with a grudge against Strafford took this opportunity to turn on him and he was taken to the Tower of London. Initially and unsuccessfully threatening him with impeachment, his foes finally got him to the scaffold by forcing Charles to put his name to an Act of Attainder – an ancient legal process that essentially found Strafford guilty of high treason without the time-consuming inconvenience of requiring his accusers to present any formal evidence of the crime. Guilt stemming from his complicity in what he knew to be a falsehood was to torture Charles ever after. How could he claim divine rule after he had ordered the execution of an innocent man? Charles would later suggest that his downfall was retribution for what he had allowed to happen to Strafford.

Events gathered pace. Hardliners in Parliament pressed on determinedly to secure the reform of royal power they felt was long

The Earl of Essex

The king raises his standard at Nottingham

overdue; and the Triennial Act was passed, stating that Parliament should sit at least once every three years and, furthermore, that it could not be dissolved without its own consent. Trouble flared in Ireland in October 1641, with a Catholic revolt against the Puritan lords justice who enforced English rule there. More anti-Royalist propaganda back home whispered that the king was somehow behind the rebellion, which left hundreds of Protestants dead. Next, Parliament presented Charles with the Grand Remonstrance, a cunningly crafted list of grievances that attempted to pass itself off as constructive criticism.

Provoked beyond endurance – as he saw it – Charles attempted one last show of strength to regain the upper hand. On 4 January 1642 he gatecrashed the House of Commons with 300 troops, intent on arresting those whom he considered to be his most offensive opponents, among them John Pym, who had introduced the Grand Remonstrance. But,

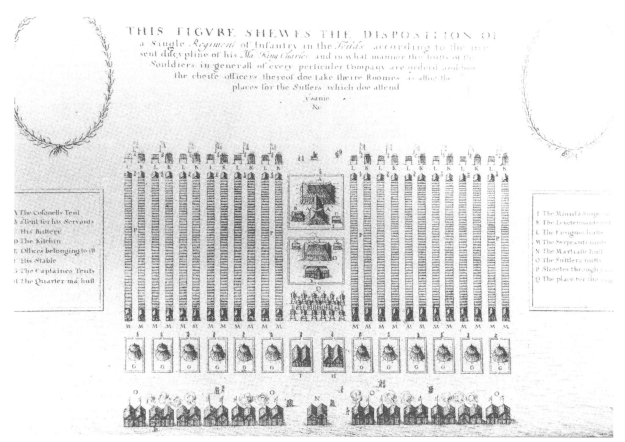

Infantry regiment of the king's army

forwarned of the king's plan, they were already in hiding in the City. On 6 January, fearing that the king was about to descend upon the City with an armed force, the populace shut the gates and took to the streets with whatever weapons they could lay their hands on. Charles fled the capital on 10 January, never to return there as a ruling monarch.

In the following months, both sides hardened in their resolve until, on 22 August, the king raised his standard at Nottingham. High winds promptly blew it down – an ill omen indeed, and one not lost on his supporters, although Charles merely intended to stay there for as long as it took to gather an army before marching on London to reclaim his throne and his country. He appealed to the population to ignore the proclamations of a parliament he himself no longer recognized – and indeed those members who felt their more hard-nosed colleagues had gone too far travelled north to side with their king. In time-honoured fashion, Charles set about raising an army by issuing 'commissions of array', the largely outmoded practice that empowered named nobles to gather fighting men together in readiness for war.

Parliament stuck to its guns and began raising its own force. It sweetened the pill of rising in defiance of the throne by declaring that those who fought with Parliament fought to free the king from the troublesome and harmful hands into which he had unwittingly fallen – a line Parliamentarians were to trot out repeatedly during the early years of the war.

Volunteers gradually rallied to both causes. Young men harbouring dreams of heroism and derring-do – and uncorrupted by the realities of killing and dying – stepped up to fight, as young men always do. Those of a religious nature – armed with a fervour more commanding than any earthly political or economic motivation – stepped up too. As the preparations for war progressed, numbers were swollen by those who chose to fight for pay or who were pressed into service against their will.

At a practical level, Parliament held some aces. It controlled the nation's principal arsenals in London and Hull, which gave it an instant advantage over Charles, who was initially dependent upon the private armouries of his supporters, which were of inconsistent quality and a finite resource. Lack of money too was to be an enduring problem for Charles. For supplementary weapons and supplies, the Royalists had to import from the Continent – and that was a problem too: from the very outset, the Royal Navy threw in its lot with Parliament, so it would always be a tricky business for the Royalists to land vessels friendly to their cause.

By September 1642 both armies, largely amateur and volunteer though they were, had recruited a smattering of trained soldiers to add a bit of professional backbone. With both forces on the move now – each with an obvious objective – a meeting to test one another's mettle was just a question of time.

Parliament stuck to its guns and began raising its own force in defiance of the throne

THE BATTLE

'O LORD! THOU KNOWEST HOW BUSY I MUST
BE THIS DAY: IF I FORGET THEE, DO NOT
THOU FORGET ME.'

Prayer recited by Sir Jacob Astley as he led the
Royalist troops into battle at Edgehill

ONCE CHARLES HAD RAISED HIS STANDARD
AT NOTTINGHAM, AN OBVIOUS OBJECTIVE
FOR HIS ARMY WAS LONDON, WHICH WAS
HELD BY PARLIAMENT. A PRIORITY FOR
THE PARLIAMENTARIAN ARMY, THEREFORE,
WAS TO PUT ITSELF BETWEEN THE
ROYALISTS AND THE CAPITAL, AND IT IS
CLEAR THAT AT THIS EARLY STAGE
EVERYONE EXPECTED THE WAR TO BE
SETTLED IN ONE DECISIVE BATTLE.

Both sides were slow to move, however, with the king busy recruiting in the Midlands and the Earl of Essex, the Parliamentarian commander, dithering in London for a full three weeks.

By 22 October the Royalist forces were at Edgecote, near Banbury, while the main Parliamentarian army was at Kineton, just eight miles to the north-west. The two sides literally bumped into one another when Royalist quartermasters looking for lodgings in the village of Wormleighton came across their Parliamentarian counterparts doing exactly the same thing and captured them. Discovering that Essex's army was at Kineton, the king was eager to do battle as soon as possible. In preparation, the Royalist army began to array itself on the high ground of Edgehill during the early hours of 23 October, spreading out along the ridge which dramatically overlooks the rolling plain below. Meanwhile the Parliamentarian army, which was still awaiting the arrival of some of its troops, including a cavalry troop led by an as yet untested Oliver Cromwell, began to deploy on the plain to the north-west of Edgehill. Before any battle could take place, however, it was apparent that the Royalists would have to come down from the high ground, as there was no way their opponents would tackle them while they held this commanding position. For purely propaganda reasons, it was in the Parliamentarians' best interests to let the Royalists make the first aggressive move; it also suited them to wait, as every passing hour brought more of Essex's scattered army on to the field. Obligingly, the Royalist army, encumbered by its heavy artillery train, made its way down the steep slope of Edgehill and formed up on the edge of the plain, just to the north-west of Radway village.

The plain across which the two armies faced one another, at a distance of just over half a mile, was relatively open across the middle but hemmed in on either side by fields surrounded by hedges and ditches. This enclosed ground was most extreme on the Royalist left and caused some difficulty for the advance of the king's cavalry positioned on that wing, under the command of Lord Wilmot. The Royalist cavalry on the right was commanded by the dashing Prince Rupert, with the infantry brigades, each made up of between three and five regiments, under the commands of Henry Wentworth, Richard Fielding and John Belasyse, from left to right, positioned to the front and Sir Nicholas Byron's and Charles Gerard's staggered behind them. As a result of an unseemly row over deployment tactics, the overall Royalist infantry commander, the Earl of Lindsey, resigned from his post and fought the battle at the head of his own regiment – a decision that would cost him his life. The role of

Oliver Cromwell

commander-in-chief was taken by Patrick Ruthven, Earl of Forth. The Royalist artillery consisted of fourteen light guns, which were probably positioned between the brigades, and six heavy pieces set back in the rear, probably not far from Radway at the foot of the slope.

The Parliamentarian infantry was drawn up in two lines, with the brigades of Sir John Meldrum and Colonel Charles Essex in the centre, the former supported by a second line of Ballard's infantry and the latter by Stapleton's and Balfour's horse. The right wing was occupied by Lord Fielding's cavalry regiment, supported on its left by two regiments of dragoons. The left wing was taken by Sir James Ramsey, whose twenty-four troops of horse were supported by 600 musketeers drawn from Ballard's second-line brigade. Half the musketeers were placed between the cavalry squadrons, where it was hoped they would break up any Royalist charge, while the other half were positioned behind hedges at right angles to the line in order to provide enfilading fire into the flank of any enemy advance. The Parliamentarian cannon were probably positioned between bodies of troops in the front line.

The Royalists' deployment took several hours, giving the Parliamentarians plenty of time to note their disposition and act accordingly. The Parliamentarians picked their ground well, placing their centre behind a ploughed field, where the soft earth would prevent cannonballs from bouncing into their lines. Although the ground on the plain looks fairly level when viewed from the ridge, there is actually a subtle incline which rises up from the base of the hill to where the Parliamentarians were positioned. Once the Royalists moved off the high ground, the topography denied them an overall view of the enemy disposition and removed the rear ranks, over the crest of the slope, from view entirely. Although the Parliamentarian army was not complete, it is thought that the two armies each comprised about 14,000 men.

The first phase of the battle was a rather ineffective artillery duel, which went marginally in favour of the Parliamentarians. The artillery fire seems to have goaded Prince Rupert to come on with his cavalry, charging Ramsey's horse on the left of the Parliamentarian line. Ramsey's men waited to receive the Royalists at the halt, firing their weapons into the mass of the oncoming enemy. Attempts to deflect the charge with musketry failed, however, with the musketeers on the flank being cleared out of the hedges by Rupert's dragoons, and the Royalists quickly managed to turn the Parliamentarian left wing, both infantry and cavalry. Ramsey's plight was not helped by the treachery of the inappropriately named Sir Faithful Fortescue, who at a pre-arranged

Opposite **Prince Rupert**

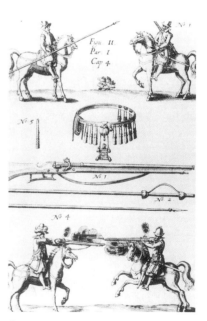

Dragoons

signal defected to the Royalist side with his entire troop of horse. Rupert's cavalry, followed by their reserve from the King's Life Guard, pursued the Parliamentarian horse into Kineton, but by failing to regroup they effectively removed themselves from the battle.

On the Royalists' left wing Wilmot's horsemen had to negotiate terrain broken by hedges and ditches, but still managed to get the better of their Parliamentarian counterparts, quickly putting to flight both Lord Fielding's horse and Fairfax's infantry. Wilmot had more success than Rupert in reining in his men and so kept some useful elements on the field.

The Royalist infantry began its advance at about the same time as the cavalry. Both Royalist lines went forward as one, with Byron's and Gerard's brigades moving up to fill the gaps between the front three brigades. At this point things did not look good for the Parliamentarians, with both their right and left wings either routed or in disarray. It was largely thanks to the two intact but small bodies of horse commanded by Stapleton and Balfour, and the departure of the Royalist cavalry, that the Parliamentarian lines were not completely broken. As the Royalist infantry came into contact with the Parliamentarian infantry, the remaining Parliamentarian cavalry units went into action, surging through gaps in their own lines. This immediately put the attacking Royalist foot on the defensive. Byron's brigade put up a fierce fight in the face of Stapleton's marauding horsemen and thanks to their discipline and the effectiveness of their pike formation they remained unbroken. But Balfour's horse met with more success, smashing through the rear of Richard Fielding's brigade and scattering them in the direction of Edgehill. Fielding himself was temporarily captured. Leaving the shattered Royalist infantrymen in their wake, Balfour's men then galloped to the Royalist rear, where they cleared the gunners away from the heavy battery and, lacking nails to plug or 'spike' the touch-holes to render the guns unusable, satisfied themselves with cutting their traces.

By now the infantry had come to 'push of pike', a polite-sounding term for the brutal business of pike-on-pike combat. The shafts of the pikes meshed, their points driving into the mass of the enemy as each side tried to break open the other's formation. On the Parliamentarian side, Ballard's brigade was heavily engaged with Belasyse and Gerard on the Royalist right, while Essex called on the second-line brigades under Robartes and Constable to assist Stapleton's and Balfour's cavalry, the latter freshly returned from their attack on the Royalist battery, in the continued assault on Byron's brigade. The fighting was fierce and turned in favour of the Parliamentarian force when the king's standard was

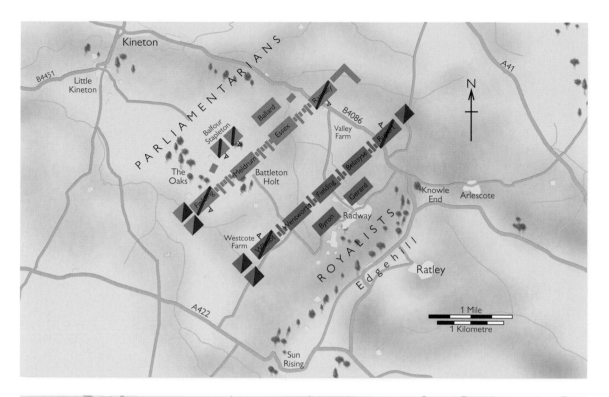

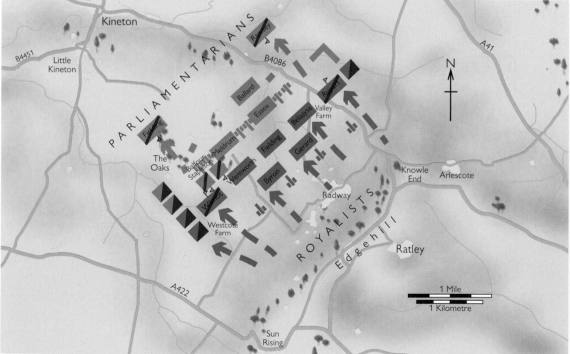

Movement of troops during the battle of Edgehill superimposed on a modern map

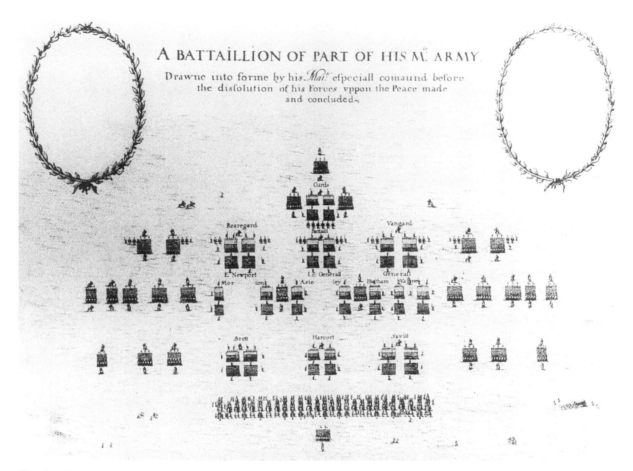

The battle deployment

captured: its bearer, Sir Edmund Verney, was cut down but, as Sir Edward Sydenham tells us, only after he had 'killed two with his own hands; whereof one had killed poor Jason [his servant] and broke the point of his standard at push of pike before he fell ...' It is said that the only part of this brave soldier to be recovered after the battle was his severed hand, still attached to the standard.

The king's standard did not remain in the possession of the enemy for long, for it was recovered by a heavily outnumbered Captain John Smith before the Parliamentarians had a chance to take it to the rear. Smith's disregard for his own safety also led him to rescue Richard Fielding. There were other acts of valour played out in the chaos of the Royalist rout. The Earl of Lindsey, who had resigned command of the army at the battle's outset, was wounded. According to King Charles's son James, who accompanied his father on the campaign with his brother Charles

The battle of Edgehill

and wrote an account of the battle after he became James II, Lindsey's son found his father 'lying in the front of his own regiment with one leg broken by a musket shot', and an attempt to rescue him coinciding with 'the charge of the enemy's horse, so that it was impossible to carry him off, he stood undauntedly with his pike in his hand bestriding his father, and in that posture wounded one of their captains in the face, and almost pushed him off his horse, but his own men at the same time giving back, he was left engaged in the midst of the enemy, choosing rather to be taken with his father, that so he might be in a condition of rendering him what service was in his power, than to save himself by leaving him in that distress'. The sacrifice was in vain and Lindsey died of his wounds.

On the Royalists' left wing, Wentworth's brigade had come through thus far without much of a struggle, and with the maelstrom whirling around Byron's brigade they left the field in good order to clear the field of fire for their recaptured guns. A fusillade of case-shot, and assaults from those Royalist cavalry units still on the field, allowed a

disengagement and general withdrawal of the Royalist line. Those units which had not been scattered during the battle, largely consisting of Gerard's and Belasyse's brigades, re-formed along a line between the Kineton road and Radway, centred in the vicinity of King's Leys Barn, where a stand-off with the Parliamentarian line was established.

The later stages of the battle had become confused and disengagement must have been a priority for both sides. Hand-to-hand fighting had been raging across the lines for nearly three hours and the onset of darkness removed any possibility of a breakthrough. Both armies re-formed to resume battle the next day, but neither side had the will and orders were given for the Royalists to retire to Edgecote, while the Parliamentarians returned to nearby Kineton.

The inexperience of both armies and the failure of command had reduced the battle of Edgehill to a chaotic struggle short on strategy. The result was inconclusive, but history has given victory to the king's army, despite the fact that at the end of the day they left the enemy in possession of the field. Despite their tenacity in the later phases of the battle, it was the Parliamentarians who had suffered the heaviest blow, losing far too many men during the initial phases of the battle. The total casualty figures are uncertain, but are estimated to be a combined total of about 1,500, with even greater numbers wounded. Many more battles would be fought before the English Civil War came to an end.

Opposite **Sir Thomas Fairfax**

Hand-to-hand fighting had been raging across the lines for nearly three hours

WHO FOUGHT HERE

BEFORE THE OUTBREAK OF THE ENGLISH
CIVIL WAR THERE HAD BEEN NO MAJOR
ARMED CONFLICT IN ENGLAND FOR A
CENTURY, AND CERTAINLY NOT ONE WHICH
COULD BE CALLED A WAR. THE DEATH OF
HENRY VIII IN 1547 MARKED THE END OF
LARGE-SCALE ENGLISH INVOLVEMENT IN
WARFARE ON THE CONTINENT,
PARTICULARLY AGAINST THE FRENCH, AND
OF THE BOUTS OF VIOLENT CONFLICT THAT
HAD FOR CENTURIES DIVIDED THE ENGLISH
AND THE SCOTS, CLIMAXING WITH THE
DECISIVE ENGLISH VICTORIES AT FLODDEN
IN 1513 AND AT PINKIE IN 1547, WITH
MINIMAL OUTBREAKS OF VIOLENCE UNTIL
THE BISHOPS' WARS BETWEEN THE SCOTS
AND ENGLISH IN 1639.

One result of this extended period of peace was a drastic reduction in the number of British males experienced in warfare and the practicalities of combat: long gone were the days when it was a legal requirement for Englishmen to be trained in the use of the bow.

But this is not to say that England had become a nation of pacifists – far from it. The late medieval tradition of communities fielding their own local militia, a sort of forerunner of today's Territorial Army, was still maintained, although few militiamen had encountered real danger since the dark days of the Spanish invasion threat, which passed with the destruction of the Armada in 1588. By the time of the Civil War these militia were known as trained bands, the best equipped and motivated of which were probably those in London. At the outbreak of war the London bands were some 6,000 strong and provided the backbone of the Parliamentarian army. A problem with all the trained bands, though, was their reluctance to fight away from their local area, the majority regarding their function as home defence. Cromwell was to overcome this problem when he established his New Model Army.

In the earlier years of his reign Charles had sent unsuccessful expeditions against the Spanish and supported the French Huguenots in their rebellion against their Catholic king. Indeed, the political and religious instability of Europe provided the climate for civil war in Britain. From the middle of the sixteenth century religion had been a major cause of conflict on the Continent, but it was often a flag of convenience which fluttered over a volatile mix of political ambition, ethnic animosity, territorial expansionism and economic pragmatism, all of which combined to make a surefire recipe for warfare.

England, and Britain as a whole, may have lacked a professional army but it did not lack professional soldiers. This was the age of the mercenary, and many of the military commanders who came to prominence in the English Civil War had previously served abroad. They had fought for various foreign powers during the Thirty Years War, a brutal conflict which raged on and off between 1618 and 1647. The Earl of Essex, commander of the Parliamentarian army at Edgehill, had served in the Dutch army, as had the Royalist Earl of Lindsey, while the Parliamentarian Sir William Waller had fought with the Venetian army against the Habsburgs and then gone on to serve in Bohemia, where along with his Royalist friend Hopton he had assisted in the rescue of James I's daughter, Elizabeth, wife of the Elector Frederick V of the Palatinate. Shortly afterwards Elizabeth gave birth to a son, Prince Rupert of the Rhine, and in one of the many cruel strokes of fate that

At the outbreak of war the London bands were some 6,000 strong and provided the backbone of the Parliamentarian army

Training instructions

1642

accompanied the Civil War, Rupert, who had seen plenty of military service by then, and his saviour, Waller, fought on opposite sides at Edgehill.

Nor was it just gentlemen and the high-born who served overseas. English regiments were employed by Catholic Spain and France and also by Protestant Sweden, the latter being particularly popular with the Scots. The strictly Protestant states of Holland, headed by a dynasty that was to favour the king during the Civil War, employed four English and four Scottish regiments of foot. This willingness to fight for either side during the Thirty Years War may have been a foretaste of things to come.

So, despite the fact that many soldiers in the Royalist and Parliamentarian armies were inexperienced at the outbreak of war, with trained bands representing the bulk of the fighting force, a number of the senior officers and other ranks had experienced combat on various occasions. Just as importantly, this small elite had also learned much about the latest innovations in strategy and tactics which had evolved on the Continent during the Thirty Years War. This was an important period in the history of warfare and some historians have even gone so far as to say that the first half of the seventeenth century witnessed a military revolution.

THE MUSKET

The half-century before the Civil War saw real advances in the development of firearms, which were fast becoming the most important battlefield weapon. At the start of the Thirty Years War the musket was a heavy, cumbersome weapon, which required support on a forked staff, so loading and firing was a tricky operation. The weapon was introduced by the Spanish in the late sixteenth century, and the one advantage of its bulk was that it was capable of firing a heavy, two-ounce ball which could deliver a devastating blow even against armour. During the first half of the seventeenth century the Swedes replaced this heavy weapon with a lighter version which did not require support from a staff, thus greatly aiding the loading process and increasing the rate of fire from about one round a minute to two. This new musket fired a 1-ounce or 1.2-ounce ball. Twelve of the latter could be made from a pound of lead – hence the term twelve-bore, which is still used as a designation for a shotgun gauge.

Muskets at this time worked on the matchlock principle, based on a cord fuse or match, which burned constantly but slowly throughout a battle. The match was mounted in a moving lever mechanism called a serpent. When the trigger was pulled the cock dropped into the priming pan and the burning end of the match ignited the powder in it, and this in turn, via the touch-hole, set off the powder inside the breech against which the ball had been rammed. The resulting explosion inside the breech forced the ball up through the barrel and out of the muzzle.

A disadvantage of matchlocks was their susceptibility to dampness, which made them useless in the rain. This problem was partly overcome by the introduction of the flintlock or firelock, which instead of a match used a flint to provide a spark. The flint-lock gained in popularity during the course of the Civil War, but at Edgehill the majority of muskets were matchlocks.

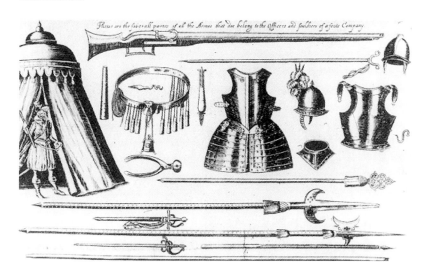

Details of infantry arms

The wheellock was another type of firearm in use at the time. It employed a key-wound spring to spin a steel wheel against a lump of iron pyrites to produce a spark, but it was expensive, difficult to repair and prone to misfires.

The inside surface of the musket barrel was smooth, not spiralled or rifled as became the norm during the nineteenth century. Rifling puts spin on a bullet, thus ensuring a long, straight flight, whereas a bullet fired from a smooth-bore weapon quickly drops and may even fly off at a slight tangent. Small numbers of rifled weapons were available, but they were very expensive and they were usually privately owned hunting weapons or fowling pieces; in experienced hands they made effective sniping weapons. As it was a smooth-bore weapon, the musket was generally not aimed at a specific target but simply pointed in the direction of the enemy. When many muskets were pointed at a massed body of the enemy at a relatively short range of no more than forty-five metres or so, aiming became an irrelevance: by the simple law of averages, enough bullets would find a target.

THE PIKE

Despite their increasing efficiency, firearms still had some way to go before they entirely dominated the battlefield. The other mainstay of the infantryman was the pike, which had been in general service in most European armies since its introduction by the Swiss in the late fifteenth century, having evolved from the shorter spear carried by the medieval foot-soldier. The standard pike was between 4.5–5.5 metres long; but as cavalrymen abandoned the lance in favour of the pistol in the mid sixteenth century, the pike could be shortened, as there was no longer a need for it to be longer than the attacking lance, and obviously no pike, whatever its length, could repel a pistol shot. Some troops adopted pikes as short as 3.5 metres as at this length they were easier to handle and transport. It was usually the tallest, strongest men who were selected to

'Hedgehogs' of pikemen at
Edgehill

carry the pike, known as the 'queen of weapons', and on the grounds of the skill required in its use it was regarded as superior to the cumbersome and smelly musket.

The pike was initially a very important offensive weapon and the outcome of most battles was decided at the 'push of pike', when opposing massed formations of pikemen went point to point. At times this could be rather like a rugby scrum, with the winning team simply pushing the weaker side back until they broke formation. At the Scottish battle of Langside in 1568, it was reported that the pikemen on both sides were so heavily armoured that the pikes inflicted little damage and the two solid walls of pikemen prevented units in the rear from coming to handstrokes. The rear ranks had to satisfy themselves with throwing broken weapons and stones over the heads of their own pikemen, and many of these missiles did little more than come to rest on the interlocked raft of pikes between the armies.

By the end of the English Civil War the pike had largely become a defensive weapon, serving to protect the musketeers from cavalry attack. In battles where experienced and efficient musketeers were deployed, it became rarer for push of pike to occur. At the beginning of the century the standard ratio between musketeers and pikemen was 1 : 1, but by the time of the war the ratio was nearer 2 : 1. Where musketeers were not so well practised, as would have been the case at Edgehill at the beginning of the war, the pike still served an important offensive role and was capable of deciding the outcome of a battle.

The Thirty Years War provided tactical and technological innovation for British soldiers serving in foreign armies. At Edgehill the Royalists – after a bitter row between their senior officers – selected the Swedish method of deployment, while their opponents employed the Dutch system. Of the two systems, the Dutch was the simpler. Whereas the Swedish system had very large bodies of men organized by regiment into brigades in arrowhead or diamond formations, the Dutch used smaller bodies of men, of regiment strength, in a more straightforward block arrangement. The Parliamentarian troops, in the Dutch style, were probably about eight ranks deep, with each regiment's pikemen flanked by its musketeers. The arrangement of the Royalist brigade, or tercio, was less simple, however, with pikemen to the front and centre and musketeers arrayed on the flanks, at the rear and behind the front body of pikes.

The Dutch style worked better for troops of limited experience. The Swedish system required large numbers of trained officers to maintain

The pike was initially a very important offensive weapon and the outcome of most battles was decided at the 'push of pike'

order, and the success of the Parliamentarians in breaking up several Royalist regiments in the thick of the fight was probably due to the inability of the king's troops to maintain their complex formation under battle conditions. The fact that the Royalists were also attacked by cavalry who appeared from between the opposing infantry regiments didn't help either: this interleaving of infantry and cavalry, rather than keeping the horse exclusively on the wings, was another feature of the Dutch system.

CAVALRY

Controversies within the Royalist high command aside, Prince Rupert's Royalist cavalry were to fight an impressive, if imperfect, battle at Edgehill. Rupert, having served as a cavalry officer in the Thirty Years War, was well acquainted with the various fashions of combat. The adoption of the pike and musket by infantry caused problems for cavalry, as both weapons effectively prevented close-quarter combat. No longer could the cavalry, with the advantages of speed, weight and height, simply charge into masses of foot-soldiers. One way to counter the threat of bullets and pike points was the use of armour. There were two principal types of cavalry at the time. One was the cuirassier, who wore substantial armour, including helmet, usually with visor, breast- and backplate, pauldrons to cover the shoulders, and tassets to protect the legs down to the knees. Although cuirassiers fought at Edgehill, they became a less frequent sight as the war progressed, as the armour was cumbersome and expensive. The commonest type of cavalryman was the arquebusier, named after the arquebus or short musket (carbine). This soldier opted for lighter armour, perhaps limited to an open helmet and breast- and backplate, usually worn over a buff coat of heavy hide. A third type of mounted soldier, not strictly classed as cavalry, was the dragoon: he was essentially a foot-soldier who used a horse to get into battle, then did most of his fighting while dismounted.

The abandonment of the lance and the adoption of firearms were the main developments in cavalry warfare during the late sixteenth and early seventeenth centuries. All cavalrymen carried firearms of some description, usually a pair of pistols in holsters either side of the saddle and an arquebus, while the dragoon who fought on foot may have carried a standard musket before these were replaced by the carbine. These firearms were usually of the wheellock or flintlock type, as matchlocks were too impractical on horseback. The sword was another favoured weapon, and at Edgehill it probably played as much of a role as the

The attack on the baggage train

firearms, both because of the tactics Rupert adopted, and because cavalry firearms were too expensive for everyone to be equipped with them.

For the effective discharge of firearms by a cavalry force, the Germans had developed the caracole system, whereby the cavalry would advance on the enemy, sometimes halting to draw the enemy's fire, and then when quite close, perhaps no more than twenty paces distant, the first rank would fire. Having discharged their weapons, the first rank then wheeled around the sides of the formation and rejoined at the rear, where they would reload their weapons. It would then be the turn of the second rank to fire. Firing would continue until the enemy were observed to be suffering, and only then would the attacking force close with sword in hand.

King Gustavus Adolphus of Sweden, who was responsible for many tactical innovations in the early seventeenth century, chose to abandon the caracole system, which by then was widespread across Europe.

Instead he opted for shock tactics, dispensing with the various manoeuvres to draw fire, and instead closing with the enemy as fast as possible, usually at the gallop. Only the front rank were allowed to fire at the enemy, and only when they were almost upon them: the charge was then carried home at sword point. Such tactics were not new but had simply fallen out of fashion once firearms were widely adopted; their purpose was partly to counter the effects of incoming fire. The key to success was to attack the enemy as fast as possible and in so doing increase the momentum of the onslaught while also minimizing the time the enemy had to fire on the attackers.

Having witnessed these Swedish tactics in action, Rupert ordered his men to advance at the gallop and to hold their fire until the last minute. The threat posed to the charge by flanking musketeers positioned in the hedges was removed by the advance deployment of dragoons. Even the mixing in of musketeers with the cavalry and cannon-fire failed to slow the Royalist charge, and in the face of a seemingly unstoppable force the Parliamentarian horse turned and fled. Sensing victory, the Royalist cavalry pursued their desperate enemy all the way to Kineton, but here they let themselves down: instead of returning to the battlefield to attack the Parliamentarians from the rear, most of them fell to looting the enemy's baggage train. There was nothing that Rupert could do to stop them, and what was perhaps the Royalists' best chance for a decisive victory was gone.

Edgehill set a clear example for later cavalry actions, and the man who learned most from it was a cavalry captain who arrived late on the battlefield. His name was Oliver Cromwell. Ironically, Cromwell, who had no prior military experience, became one of Britain's greatest military leaders. At Marston Moor just over two years later, having installed a strong sense of discipline into his troops, Cromwell routed the entire Royalist right flank, and instead of pursuing them pointlessly his men returned to the field to continue the fight against the rest of the enemy forces.

The key to success was to attack the enemy as fast as possible and in so doing increase the momentum of the onslaught

THE AFTERMATH

THE FIRST PITCHED BATTLE OF THE
ENGLISH CIVIL WAR HAD ENDED IN WHAT
CAN REASONABLY BE DESCRIBED AS A
DRAW. NEITHER SIDE HAD CONVERTED ITS
CHANCES FOR VICTORY, AND THOUGH THE
ROYALISTS HAD PROBABLY HAD THE
BETTER OF THE FIGHT, THERE WAS NO
SENSE OF TRIUMPH AMONG THE KING'S
MEN. AND EVEN FOR SOLDIERS HARDENED
BY FIGHTING ON THE CONTINENT, THE
BATTLE PRESENTED A NEW EXPERIENCE:
EDGEHILL WAS THE FIRST TASTE OF
MAKING WAR ON FRIENDS AND NEIGHBOURS,
ON FELLOW COUNTRYMEN – AND THE
INDECISIVE CONCLUSION MEANT THERE
WOULD BE MORE OF THE SAME TO COME.

Fellow countrymen or not, the fallen were as ill treated as strangers. As was commonplace, survivors scoured the field for valuables and equipment that could be used again. It was not only the dead who were stripped of their clothes, weapons and other belongings, but the gravely wounded and dying too. No lesser observer than the future James II noted one such example of cruelty: horribly injured, with seventeen wounds upon his body, the Royalist Sir Gervase Scrope was left for dead. A Parliamentarian soldier found and stripped him, taking away all that was of value. But in doing so, he unwittingly saved his life. The night following the battle was a bitterly cold one, and the low temperature, exacerbated for those wounded who had been stripped naked, made all the difference: the surgeons of the time, according to the Earl of Clarendon, were convinced that the wounded who survived 'owed their lives to the inhumanity of those who stripped them, and to the coldness of the nights, which stopped their blood better than all their skill and medicaments could have done'. Their metabolisms were slowed to a point where their blood loss was minimized. Similar reports emerged from the Falklands War: severely low temperatures meant that wounded men who might otherwise have died were found dangerously chilled but very much alive; again, their core temperatures had dropped to a point where bleeding and other key bodily processes were crucially slowed. So when Scrope's son, Adrian, set out in search of his father's corpse, he was amazed to find him still among the living – if only just. Scrope subsequently recovered, though he wore one arm in a sling thereafter.

By contrast the tale of Captain Henry Bellingham is tragic. He survived the battle and was found alive among the corpses three days later, with twenty wounds. Carried to safety by a friend, he might have lived, had his surgeons not overlooked a wound to his thigh and failed to clean it. And so despite having been spared death by the same low temperature that saved Scrope, he died at Oxford ten days later of an infection.

For the first few days after the battle, as both sides gradually realized that the chance to settle matters had been missed and they were in for a long haul, neither Royalists nor Parliamentarians seemed to know quite what to do next. By 27 October Charles had moved only as far as the nearby town of Banbury, and though Prince Rupert made an understandable plea for a dash towards the capital, the king instead settled for setting up his headquarters at Oxford. In London a force in excess of 25,000 men was assembled to face whatever Charles might throw at it. He ordered Rupert to take Brentford, which the prince duly

When Adrian set out in search of his father's corpse, he was amazed to find him still among the living

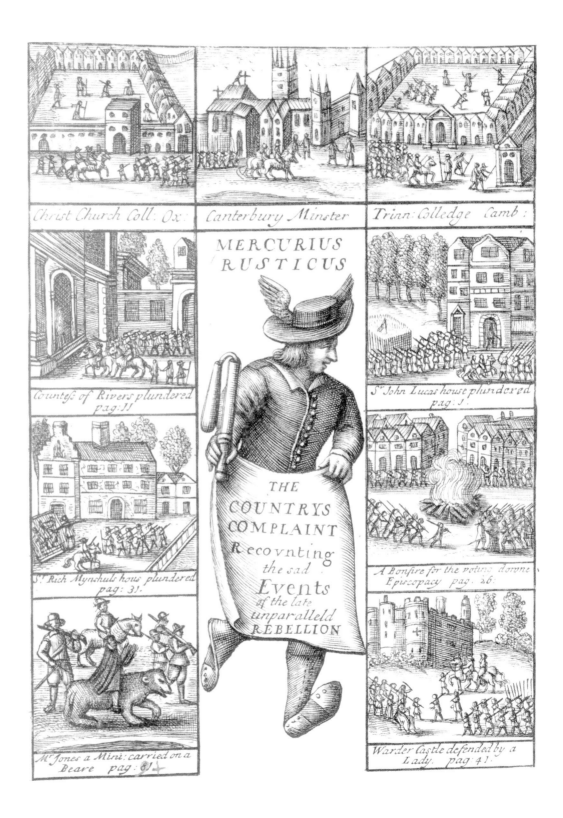

Christ Church Coll: Ox.

Canterbury Minster

Trinn: Colledge Camb:

MERCURIUS RUSTICUS

Countess of Rivers plundered pag:11

Sr John Lucas house plundered pag:1.

THE COUNTRYS COMPLAINT Recovnting the sad Events of the late unparalleld REBELLION

Sr Rich Mynshulls hous plundered pag: 31.

A Bonfire for the voting downe Episcopacy pag: 26.

Mr Jones a Mini: carried on a Beare pag: 61.

Warder Castle defended by a Lady. pag: 41.

did, swooping upon the garrison there at dawn and slaughtering them almost to a man. The prospect of facing the massed Parliamentarian force at Turnham Green, however, proved wholly unappetizing and he shied away from the confrontation.

And bar the shouting, that was that for the campaign of 1642. For now, Charles controlled the north and west, while Parliament held sway over the south and east. In fact the aftermath of Edgehill is the entire saga of the English Civil War. It was settled in the end as much by attrition as by set-piece battles such as Marston Moor and Naseby. Each side fought for the control of towns and cities – their populations and the resources they commanded – and it was mastery of siege warfare rather than of pike and musket that would make the difference.

The legendary Parliamentarian commander Oliver Cromwell – having deservedly attracted the right kind of attention for his battle-winning control of his cavalry at Marston Moor in 1644 – steadily rose to dominance. He was given charge of the New Model Army of truly professional soldiers in 1645, which he used to devastating effect. By the end of 1646, Charles was a prisoner. When the king escaped his captors in 1648 and struck up an alliance with the Scots, it was Cromwell and his New Model Army that crushed him once and for all at the battle of Preston. Charles was imprisoned once again, and by now the hardliners in Parliament were coming to the conclusion that this monarch was an infected limb likely to spread a rebellious disease into the body of the nation for as long as he remained alive. Charles was beheaded at Whitehall on 30 January 1649. What had hitherto been unimaginable had come to pass: the king had been executed by order of Parliament and a republic had replaced the monarchy.

War broke out again in 1650, when Charles's own son, Charles II, sought to oust Cromwell and his republic and put himself on the throne. Matters came to a conclusion at Worcester on 3 September 1651, when the king-in-waiting was defeated and driven into exile. Cromwell was proclaimed Lord Protector and conducted himself much like a king in any case. He died in 1658 and was treated to what was effectively a royal funeral and burial in Westminster Abbey. Just two years later, the Restoration put Charles II on the throne so reluctantly vacated by his father. The bodies of Cromwell and other prominent Parliamentarians were promptly exhumed on his direct orders and taken to Tyburn, where they were beheaded in a bizarre act of posthumous revenge.

The republic and its Lord Protector were dead: long live the king.

Opposite **Contemporary pamphlet showing events during the English Civil War**

The king had been executed by order of Parliament and a republic had replaced the monarchy

the Dig

Old Radway church

English villages are renowned for their pretty churches and peaceful churchyards, and Radway village, which nestles cosily at the foot of the wooded slopes of Edgehill, is no exception. The church is a sturdy building with a pointed spire and stained-glass windows, and is decorated with carved angelic faces and the odd gargoyle. The graveyard is well kept and of special interest because it contains the last resting place of a lady who was reputedly the first victim of a road-traffic accident in Britain. Williamina Macleod died in 1899 when the car in which she was a passenger careered off the steep stretch of road which runs down the side of Edgehill.

Inside the church, near the altar, there is an old tomb with a worn recumbent figure, perhaps of a medieval knight, carved into the white stone. When we first visited the church, we assumed that like the knight the building was hundreds of years old. This sense of antiquity was reinforced by a second funerary sculpture, in a niche in the wall next to the font. This is a more elaborate figure, carved in the form of a mustachioed gentleman adopting a relaxed pose, with one leg bent at the knee as he reclines back on his right arm on a bed. Although clearly not as old as the apparently medieval tombstone near the altar, the figure has been through the wars, as his left hand is missing and both his legs have been chopped off at the knee – one broken foot rests beside the statue. He is also missing his hat, which we assume was of the wide-brimmed Cavalier style. An ornately carved stone plaque hangs beside the sculpture, and the inscription says that the man is Captain Henry Kingsmill, who fought on the Royalist side and was killed at the battle of Edgehill. The eulogy explains that the poor soul was killed by a cannonball and as we looked at the fragmented state of the statue it was not

Gravestones line the path past the old churchyard

hard to imagine what a terrible death this must have been. The statue was commissioned as a lasting memorial by Kingsmill's grieving mother and was erected in 1670. From the inscription, however, it was apparent that the statue had not always occupied its present position, but had once marked the soldier's grave somewhere outside the church; the medieval tomb must also have been outside at some point – hence its weather-worn appearance.

On our way out of the church we saw a pair of old framed drawings hanging on the wall by the door. The drawings were renditions of another church, and as we studied them it became clear that all was not as it seemed with Radway church. The drawings are dated 1821 and 1845. Both claim to show the same building, but it has changed much in the years separating the renditions. The earlier drawing shows a fairly simple stone building with a small timber bell-tower; the other depicts a far more elaborate and presumably larger building, and the simple little bell-tower has turned into a substantial square tower. While the first building has an elegant simplicity, the second is fussy and really quite ugly.

But the real mystery was that these drawings referred to old Radway church, and neither of them

resembled the building we were standing in. So presumably there was another church in the village. It was only when we talked to the vicar and did some background reading that we discovered that the church we had visited was not as old as it looked and had been built as recently as the 1860s. The good people of Radway had become disenchanted with their old church and decided to build another one – and from what we had seen in the drawings we couldn't blame them for wanting to move. The two sculptures in the new church had been brought from the original church, where at some point, we guessed, they had been located in the graveyard. So where was this old church? Our inquiries revealed that it had been demolished in 1865, and the stone from the old church had been used to build the new one. The old carvings and gargoyles had added to the ancient appearance of the nineteenth-century building.

Old maps show the site of the original church – like the new one, it was known as St Peter's – to be about half a mile to the south of the present church, on the other side of the village cricket ground. Here, in a sheltered spot surrounded by trees and terraced cottages, was a small grass-covered clearing. There was no obvious evidence of the church, but a line of

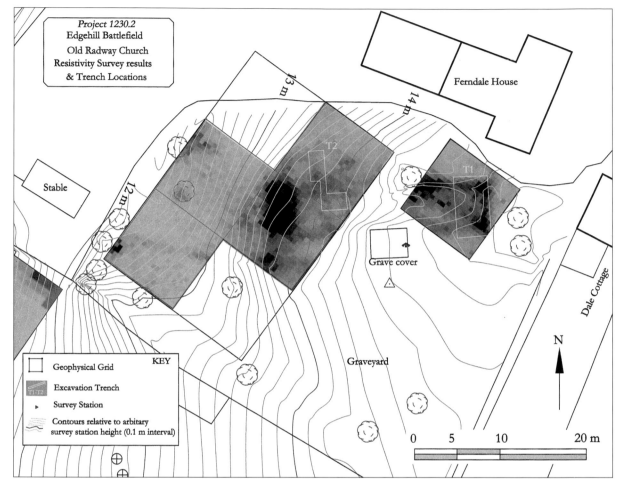

Geophysical survey of old Radway church, showing traces of a rectangular building

gravestones marked the edge of a footpath skirting one side of the clearing and giving access to a paddock beyond. These gravestones, many of which bear the winged-cherub motif typical of sixteenth- and seventeenth-century grave-markers, were once distributed across the open ground, which had been the graveyard enclosing the now vanished church. In the centre of the clearing, which sloped down towards the cricket ground, was a solitary stone monument still in its original position. This was the top of the burial vault for the Miller family, several of whom had died overseas in military service in the nineteenth century.

A cross on the old Ordnance Survey map indicated

that the church had been in the corner of the clearing, close to the footpath, and this was also suggested by the lumps and bumps just visible on the ground. To check whether there was any buried evidence for the church, we set our friend Iain Banks the task of carrying out a geophysical survey across the area. The results were dramatic: the geophysical plots clearly showed the remains of a rectangular building set in an east–west orientation.

Here, then, was the church, which had borne witness to the terrible events of that bloody day in 1642. Although the battle took place some distance from the village, the Royalist army must have passed through it after making its way down the slope of Edgehill towards the Parliamentarians. That the events of that day left a mark on the village was made obvious when local people, who showed a great interest in our work, came forward to show us musket-balls and even a cannonball which they had found in their gardens, though many of them were totally unaware that there had ever been a church in this quiet little spot. How many of the men who fought that day had prayed in the church before the battle? How many had taken shelter there in the battle's aftermath, perhaps to have their wounds tended? And how many men slain on the battlefield had found their final resting place in the churchyard? Although we knew that at least one mass grave had been created on the site of the battlefield, it is likely that some of the dead would have been buried in local churchyards and it appeared that poor Captain Kingsmill, for one, had been buried in Radway. We could not resist the temptation to investigate the remains of the church, and the only way of doing this was by excavation.

We opened our main trench across what the geophysical survey suggested was the east end of the church, where the altar would have been located. Our efforts were soon rewarded. The line of the walls was marked by large stone slabs, making up the lower courses of the wall, which fortunately had not been grubbed out when the building had been demolished. The material was ironstone, the same locally quarried red stone from which the houses and the new church had been built. We found the end of the building, with both corners reinforced by thick buttresses – stone projections which supported the walls and could be seen on both of the drawings of the church. The wall was over a metre thick, with finely dressed stone on the inside and outside, and a rough rubble core.

Our research told us that the first historical reference to the church was in 1291, when the church was within the domain of the abbey of Stoneleigh. From the late fourteenth century the church was served by one of the monks from the abbey, and a secular priest was appointed some time around 1535. Although the church is not mentioned in the Domesday Book of 1086, there are reports that fragments of a Norman piscina – a

Excavating old Radway church

stone basin for rinsing altar vessels – were recovered from the foundations during its demolition. It was obvious that the church had a long and venerable history and it seemed rather sad, as we excavated its few remains, that it came to such an inglorious end after all that time.

We dug down into the interior, removing earth and rubble and looking for any trace of the floor. Our digging revealed bones, ribs and fragments of skull – human remains. These may have come from the graveyard, originally, but they had been disturbed long before our intrusion. They may even have come from a charnel pit beneath the church, where bones disturbed by gravediggers were sometimes collected together. Today these bones are just anonymous fragments, broken pieces of past lives. Were they villagers who had died peacefully, or is it possible they were casualties of the battle? These were the thoughts that filled our minds as we carefully buried the bones once again.

Our excavation had revealed a fairly small but substantially built church, which had more in common with the earlier of the two drawings than the rather fussy edifice portrayed in the second. Weighing up the evidence, we concluded that the second drawing was not a true depiction of the church but a suggestion of what it could have looked like if the old church had been modified – an architect's proposal, if you like. It seems likely that the good people of Radway, perhaps finding the old church too small for their needs, decided to convert it into a larger building. An architect's drawing was then produced, but it was ultimately decided to abandon entirely the old church, and build from scratch on a new site. The old church lived on in the new building, in the form of recycled stones and relocated monuments. But although we had learned much about the church and its strange history, we never did find Captain Kingsmill's hat.

Metal-detecting the battlefield

The church was fascinating and it was a real thrill to show today's villagers where their ancestors once worshipped, but we were eager to get on to the battlefield itself, where we were going to carry out a metal-detector survey. When first considering Edgehill as a candidate for investigation, we were disappointed to discover that a massive Ministry of Defence depot occupied a good portion of the site. Furthermore, the farmland around the depot was also the property of the MoD, who quite rightly have a strict policy against metal-detecting on government-owned land. Even though things didn't look too promising at first, we nevertheless visited the depot and explained our intentions to the base commander. To our relief, Colonel

Ingle and the rest of his staff were very interested in our proposed work and went out of their way to provide us with special permission to carry out our survey.

The army shared our eagerness to discover more about the battle – it was, after all, their military predecessors who had fought and died there 260 years ago. But we were not the first to show an interest in the site. In 1979, just before the depot underwent substantial extension, an army officer stationed there, Captain Scott, took the opportunity to use his own metal detector to recover artefacts related to the battle. On many occasions when we visit a battlefield we find that metal-detector users have already been there, and this is not usually good news, as the locations of artefacts discovered by amateur detectorists are often not recorded and so we lose a lot of valuable information, though we hope this situation is slowly improving. But, to our delight, we found that Captain Scott was an exception: not only did he search areas that were later destroyed by the camp extension, but he also went to the trouble of carefully recording the locations of his finds and plotting them on a map. He forwarded the map and the finds to the county archaeologist's office. We owe Captain Scott a big debt for his efforts and will add his findings to our own when we write the final report on the site.

After studying accounts of the battle, the first area we selected for metal-detector survey were the fields just outside the southern perimeter of the depot, quite close to the site of the battlefield grave at Graveground Coppice. It was clear from Captain Scott's map that battlefield finds had come from this area, so we were keen to see whether we could find more. Our topographic surveyor John Arthur, with his trusty total

Musket-balls – the lower of the two has hit something hard!

station electronic distance measurer (EDM), set out a line of grids leading from the perimeter fence and heading off into the next field, towards the high ground of Edgehill. With high hopes our volunteers kicked off at the fence line, and it wasn't long before the detectors started beeping as buried pieces of metal revealed themselves. One of the first finds was nothing to do with the battle, but military nonetheless: it was a cap badge bearing a crossed shovel and rifle, the insignia of the Pioneer Corps, the regiment which had built the first ammunition dump on the site in the Second World War. At first, other signals near the fence proved to be nothing more than lengths of fencing wire, but soon our

A button from a buff jacket cuff

A strap buckle

high expectations began to be fulfilled: first one musket-ball, then another, then another! These heavy lead spheres were scattered quite densely in the field just to the east of the fence; some had retained their spherical form, while others were almost completely flattened. These wasted balls had found their targets, the hot metal spreading out as it hit armour or bone. Here was the reality of warfare for the battlefield archaeologist: we have found many musket-balls over the years, but each time we hold one, especially if it has been distorted through impact, it still sends a shiver down our spines.

But there weren't just musket-balls. Pieces of grapeshot and caseshot showed that the artillery too had been active on this part of the field. There were buttons, several of them silver-plated and etched with ornate designs, which may have been attached to the clothes of well-to-do officers, while plainer buttons fastened the more modest attire of the rank and file.

More and more battlefield relics came to light – pieces of horse harness, knife blades, buckles and even possible musket fittings, all demonstrating beyond doubt that this area had been the scene of heavy fighting.

As we moved away from the fence the finds, especially the musket-balls, began to dry up. We wondered whether we had been on the edge of the battlefield scatter, with the remainder lost under the depot's bunkers and mounds on the other side of the fence where the armed guards and their dogs roamed. But then, just as we were getting a little downhearted, the detectors started singing again – more musket-balls. After finding a roughly equal amount to the last scatter, we realized what we were looking at: the musket-balls marked the position of the two armies as they faced one another as the battle entered its crucial stage, with Parliamentarian and Royalist musketeers so close that they would literally be able to see the whites of one another's eyes. The empty ground separating the two scatters was the space over which the balls were fired, some finding their targets among the press of men, others falling to the ground at the end of their flight or dropped by fumbling fingers as muskets were reloaded in the heat of battle. We extended our search by putting in another line of grids next to that already completed, and came up with the same pattern. We had found the front line. We were standing on the killing ground.

The ford at the river Dene

Having established the position at which at least part of the battle had taken place, we moved our attention to the village of Kineton, where the Parliamentarian army had billeted on the eve of battle. The road from the village to the battlefield passes over the river Dene just outside the village, and in the nineteenth century workmen building a sluice came across several skeletons close to the riverbank. Along with the skeletons, armour

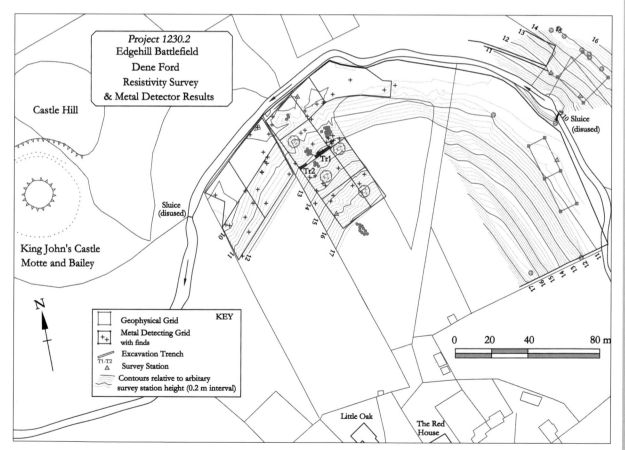

Location of metal-detector finds and trenches at Dene river

was also uncovered, but we have no idea what happened to the bones or the armour after their discovery. The site of burial, next to the river, has suggested to some historians that these men were killed defending a ford across the river as Royalist cavalry, having routed most of the Parliamentarian left flank, came charging into the village and pillaged the baggage train. Using descriptions passed down by the workmen, we tried to locate the burial site, which seemed to be some distance to the west of the present bridge crossing the river and carrying the road, known as Bridge Street, into the village. Armed with old maps we walked the ground, looking for any signs of a crossing-point or trackway. There was a suspicious double line of trees on the map, which may have marked some sort of thoroughfare, and the sloping ground on either side of the trees was covered by the undulations of ridge and furrow which survive as evidence of earlier ploughing. On the other side of the stream, on high ground now occupied by the village, is the site of King John's castle, a motte-and-bailey fort probably dating back to the Norman period. It is not unusual to find river crossing-points and roads close to fortified sites such as this, and, together with the tree-lined avenue, this was a good indicator that we may have been close to a ford that pre-dated the nineteenth-century bridge. We put in some geophysics grids to see if we could come up with signs of grave pits or a made road, but nothing of interest showed up.

Just to check, we put a long trench in place between the trees, where we thought a track most likely. We found nothing except scraps of pottery, but our excitement rose when we came across a small lead ball, smaller than the musket-balls we had been finding: this belonged to a different kind of weapon, perhaps a pistol, the type of firearm carried by cavalry of the time.

What distinguished this ball were the clearly visible casting sprue and seam. These are created during the moulding process, when lead seeps through the gap between the two halves of the mould, creating the seam, and is left in the channel through which the lead is poured, creating the sprue. In ideal circumstances the ball would be hand-finished, the sprue being snipped from the ball and the seam polished away, but that had not been done here. At first we thought that the presence of a sprue on a musket-ball must be clear evidence that it had never been fired, as it clearly distorts the shape of the bullet and must surely cause damage to the inside of the barrel. However we later found out from firearms expert Martin Hinchcliffe, of the Royal Armouries, that musket-balls could be fired with the sprue in place as long as the 'tail' of the sprue was loaded breech first, thus preventing it from

Johnny A. surveys the scene

Fragment of a soldier's iron cooking-pot

A gaming piece fashioned from a piece of lead caseshot

touching the sides of the barrel as it was fired.

We instigated a metal-detector survey around the trench and down towards the river, and we came up with some amazing results. We found upwards of a dozen small lead balls, all displaying a clear sprue and seam. Taken together, the evidence pointed to pistol-balls that had not been fired – we didn't find a single flattened or distorted ball, which is normal when the scatter represents fired balls. We also found several lumps of lead waste, which had probably been spilled on the ground during casting, and thus provided good evidence that the balls were actually being made on the site. In addition we found a couple of old pewter spoons, which are the sort of domestic objects you expect in a camp rather than on a battlefield. There were a couple of cylinder-shaped pieces of lead – probably caseshot, which was designed to be fired en masse from a cannon. Even these items of destruction had a more peaceable appearance: one of them had possibly been converted into a gaming piece by having a series of lines incised into one end.

All the evidence from the riverside points to a Parliamentarian camp, perhaps related to the baggage train or guarding the ford, but certainly alongside the road that led to the battlefield. Not only do we think we have a camp, but we strongly believe that the exclusive presence of pistol-sized balls indicates that it is a cavalry camp. Direct evidence of fighting, in the form of fired musket-balls, is lacking, but the fact that so many unfired balls were dropped suggests that the place was vacated in a hurry, possibly during the rout into the village. Even though we found no trace of graves or evidence of a manufactured road surface, we are delighted that metal-detecting provided us with meaningful results and allowed us to sketch in another episode of the epic battle of Edgehill.

King's Leys barn

King's Leys Barn, as the name suggests, is a place traditionally identified with the battle: the royal connection probably relates to the story that the king spent the night after the battle in the barn before he and his army departed the field. But there is also another story that relates to the barn, concerning the king's sons Charles (the Prince of Wales and future Charles II) and James (the Duke of York and future King James II) while they were accompanying their father on the campaign. In his account of the battle, James writes:

> *Sr. Will. Howard went off with the Prince and Duke pursuant to his orders (to get them out of harms way), and they had not gone above musket shott from the place, when they saw a body of horse advancing directly towards them from the left hand of the King's foot; upon which sending to see what they were, and finding them to be the Enemy, they drew behind a little barn not far distant from them, which was incompassed by a hedge. In this barn severall of the King's wounded men were then dressing, but the Enemy observing the King's men to be within the inclosure, drew immediately back without ingaging them, by which means the Prince and the Duke escaped the evident of being taken; for had they charged that small party they could not have fail'd of beating them, considering the vast advantage of their numbers.*

The mounted Parliamentarians were probably Balfour's horse returning to their own lines after their successful foray against the Royalist guns.

The barn presented us with an irresistible target. Most of the buildings we have previously investigated,

The well-made wall at King's Leys barn

including old Radway church, sat on the sidelines of battlefields, but the barn was a very rare instance of a building actually located on a battlefield and is recorded in an eyewitness account. Once again, the problem was that the building is no longer standing, having been demolished some time in the early twentieth century. A clue to its whereabouts is provided by the place name King's Leys spinney, which is given to a clump of trees to the north of Radway village. On the first (Victorian) edition of the Ordnance Survey map of the site, the barn does not appear alone: there are three buildings on the site, all clustered round a small courtyard with a larger enclosed yard attached to the north. Further evidence of enclosure, as suggested in James's account, is provided by a long hedge which passes along the eastern side of the building cluster, running north to join the stand of trees at King's Leys spinney. The buildings probably represent a farmstead, and may have included a house as well as a barn.

Our first visit to the site was in the company of a

Hard at work at King's Leys barn

local man who remembered playing in the ruins of the barn as a child in the 1950s. We were encouraged when he walked us to a spot in a massive open field and told us that the barn had been located where we were standing. There were no remains to be seen, but we could discern a line of discoloured grass which followed the line of the long hedge shown on the map. We were confident that geophysics would find the buried remains of the barn.

As we took a closer look at our surroundings, however, our hopes began to fade: about fifty metres from where we stood was a large conical mound, the only upstanding feature in a field that was otherwise as flat as a pancake. We sensed trouble. 'What's that mound?' we asked, pointing to what was clearly a man-made hillock. 'Oh that's where the army dumped the rubble from the buildings that were here during the war,' our friend replied. Fine, but could they have dumped the rubble on the barn? He was adamant that the barn had been where we were standing and that the rubble did not cover the site. We took a look at the mound, which consisted of large chunks of concrete and fragmented lumps of brick wall. Mixed in among the obviously modern debris were large stone blocks that looked as though they might have come from an earlier building. Similar stones could be seen protruding from the soil

out of the woods: the mound contained a number of impressive burrows that had been excavated by badgers, and badgers are protected by law. If there was any risk of scaring them away from their sett by using a mechanical excavator or even digging by hand, the site would be out of bounds to us.

We had the mound inspected by a ranger from the Badger Preservation Society, and to our relief he informed us that the sett was not being used at the present, and that in any case our work would be too far away to disturb our fellow furry diggers. With the coast clear, the next phase of the operation was to send in that other furry digger – Iain and his geophysics kit. When he returned with his results we couldn't have been happier: the plot clearly showed the dark outlines of rectangular buildings running out from under the edge of the mound. Substantial portions of the buildings were available for excavation.

We excavated four trenches, two over the remains of buildings on the north edge of the mound and two over the lines of the hedge and enclosure further to the north. In the trenches near the mound we found the remains of two buildings, both of them well made with thick, rubble-filled walls. There was no evidence that floors or other refinements had survived, but the effort that had gone into the walls suggested that we were looking at the site of a farmstead, with one of the buildings, possibly the smaller of the two, being a house and the other a barn.

Metal-detecting in the field around the mound produced a light scatter of musket-balls, but not enough to suggest that fighting around the buildings had been heavy. One of the most impressive finds was a bronze prick spur from a horseman's boot, which tied in

around the base of the mound. We had grave suspicions that the rubble mound had indeed been dumped on the barn, and if so there was no way we could move what must have amounted to tons and tons of rubble.

We had to wait until we got back to the office to see if our fears were justified. We had paced out some measurements in the field, from the spinney to the mound, and we checked these against the distance between the barn and the spinney shown on the map. They matched exactly. The barn was definitely under the mound! Memory had played tricks on our local guide.

But there was still some hope. According to the map, the area covered by the buildings was greater than that covered by the mound, and the stones protruding from the field suggested that parts of the buildings had escaped burial and extended outwards from the edges of the mound. It looked as though the rubble had been piled in a small courtyard, which at the time may have been enclosed by the ruined walls of the buildings, creating a handy stone-built skip. But we still weren't

A prick spur

nicely with James's account of the cavalrymen in the vicinity of the barn. When handling this spur, it was impossible to dissociate it, in the mind's eye at least, from a story told by Sir John Hinton, who belonged to the same party that included the two young princes. According to Hinton, the incident at the barn was hotter than James remembered it, for as the party came within 'half a musket shott' of the body of Parliamentarian horse, one of Balfour's men broke ranks and charged towards the royals. Prince Charles, totally unflustered, drew his pistol and was quite prepared to take on his foe, but Hinton, a faithful bodyguard, went forward to face the oncoming horseman. Pistol shots were exchanged, but only Hinton's bullet found its mark and the Parliamentarian tumbled from his horse. Hinton then tackled the dismounted rider with his sword, but the man was heavily armoured and Hinton's sword did little damage. Then another Royalist stepped in and finished off the fellow with his pole-axe. Could the spur possibly have belonged to that rash Parliamentarian? Our experience as archaeologists tells us the chances are against it, but what if?

It seems likely that the barn, although witness to the suffering of the wounded men inside it and the adventures of the young princes close by, remained behind the Royalist line throughout the fighting, and the two sides came to a halt somewhere between the barn and the MoD base as darkness put an end to further fighting. The barn's location would have made it an ideal command centre and dressing station, as suggested by James. Ironically, the fact that had impeded us – that the building remains were buried beneath the mound – had protected them from being ploughed away, and it would be encouraging to think that they will always be there, a buried memory of the battle of Edgehill.

Archaeological Techniques:
Fieldwalking

Of all the techniques employed by archaeologists to find clues about what people got up to in the past, fieldwalking is probably the one that comes most naturally. Surely everyone who has ever taken a stroll across a ploughed field has found their glance drifting towards the ground from time to time, their attention caught by the glint of quartz or a brightly coloured pebble? Perhaps it's a trait that humans share with magpies; or maybe the millennia our ancestors spent foraging for food and other necessities have left us with an instinctive urge to scour the ground. The number-one ally of the fieldwalker, without which the pursuit would be fruitless, is the humble plough. Material buried by the passage of time will remain buried unless some activity disturbs the ground. Ploughing is designed to loosen and aerate the top layer of soil. The shape of the ploughshare ensures that the soil that lies several inches underground is pulled to the surface and flipped over. Conveniently for archaeologists, when ploughing takes place over an archaeological site, buried artefacts are pulled to the surface as well. This provides us with our own harvest – of finds. Every time a field is ploughed, more and more buried material is gradually freed from the hidden archaeological layer in which it was sealed.

Many archaeological sites have been discovered because an observant farmer has noticed telltale artefacts exposed in the wake of his tractor and informed the relevant authorities.

The advent of more sophisticated (not to mention technologically dependent) prospecting techniques such as geophysical survey has resulted in fieldwalking being somewhat sidelined in recent years. But the primary tool of the archaeologist has to be his or her eyes, and fieldwalking is still a wonderfully simple and effective way to use them.

To ensure that the results of fieldwalking are of value, it is vital to bring order to what would otherwise be random treasure-hunting. Television news footage of police undertaking a fingertip search of a crime scene – with a shoulder-to-shoulder line of officers working their way slowly over an area in search of clues – gives a helpful image of the way archaeological fieldwalking is conducted. First, the field to be walked is surveyed by a topographic surveyor and a regular grid pattern of squares laid out with marker poles. The walkers – usually volunteers – assemble in a line a few metres apart from

One of the sites we were interested in finding at Edgehill was the Parliamentarian baggage train. Every army has to carry with it not only weapons but also all the paraphernalia needed for thousands of men to exist on campaign. The baggage train at Edgehill probably included hundreds of wagons full of food, cooking utensils, clothing, blacksmithing facilities, personal possessions, livestock fodder, and all the other bits and pieces required by an army. An enemy baggage train was always a tempting target, and pillaging the enemy's possessions was a long-standing tradition for all armies. But it was one that needed to be stamped out. At Edgehill the Royalist cavalry lost the initiative when they fell to looting rather than returning to the battlefield to finish what they had started.

Contemporary accounts inform us that the baggage train was located in and around the village of Kineton, where the Parliamentarian army had spent the night before the battle. When examining the local Sites and Monuments Record we had come across a note referring to a scatter of pottery in a field quite close to the village and behind the position where the armies faced one another in battle. Could this be the site of part of the baggage train? To our delight we discovered that the crop in the field had been harvested by the time we arrived, which allowed us to try fieldwalking.

Being small in number we recruited an army of our own and on the appointed day around thirty Cubs and Brownies arrived to help us with our work. Once John Arthur had set out the grids, we lined up the kids and at the count of three, with eyes glued to the ground, they advanced slowly across the field. Everyone carried a plastic bag, into which they dropped anything of interest – mostly pottery and metal. Once the line

each other. The line moves forward slowly and the walkers, armed with polythene bags, simply collect whatever artefacts they find within the part of the grid assigned to them. The bags are numbered and labelled and their contents are later plotted on a plan of the field, which reveals any concentrations of finds (flakes of flint, pottery sherds, fragments of floor tiles or whatever) that may point to areas of human activity.

A coin of the period

reached the end of the grid, the bags – many of which were full to bursting – were left on the ground, new bags were issued and the line began walking the next grid. This process continued all the way across the field. Once the fieldwalkers had passed over the ground, the metal detectorists went in to find items buried beneath the surface.

By the end of the day, thanks to our young volunteers' keen eyes, we had dozens of bags full of goodies. It will take a lot of work to process all this material back in the lab and, as with metal-detecting, quite a bit of it will be of no interest – bits of stone, modern pottery and all the usual junk that ends up in farmers' fields. But among the rejects there are some real treasures. We found quite a lot of slipware, the colourful glazed pottery that was in use at the time of the battle; the odd coin; buckles and buttons; but – tellingly – only one or two musket-balls, which supported the fact that we were away from an area where fighting took place. All this material may indicate that part of the baggage train was here at the time of the battle, but we need to do a lot more analysis before we can say for sure. But it wasn't just seventeenth-century material we discovered: there was a beautiful Roman brooch and some Roman pottery, good evidence that there is a Roman settlement somewhere close by. The whole team certainly had had a rewarding day.

Conclusion

When we arrive at a battle site and look out over the modern landscape for the first time, we always wish we could see the place through the eyes of the men who actually fought there. We see the roads and the power-lines, the houses and the barbed-wire fences, but we try hard to look beyond that to the terrain that was the scene of such drama and horror. Having visualized it in our imaginations, we try to prove to ourselves that the landscape we are searching for has not vanished completely, and that little pockets of it are out there just waiting to be uncovered. As a result of our work on the battlefield of Edgehill, we came close to realizing that dream. Our carefully selected array of archaeological techniques caused crucial fragments of the battlescape to reappear, one after another.

In the heart of the picture-postcard village of Radway, on a patch of ground tucked away behind some beautiful houses, we had been looking for a mysteriously vanished church. Churches, once built, tend to survive, as long as there is a congregation in need of a place of worship. Even when circumstances lead to their abandonment and ruin, the very solid nature of their construction usually means that remains are visible in the landscape long after the population that used it has disappeared. In the old churchyard at Radway, though, there was only a slight bump in the grass to show where that long-lost place of worship had once stood. Nonetheless, we found it. Our carefully positioned trench revealed that while all surface traces had been removed, the lower courses of plastered walls survived intact just beneath the grass. It was deeply satisfying to see this first part of our battlescape revealed once more – and it was clear that many of the villagers who came to inspect our work were delighted too.

At King's Leys Barn it was a similar story, out of even more amazing circumstances. Not only did every vestige of the building complex seem to have been scalped away, but also a massive mound of rubble had been dumped on to the very spot where it had once stood. The rubble had more recently been colonized by a population of badgers and, all in all, it had left us feeling pretty discouraged about the chances of finding anything of value there. Once again though, geophysical survey followed by carefully targeted excavation revealed a truly amazing survival. Far from damaging the remains, the very presence of the rubble mound seemed to have sealed and protected them. Here were traces of buildings around which some fighting had taken place. The Royalist army had begun their advance from close by and had also exploited its potential as a temporary hospital. They had then fallen back to this location as the battle drew to a conclusion and both sides fought one another to a standstill. Charles's young sons had taken cover in the buildings during the battle, and some accounts have the king and his lads spending the following night there. At Culloden and other places we had gone in search of buildings that played a part in great battles: at Edgehill, we succeeded in finding one.

Metal-detecting too proved to be as revealing as we could have hoped. Beside Dene river, where we searched for the ford, our finds were enough to convince us that we had located a camp used by Parliamentarian soldiers. Perhaps they were there to guard a nearby crossing-point just beyond our area of investigation. Maybe they fled at the sight of the Royalist cavalry under the command of Prince Rupert. On the battlefield itself we found the point at which the two great armies clashed, and from the pattern of the finds we could even see the position of the opposing musketeers as they fired at one another.

We have learned from experience that battlefields are always reluctant to reveal their secrets. Battlefield archaeology is developing the techniques to prise some of those secrets free, and at Edgehill, we struck gold.

SEDGEMOOR 1685

SEDGEMOOR

1685

LYME REGIS, WITH THE SEA BEFORE IT AND THE DORSET DOWNS RISING UP BEHIND, IS A PRETTY LITTLE TOWN. ONCE A SAFE HAVEN FOR FISHERMEN, IT IS NOW A MAGNET FOR TOURISTS, WHO STROLL THROUGH ITS NARROW STREETS IN THEIR THOUSANDS AND INVADE ITS BEACHES DURING THE SUMMER MONTHS.

On either side of the town the buildings give way to steep, friable cliffs which regularly release the fossilized remains of animals millions of years old. If you pick your way through the boulders and stones that litter the beach you are likely to see spiralling ammonites the size of coffee tables. Since their discovery in the nineteenth century, fossils have become almost an industry in Lyme and fossil shops do a roaring trade in geological hammers and collectors' specimens. But it is a man-made landmark and not these natural ancient wonders for which the town is probably best known: the Cobb, a great stone buttress that curves out from the shore shielding the small harbour that has for centuries protected the town's fishing fleet from winter storms.

You may recall a scene from the film *The French Lieutenant's Woman*, based on the book of the same name, in which Meryl Streep, head bowed, battles her way along the Cobb, her frame wrapped in a wind-whipped cloak in protection against waves as high as houses. The author of that book, John Fowles, lives somewhere in Lyme – he's an old man now and something of a legend. An interesting feature of the book is that it has two endings and readers are left to decide which they prefer. Fitting really, as the story of the battle of Sedgemoor, which begins at Lyme Regis, has two endings too, at least as far as some people at the time were concerned.

The Monmouth Rebellion, which culminated in the battle of Sedgemoor, began in earnest when James Scott, Duke of Monmouth and nephew of James II, landed at Lyme Regis on 11 June 1685. Bringing with him only eighty-two men and a small arsenal, Monmouth came ashore on the evening of the eleventh, landing on the shingle beach not far from the Cobb. A town official, in no doubt about his intentions and having no powder for the town's cannon, tried to convince the captain of an armed ship in the harbour to open fire, but to no avail. So the mayor mounted his horse and fled the town to warn the outside world, thus setting in train the downfall of Monmouth and his cause. But not everyone was horrified by Monmouth's arrival: many of the townsfolk cheered him and thronged around him to hear a declaration in which he set out his grievances against his uncle, James II, including an accusation that he poisoned his own brother, Charles II. His audience's belief in the Protestant duke and their suspicions of the king and his Catholic religion were such that before Monmouth's speech was finished people were falling over themselves to join the rebellion. For three days Lyme Regis became a recruiting centre, with people from all around hurrying to pledge allegiance to Monmouth's cause. The stakes were

For three days Lyme Regis became a recruiting centre, with people from all around hurrying to pledge allegiance to Monmouth's cause

James Scott, Duke of Monmouth

1685

high in this all-or-nothing venture, with the British Crown the reward for success and the executioner's axe the penalty for failure.

The next days and weeks saw the rebel army's ranks swell by thousands as it progressed through the counties of the south-west. There was little time for training and weapons were in short supply. But even so, the army successfully put to flight local militia standing for the king during several skirmishes. James soon had no option but to deploy almost half the British army against his nephew. It was only a matter of time before the two sides would come face to face for the final showdown.

Not surprisingly, the discipline and training of the king's regular army gave them a strong upper hand against Monmouth's keen but

Sodalis, **the Duke of Monmouth's ship**

green amateurs, and although the contest was for a while a close-run thing the defeat of the rebellion was perhaps inevitable. The battle of Sedgemoor, just thirty miles to the north of Lyme Regis, was a fast and furious affair and its aftermath harsh and unforgiving: in the so-called 'Bloody Assizes' Judge Jeffreys condemned hundreds of men to the gallows and to transportation, and Monmouth himself was beheaded.

So ended the Monmouth Rebellion – or perhaps not quite. Soon after Monmouth's execution rumours began to circulate that Monmouth was still alive. It was an impostor standing in for the duke who had been executed, the story went. The rumours spread throughout the West Country, and like a seventeenth-century Elvis the duke was seen in several locations, alive and well and believed to be planning to complete the work he had set out to do when he landed at Lyme Regis. Here, like the end of Fowles's book, we have an alternative ending. But do history and archaeology allow us the same privileges as those of a novelist's imagination?

BACKGROUND

THE SOPORIFIC ATMOSPHERE IN THE
SOUTH-WEST TODAY — IN CORNWALL,
DEVON, SOMERSET, DORSET AND WILTSHIRE
— COULD FOOL ANYONE INTO BELIEVING
THERE WAS NEVER MUCH MORE GOING ON
HERE THAN CREAM TEAS, SUMMERTIME
HOLIDAY TRADE AND A PREPONDERANCE OF
COMFORTABLY OFF RETIRED FOLK. A QUICK
LOOK AT THE REGION'S HISTORY,
HOWEVER, REVEALS THAT IT WAS NOT
ALWAYS LIKE THIS. THE REBELS WHO ROSE
IN SUPPORT OF THE DUKE OF MONMOUTH
CAME FROM A TRADITION OF INDEPENDENT
THINKING AMONG THE PEOPLE THERE.

During the Civil War of the 1640s, for instance, it was here that the famous 'clubmen' formed themselves – armed gangs willing to take on soldiers of either side in order to keep their towns and villages out of the war.

Later, Wiltshire-man John Penruddock led local people in opposition to Oliver Cromwell's Protectorate. Intended to be part of a nationwide Royalist coup, the movement found its feet only in the south-west before being crushed by the state.

When Monmouth landed at Lyme, then, he knowingly set his feet into a hotbed of anti-establishment sentiment for he was no stranger to this place or to these folk. He had last visited the area in 1680 in the thick of the Exclusion Crisis of 1679–81. Protestant Dissenters there, whose impassioned opposition to a succession of Catholic monarchs had found much support in the south-west, had sought unsuccessfully to bar his uncle, James, then Duke of York, from succeeding his elder brother Charles II. A bastard son of Charles II he may have been – born as he was to Lucy Walters, one of the king's mistresses. But he was a Protestant and that, added to the fact that he was the king's eldest son, gave him a legitimacy that birth on the wrong side of the blankets could not take away.

Charles was loudly fond of this eldest of his many illegitimate children, but this royal affection was dangerously eroded in the years following Monmouth's triumphal tour by his association with men opposed not only to James but also to Charles. Monmouth was astute enough to remove himself from England for a while and was in self-imposed exile in the Low Countries at the time of Charles's death and James's accession.

While away, he spent more time in the company of opponents of James, including the Earl of Argyll, chief of the influential clan Campbell. Anti-Catholics, Whig politicians, Dissenters and Covenanters in Scotland, in need of a focus for their opposition to James, successfully recruited their preferred figurehead. For all these malcontents, the game was afoot. A Protestant claimant to the throne would find support too among the Presbyterian Covenanters of Scotland, and Argyll sailed to Scotland to raise a rebel army there while Monmouth made for England.

EARLY DAYS

After his arrival and initial recruiting at Lyme Regis, Monmouth moved through those counties where his popularity was still high following his visit in 1680, hoping to swell his ranks. As he made his way through Axminster, Chard and Ilminster towards Taunton, he recruited rebels

The ladies of Taunton receive the Duke of Monmouth

1685

from trades such as weaving, cloth-making and carpentry. By the end of June, he had gathered nearly 5,000 men to his cause. He divided this force into five regiments, each distinguished in true *Reservoir Dogs* style by its own colour: Red led by Colonel Wade; Yellow, Colonel Matthews; White, Colonel Foukes; Green, Colonel Holmes; and Blue, Colonel Bovet. Although poorly armed and, in comparison to the professional soldiers of James's standing army, poorly trained, Monmouth's men were undoubtedly enthusiastic and well motivated. In the face of this tradesmen's army James's militia of part-time soldiers was to prove ineffectual at best and cowardly at worst during the early days and weeks of the affair. The rebels clashed with these locally raised bands at Bridport in an inconclusive skirmish that bolstered the confidence of the duke's men – first blood to the rebels. By the time the rebels approached Taunton, the resolve of the king's men appears to have collapsed completely: they fled from the town, leaving their valuable stores and ammunition at the duke's disposal. Here, among the spoils of war, Monmouth was proclaimed king. Hopes among the rank and file for the success of the rebellion must have been high.

Monmouth next turned his attention to Bristol, which was then the country's second city. As a strategic move, it was a good one. He had spent too long in Taunton, however, and Bristol had been put on alert and its defences strengthened. By this time James had deployed over 4,000 men of his standing army. Rebels and government forces briefly clashed at Keynsham, close to the city, on 26 June in an inconclusive cavalry engagement. A group of prisoners taken by the rebels claimed under interrogation – wrongly – that the the king's army was just a few miles away. Monmouth took them at their word and withdrew his force in the direction of the Wiltshire border.

Royalists and rebels clashed again at Norton St Phillips. Here the king's advance guard was commanded by Monmouth's half-brother, the Duke of Grafton. Using a barricade and hedgerows as cover, the rebels set up an effective hail of musketry which pushed back the oncoming Royalist infantry. The fight was then reduced to a largely ineffectual artillery bombardment on both sides. As evening drew on and the weather worsened, with rain turning the lanes to muddy watercourses, both sides withdrew, the rebels lighting bonfires to fool the opposition into thinking that they were still in position. Although both sides seem to have suffered about twenty dead, Monmouth came out on top as far as tactical use of the terrain was concerned. He made for Bradford-on-Avon, where his men had a well-deserved rest, before moving on to Frome.

Here the duke received the crushing news that Argyll's efforts in Scotland had failed. Monmouth was now on his own. The council at which he discussed possible options with his commanders must have been a gloomy affair – he even suggested that the army disband while he returned to the Continent. The situation was not helped by the king offering a pardon to any rebel recruited in England if he laid down his arms.

Nevertheless, the decision was made to continue with the rebellion. With the hope of more recruits, a promise of supplies of arms from the Continent and support from Protestants in Ireland, the duke also took strength from the possibility of risings in Cheshire. Following the removal of much of the London garrison, there was even hope of support there. These were all to prove false hopes, however, and when on 3 July the rebel army arrived in the village of Bridgwater it was to face its final challenge alone.

Here the duke received the crushing news that Argyll's efforts in Scotland had failed. Monmouth was now on his own

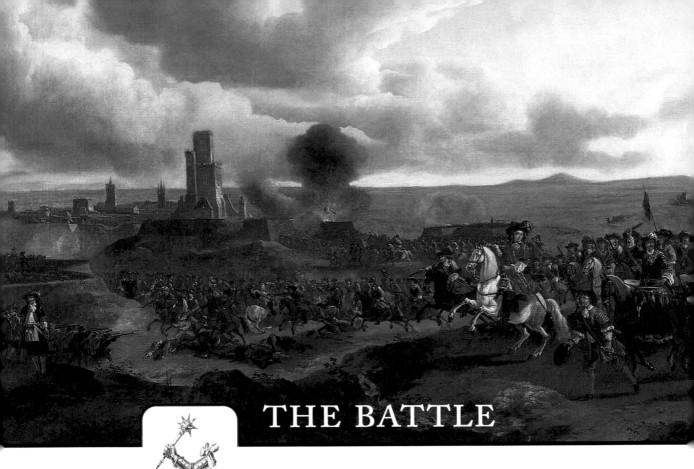

THE BATTLE

THE ROYALIST FORCE, NOW SHADOWING
THE REBELS' EVERY MOVE, CAMPED ABOUT
THREE MILES AWAY FROM MONMOUTH
ACROSS OPEN MOORLAND. THE INFANTRY
WERE CAMPED ON OPEN GROUND BETWEEN
THE VILLAGE OF WESTONZOYLAND AND A
WIDE DRAINAGE DITCH KNOWN AS THE
BUSSEX RHINE (PRONOUNCED 'REEN'). THE
MILITIA UNITS AND THE CAVALRY, WHO
WERE WITHOUT TENTS, WERE QUARTERED
IN THE VILLAGE ITSELF, ALONG WITH
THEIR COMMANDER. LORD FEVERSHAM
PONDERED HIS ENEMY'S NEXT MOVE:
WOULD THE DUKE MAKE A RUN FOR IT, OR
STAY PUT AND SIT OUT A SIEGE?

Feversham's informants told him that the latter was the most likely possibility – although they may have been deceived by a deliberate ruse on Monmouth's part, which he reinforced by sending out for extra food and entrenching tools. Feversham called up his heavy guns, but also kept the artillery close to the road in case Monmouth decided to make a run for it.

In the event, though, Monmouth chose neither to sit tight nor to flee. He had the necessary numbers of men, who were keen to fight, but he was aware that a face-to-face encounter over open ground in daylight against professional soldiers would place his scarcely trained volunteers at a fatal disadvantage. Instead, he had to exploit the element of surprise. Having climbed the church tower at Bridgwater and surveyed his enemy through an eyeglass, he hit upon the idea of launching an all-out attack – by night.

THE ENEMY HAS COME!

On the night of 5 July, Monmouth led his men out of Bridgwater. To avoid the roads, which were all heavily patrolled by Royalist cavalry, they set out over the moor. Silence among the men was essential. Horse furniture and hooves were muffled by rags and each man was under orders to club down the man in front if he so much as made a sound. A ground fog swirled around the rebels as they made their way in the dark across the broken ground. Their six-mile route was far from direct and even the local man employed to find them a path struggled to make headway. Precious time was wasted while he searched for the stepping stones across the Langmoor Rhine, a drainage ditch which, along with the Bussex Rhine, cut across their approach to the Royalist army. The delay, though, saved the rebels from meeting a Royalist mounted patrol on its way to Bridgwater, with orders to check that the rebel army were still there.

But the duke's good fortune did not hold for long as, when he and his men were about a mile short of the Royalist position, a pistol shot rang out in the darkness. Opinions were to vary as to whether the shot was discharged by a rebel – unnerved perhaps by a shadow moving in the mist – or by a watchful Royalist sentry. In any case, a mounted Royalist soldier galloped back to the camp where his comrades lay sleeping, and shouted the alarm: 'Beat your drums, beat your drums, the enemy has come!' Monmouth realized that any chance of deploying his entire force in a disciplined fashion was gone. Speed was now of the essence if any form of surprise was to be maintained and, making the best of it, he sent

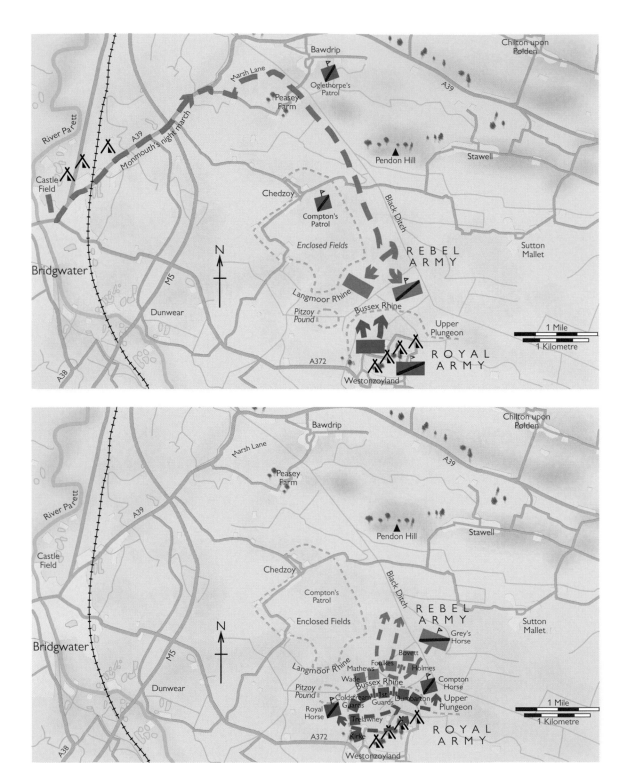

Movement of troops during the battle of Sedgemoor superimposed on a modern map

forward his cavalry. The infantry followed, making all possible haste. Spread back in single file for well over a mile, they hurried forward through the darkness in their regiments to form up facing the enemy.

As the rebel cavalry galloped towards the enemy, in anything but a coherent charge, the Royalist troops struggled into their uniforms and quickly fell into ranks in front of their tents behind the Bussex Rhine. Lord Grey, at the head of the rebel cavalry, looked for a way across the Rhine – it is said that they were seeking a causeway known as the Upper Plungeon – but when he found the crossing his path was blocked by 150 of the king's cavalry under the command of Sir Francis Compton. Muzzles flashed fire as pistol shots were exchanged; several of the king's officers were wounded and one of the balls found its mark in Compton's chest. Captain Sands took his place and, despite taking a pistol-ball himself, successfully defended the crossing against a regrouped force of rebel horse led by Captain Jones. Meanwhile, Grey restored order to the disarrayed horse and, turning them to the right, led them across the front of the Rhine, searching for another way across. In doing so he exposed his men to the Royalist front and musket volleys brought down horses and riders alike. Those who stayed mounted snatched their reins to the right and spurred away from the Rhine and back towards their own advancing infantry.

Feversham's well-disciplined men were by now fully deployed between the lines of their tents and the Bussex Rhine, which separated them from their foe. Dumbarton's Royal Scots Regiment, under Colonel Douglas, had the right. To his left were the 1st Foot Guards, under the Duke of Grafton; then the 2nd Foot Guards under Colonel Sackville; Trelawney's regiment under Colonel Churchill and Kirke's regiment on the extreme left. The Royalist horse were in the village of Westonzoyland and the artillery train strung out along the Bridgwater road. Even so, with not all the troops at his disposal present, Feversham was out-numbered. He had around 2,500 men with whom to fight the rebel force – which, though by the time of battle it had shrunk from its height of 5,000, was still probably over 3,000 strong – and the initiative was not his. Professional army or not, half an hour after that first pistol shot the outcome of Sedgemoor was anyone's guess.

The first of the duke's infantry began to arrive on the scene under the command of Wade, the most able of Monmouth's officers. His was a difficult task – to deploy his men in total darkness so that they faced the enemy. Using the glowing matchlocks from the enemy's right as a guide, he wheeled his men to the right, filing them out towards the royal army's

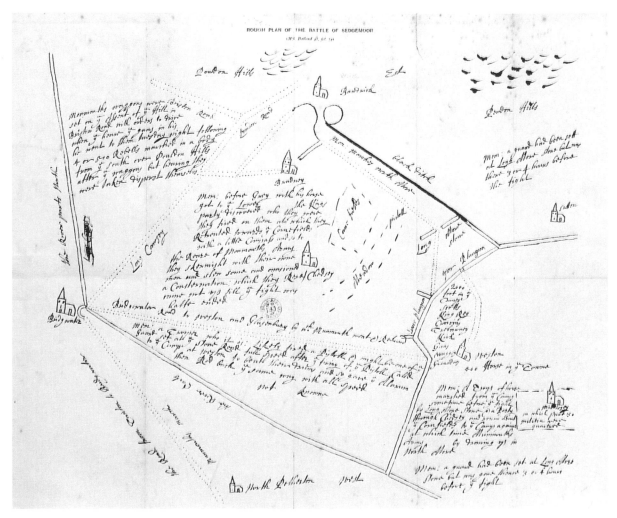

Paschall's map of the battlefield

left. Alas, he underestimated the distance – perhaps because those soldiers on the left were armed with firelocks rather than matchlocks and so invisible in the dark – and brought the deployment to halt only halfway along the face of the Royalist line. This left his front outflanked by the Royalist left and at least a third of his force unable to join on to the left of their own front. Correspondingly, though, the rebel left now outflanked the Royalist right and once battle had commenced, the senior officer in the camp, Churchill (later the Duke of Marlborough), moved regiments from the left behind their own line to create a new right and so come face to face with the reduced rebel line.

Wade's next move was surely to advance his Red regiment across the

John Churchill, 1st Duke of
Marlborough

Rhine to join in hand-to-hand fighting with the king's troops, where the
rebels' greater numbers might carry the night. Instead they became
frozen to the spot and those with firearms – hundreds of men were
armed only with scythe blades attached to the ends of poles – opened
fire with their muskets. As ball after ball was sent towards the royal line,
Colonel Matthews's Yellow regiment following suit, the king's army
showed its mettle, each regiment standing at attention, staring out
towards the flashing muskets on the other side of the Rhine. Officers gave
orders that not a single shot was to be returned and here and there men
fell to the ground as missiles found their targets. It was the best part of
two hours before the rebel muskets were silenced by lack of ammunition.

As the rebels' fusillade began, their gunners (by now having only three light pieces in their armoury, having abandoned one during the advance) positioned themselves. The cannon were aimed towards the royal right and soon men in that part of the line were cut down. The three light field pieces, however, could only do so much. By the time dawn began to break it was obvious that the rebels had let opportunity slip from their hands. By then the royal artillery had brought sixteen guns into action. With accurate counter battery fire they took out the rebel guns and then began to cut swathes through the ranks of infantry. Monmouth left the field with several of his followers.

Then the order was given and, with their enemy now clearly visible in the dawn light, the king's officers drew their swords, urging their men into attack. With bayonets fixed the royal line surged like a single great beast. Down into the Rhine they went, the water barely wetting their calves, and up the other side. Choreographed to the second, the royal cavalry crossed both the Upper and Lower Plungeons and pounded towards both the left and right of the rebel position. Monmouth's scythemen were broken in an instant and the slaughter began.

Escape was now the only option left open to the rebels. They turned and fled, many to be cut down by horsemen, who easily outpaced them. Some came to grief in other ditches, shot down into the mire as they struggled to get across. Those who made it into the cornfield on the opposite side were hunted down and put to the sword. For hours the pursuit and killing continued: the retribution had begun. Well before the morning of 6 July had come to an end, the best part of 1,500 rebels, almost half of Monmouth's entire army, lay dead. Monmouth was captured two days after the battle – found hiding in a ditch – and he too met a bloody end.

A contemporary playing-card depicting the battle

The morning of Sedgemoor

WHO FOUGHT HERE

REBELS ARE NOTHING IF NOT DARING
GAMBLERS. TO SUPPORT A CHALLENGE TO
THE COUNTRY'S LEADERSHIP IS TO RISK
ALL. MOST, IF NOT ALL, OF THOSE WHO
RALLIED TO THE DUKE OF MONMOUTH CAN
HAVE BEEN IN LITTLE DOUBT ABOUT THE
FATE THAT AWAITED THEM IF THE BID
WERE TO FAIL: BLOODY DEATH IN BATTLE
OR CAPTURE FOLLOWED BY TRIAL AND
AWFUL PUNISHMENT FOR TREASON.
SO WHO WERE THEY? WHAT DO WE KNOW
OF THE BACKGROUNDS AND CHARACTERS OF
THE THOUSANDS WHO TOOK SUCH A RISK,
LEAVING BEHIND THEIR ORDINARY LIVES
AND SETTING OUT IN 1685 IN THE HOPE OF
TOPPLING THE KING?

In the weeks following the battle, parish leaders were ordered to draw up lists of all who had been absent from home during the weeks of the rebellion. Over 2,600 names appeared on those lists. Given that a few people would have been able to call in the kinds of favour needed to be kept off such a list, it may be that there were around 3,000 rebels, though figures as high as 5,000 are regularly quoted.

Almost all of them came from Somerset, the rest from neighbouring Devon, Cornwall, Dorset and Wiltshire. They were almost all from the lower classes – Lord Grey was the only titled man to join the rebels and the vast majority of the gentry stayed away in droves. They were poor, although the poor in the south-west were no worse off than the poor elsewhere: the towns were overpopulated, but only because local crafts and trades like cloth weaving, glove making, lace making and stocking knitting held out hope of employment; and the rich farmland promised work on arable and dairy farms and in the orchards and market gardens. It would be a mistake, however, to think that poor in this case meant ignorant or gullible. Literacy was not exclusive to the wealthy or the gentry by this time. Inventories compiled in the years immediately before the rebellion show that books were among the possessions of comparatively poor craftsmen such as weavers. The common folk who followed the duke did so because they believed – because they had been exposed to pamphlets and other sources of contemporary politics and ideas – that he offered hope of a better life. The Protestants among them believed too that the duke promised security from a religion they feared. Not only was there widespread support in the region for Exclusion, but rumours of a 'popish plot' to force Catholicism on Anglicans – the religious majority in England – had been circulating for some time and passions were running high.

As in so many wars, most of the volunteers were also young. Many of the rebels were men in their teens or early twenties – young men without positions in society, perhaps without jobs or dependants. They had nothing to lose but their lives. There were also family men in their thirties and forties, ready and willing to leave their homes and work in support of Monmouth's ambition.

It is vital to remember that the Duke of Monmouth would not have planned to fight his way to London and the throne with this army of commoners. He had little money and the need for rapid advance through the country left him and his few officers little time in which to train and supply a credible force. While he was able to collect some arms along the way – from fleeing militiamen and others – he was by no means able to

The common folk who followed the duke did so because they believed that he offered hope of a better life

ITY OF LONDON TOWARDS HIS CORONATION
The Duke of York's Horse Guard. Confisting of

'The Horse Guards' from Ogilby's
Coronation of Charles II

equip all who came to his side, which is why, famously, many were armed simply with scythe blades fixed to long poles. The duke was more than enough of a strategist to realize that he depended not upon military might but upon popularity to carry him into power. His volunteers would be the rallying point for this popularity rather than the means with which to smash a professional army. That his men stood by him – there was hardly a deserter among them during weeks of campaign – says much about the duke as an inspirational leader and about the men who answered his call.

A STANDING ARMY

A further reason to believe the duke planned not to fight but to be carried to the throne by a wave of popular support, and to admire the bravery of his supporters, is the fact that they faced professional soldiers. The duke's rebels were the first in British history to fight against a standing army. Whereas in earlier times a monarch had relied upon his right to demand military service from his people in time of need, by 1685 war was the job of men who trained and prepared for nothing else. Oliver Cromwell's New Model Army, formed in 1645 to help Parliament defeat the Royalists, and notorious for its discipline and its religious zeal, had sown the seeds from which professional soldiery and the concept of the modern army grew.

The standing army available to the king at that time was about 9,000 strong. This was a small force compared to the armies of seventeenth-century Continental powers, and an illustration of the way ambitious men sometimes viewed the defence of the realm at this time – with a dismissiveness bordering on contempt. James deployed almost half these to suppress the rebellion. Small as it was, though, it was still professional.

WEAPONS

Traditional history has often painted the Monmouth Rebellion as a quixotic adventure: well meant, but doomed. As part of this picture, in the oral tradition at least, much has been made of the duke's 'scythemen' – doughty men of toil armed with nothing more than Protestant zeal and the scythes from their own tool stores, tied to poles. The abiding impression to be had from the folk myth is of a rebel army less than blessed with the paraphernalia of war. In fact, however, while Monmouth undoubtedly lacked the time to train his ad hoc army fully for the job in hand, the quality of the equipment he had at his disposal was at least equal, and possibly superior, to that of the royal army.

Among the fighting men Monmouth landed with in Dorset were a handful of Dutch gunners trained in the use of four light field guns, the extent of his artillery train. He had spent part of his meagre budget (apparently even his mistress, Lady Henrietta Wentworth, had pawned her jewels to boost the campaign coffers) on 1,500 'foot arms' and 1,500 cuirasses. The latter was armour for the cavalry he had yet to raise but in fact it was never unloaded. It was later captured, along with the ship that had carried it from the Low Countries, by an English navy vessel. The term 'foot arms' describes the two kinds of weapon with which infantry were equipped at the time: muskets and pikes.

At the time of the rising, the musket was going through a transition from the matchlock type that had long been the staple, with the powder being ignited by the smouldering end of a two-foot length of cord – the matchcord – impregnated with saltpetre. These weapons were not only slow to use, often unreliable and useless in wind and rain, but, given the matchlock's propensity to spark, one might also accidentally ignite the powder in a musketeer's bandoleer or in barrels near by. Just to add insult to injury, the glow of the little orange lights of many matchlocks could give away the position of a party of musketeers working under cover of darkness – as indeed happened to the Royalist troops at Sedgemoor. Since the Royalist troops did not report the rebels giving away their own positions in the same way, it is possible that most if not

Pikemen

1685

all of Monmouth's men were armed with the new type of musket, the flintlock. In this evolution the matchcord was replaced with a piece of flint and a simple trigger mechanism caused the flint to strike against steel, creating a shower of sparks that ignited the powder. If it was the case that some of Monmouth's men were armed with the flintlock, they had an advantage over their opponents, most of whom seem to have been armed with matchlocks. Only those Royalist soldiers fighting from horseback – the Guards, for instance – would certainly have been using

flintlocks, as using the matchlock was an impossibility from the moving firing platform of a horse. Unfortunately for the duke, though, whether his muskets were matchlocks or flintlocks, he did not have enough of them to equip more than half of his men.

The bayonet probably made an early appearance at the battle of Sedgemoor. The English Royal Fusiliers, raised in 1685, had muskets and bayonets issued to them and bayonets had been used on the Continent by regiments of the French Fusiliers since 1671. In its earliest manifestation, as used at Sedgemoor, the bayonet was little more than a knife 'plugged' into the barrel of the musket – the so-called 'plug bayonet'. This had the obvious handicap of rendering the musket unusable as a firearm, but at least it enabled the musketeer to defend himself if his enemy was going to close with him before he could reload. The next evolution – the ring or socket bayonet which slotted around the outside of the barrel and allowed continued firing – did not come into common use in Britain until the early 1690s.

The bayonet probably made an early appearance at the battle of Sedgemoor

THE AFTERMATH

THE BLOODY ASSIZES

'WE HAVE BY SAD AND LONG EXPERIENCE
FOUND THE MISCHIEVOUS AND FATAL
EFFECTS OF TOO MUCH LENITY AND
INDULGENCE, WHICH MEETING WITH THE
INCORRIGIBLE ILL NATURE OF THE SECTARIES
AND PHANATICKS, DID CERTAINLY BEGET
AND NOURISH THIS LATE IMPUDENT
REBELLION; WHICH A FEW GENTLESTROKES
OF JUSTICE WOULD AT FIRST HAPPILY HAVE
PREVENTED; SO THAT THE SWORD WHICH
HATH BEEN DEFINITELY UNSHEATHED, AND
HATH BEEN (THANKS TO ALMIGHTY GOD)
SO SUCCESSFUL, MUST FOR SOME TIME BE
NECESSARILY KEPT UNSHEATHED, IN THE
EXECUTION OF THE LAWS, TILL THIS
GENERATION OF IMPENITENT AND
DESPERATE REBELS BE ALL CUT OFF . . .'

Statement by the Devon Justices of the Peace, 15 October 1685

The merciless nature of the punishments inflicted upon the captured rebels after the battle of Sedgemoor has entered English folklore. Rebellion against the monarch was among the blackest of sins imaginable in the seventeenth century – and yet the horror with which the Bloody Assizes are recalled testifies to a special harshness.

Here was a government determined to stamp out once and for all any smouldering appetite for revolt. The Bloody Assizes, directed by Judge George Jeffreys three months after the battle, ordered the hanging of more than 250 rebels and the transportation to the West Indies of nearly 900 more. More than 100 died of their wounds in custody and of smallpox and other diseases caught during their incarceration in sordid conditions prior to any trial.

Even those only indirectly involved were punished. Dame Alice Lisle, for instance, a respected woman in her seventies, harboured two rebels in her home in the aftermath of the fighting. She was found guilty of high treason and sentenced to be burned at the stake. After special pleading on her behalf, she was dispatched by simple beheading.

The same fate awaited Monmouth. He was taken to the scaffold in London and placed under the axe of the veteran executioner Jack Ketch. Upon examination of the axe the duke, who faced his fate bravely, expressed doubts that it was sharp enough for the job at hand. Ketch replied that it was both sharp and heavy enough to remove the duke's head cleanly. He was wrong, and in the event after at least five axe blows Ketch had to resort to his knife to finish the job. The crowd was in uproar and Ketch was lucky to get away without being lynched.

Contemporary playing-cards depicting the Earl of Argyle's execution and the Bloody Assizes

the Dig

Feversham's HQ

We knew from accounts written soon after the battle that James's army, under the command of French-born Louis Duras, 1st Earl of Feversham, arrived at the village of Westonzoyland on Sunday 5 July, having marched from Somerton. On arrival a priority for the commanders would have been the dispersal of the men into whatever accommodation was available. Exact figures are hard to come by, but it is likely that Feversham's force at the battle of Sedgemoor numbered about 2,500 men. Of these perhaps 1,000 were cavalry, which meant space was needed for horses as well. There was also an artillery train of twenty-six guns and the supplies required by an army on the move. This then was a formidable body of men, animals and equipment and all of it had to be distributed, close enough at hand to be quickly drawn together again the following day. A further 1,500 men, forming three regiments of royal militia, were stationed a mile or more away to the south in the villages of Middlezoy and Othery.

The bulk of the foot-soldiers of the main force were put up in a tented camp hastily erected on the edge of the moor on the fringe of Westonzoyland, behind the Bussex Rhine. The cavalry and dragoons however, lacking tents, together with the rest of the infantry, had to be found beds in the homes and other buildings of the village itself. In his detailed 'narrative' of the events of July 1685, Andrew Paschall, Rector of Chedzoy, noted, '500 horse quarter in the town.' Senior officers helped themselves to billets in the best homes, including the inn, which still occupies the same site today. Feversham, his second-in-command John, Lord Churchill, and their closest aides set up their headquarters in the buildings of Weston Court on the high street. Paschall notes, 'The Lord General [Feversham] was on his campaign bed set up in the

parlour at Weston Court.' All in all the locals must have been thrilled.

Having looked at the available maps, we knew that Weston Court had been a sizeable place at one time. A large complex of substantial buildings had been put through various developments and redevelopments before disappearing from the maps around the twentieth century. As a key part of our project, we wanted to see what archaeological traces of those buildings remained – and in so doing learn more about the landscape that had provided the backdrop for the battle that brought Monmouth's rebellion to a bloody end.

The site of the main buildings of the place – where, presumably, Feversham would have lodged – is now covered by the more modern homes that front the main road through the village, opposite St Mary's church.

Clearly there was no hope of finding anything related to the royal army's occupation there. But our eyes were drawn to the open ground to the rear of those buildings: an inviting paddock, the surface of which was pock-marked with the familiar 'lumps and bumps' that always seem to speak to us of hidden historical treasures. It was with hungry eyes that we surveyed the uneven ground upon which horses now grazed. And what about the large and recently renovated barn that dominated it? Did any of the structure date to 1685, or had it been built more recently from dressed masonry scavenged from the ruins of older buildings?

The secrets of the paddock had to remain hidden from us, as we were unable to secure permission to investigate it. We had to content ourselves instead with examining the lower paddock behind it. It has to be said

Opposite Trenches in the lower paddock

that initially we were disheartened. The site was some distance from the ground once occupied by the Weston Court buildings and it seemed a long shot indeed to be looking for traces of Feversham's sojourn here. The lower paddock had a 'landscaped' and manicured appearance: an artificially level terrace gave way, down a gentle slope, towards what appeared to be a man-made – or at least man-maintained – fishpond.

Optimism is one of the archaeologist's most valuable tools, however, and we were determined to coax out any secrets the ground was holding. Iain Banks, our geophysicist and lead archaeologist, hit the ground strolling (the pace required by his craft) and gradually built up a picture of the subsoil features. Given that it was high summer, when the grass was not quite as high as an elephant's eye but not far from it, his results were a testimony to his methodical style. His first printouts showed linear features – straight lines – cutting across the slope. He also located a circular feature about four to five metres across. We suspected that we were looking at man-made structures related to a landscaped garden post-dating 1685 by a century or more – perhaps a trackway leading towards and around a decorative pond – hardly what we wanted from the kind of manor we thought Feversham had bedded down in. The terrace or plateau higher up the slope, and closest to the barbed-wire fence separating us from the upper paddock, was initially just as discouraging to the naked eye. Were we not just looking at more of the efforts of an eighteenth- or perhaps even nineteenth-century gardener?

Fortunately for us, Banksie was not easily put off. The closer he got to the fence, up on the terrace, the more interesting his geophysical survey readings became. His magnetometer found traces of burning beneath the ground surface – results which, backed up by his instincts, suggested to him that he was pinpointing areas of buried brick. A magnetometer is sensitive to bricks because they are fired in a kiln – they are basically burnt soil. We were beginning to think that the tantalizing spread of lumps and bumps in the upper paddock, which had the appearance of building rubble levelled long ago and buried beneath the grass, might reach across into the ground we were investigating. More recent landscaping had made the lumps harder to see but their traces might still be there. In short, it was possible that the buildings of Weston Court had extended as far as the area of our lower paddock. We still had a chance of glimpsing some fragments of Feversham's landscape.

Using the geophysical plots as our guide, we set to work opening up trenches over three of the most tempting anomalies – areas that looked as if they might feature building remains. As this was carefully maintained pastureland and the owners had asked us not to use a mechanical digger here, we cut the turf with spades, making careful piles of the green rectangles so that we could put them back in place once our work was done. Then we began a careful clean-up of the exposed ground surface. To our dismay, two of the three areas contained something that we archaeologists tend to find quite a lot of, and for which we have a highly descriptive technical expression – wall-to-wall bugger-all! There was not so much as a sherd of seventeenth-century pottery to give us a hint that we were on Feversham's trail.

To begin with, the third trench seemed to be the same. Finding a spread of hard-packed stone, we

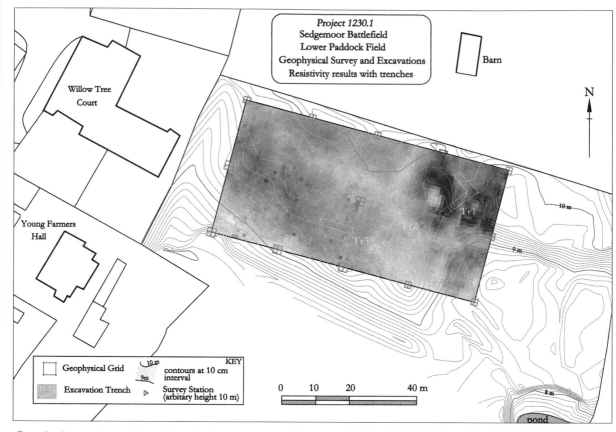

Project 1230.1
Sedgemoor Battlefield
Lower Paddock Field
Geophysical Survey and Excavations
Resistivity results with trenches

KEY
☐ Geophysical Grid   contours at 10 cm interval
▦ Excavation Trench   ▷ Survey Station (arbitrary height 10 m)

0   10   20   40 m

Geophysics and trench locations in the lower paddock – building in Tr 1

thought for an hour or two that we might have found a floor surface, but closer inspection persuaded us that it was just hard standing related to the eighteenth- or nineteenth-century landscaping. A scarcely visible linear bump on the surface that we hoped was a wall was soon revealed as nothing more than a possible field boundary. We were on the point of writing off our trench as a bad job when Banksie decided on a death-or-glory effort. Left to his own devices, he's as dogged as they come and never happier than when he's left alone on site to investigate his own theories – and today was no exception. Armed initially with mattock and shovel, and later with trowel and brush, he punched a narrow slot trench through the hard standing. Working steadily downwards, he finally found what he had expected to be there all along, thirty to forty centimetres deeper

than we had first thought. There it was: a section of massively built, mortared wall running diagonally across our trench. To our eyes, it was beautiful. It was also proof positive that the buildings related to Weston Court had once extended at least as far as the lower paddock and perhaps this substantial structure had been a fixture on the wider landscape over which the battle of Sedgemoor had raged. Even more fascinating for us, the wall Banksie had found was part of a building that had not featured on any of the early maps we had looked at.

Here, then, was part of what keeps us fascinated by this battlefield archaeology thing that we do. We had arrived at the site of two paddocks – one a quietly neglected exercise area for horses, the other visited occasionally by sheep, and the two separated by a barbed-wire fence. Nothing about either would suggest to the casual observer that here there had once been a large complex of buildings, occupied for long periods by one of the area's wealthiest families – and for part of one night by a battlefield commander, his aides and his senior officers. Churchill and the rest were housed in the buildings around Feversham, their cavalrymen, their dragoons and their horses close by. Then somewhere in the distance of that night of 5 July 1685, a shot rang out, followed by the call to arms that roused them all from their rest and sent them stumbling out into the dark to face the enemy . . . Part of our picture of that lost landscape comes from old maps, part from our imagination, fuelled by historical accounts – and part now from the slot trench so stubbornly excavated by Banksie. It is just a section of a wall, long buried beneath a carefully tended garden. But it is a vital find. At the very least, it adds detail to our picture of the village as it was around the time when the royal army of James II arrived to crush a dangerous rebellion.

Rediscovering the Bussex Rhine

In war, as in so much else, the devil is in the details. The simple facts are that the Monmouth Rebellion failed and the battle at Sedgemoor left more than 1,500 rebels dead. A look at the details, however, the minutiae affecting decisions made on the spur of the moment and under appalling pressure, reminds us that Monmouth missed his objective at Sedgemoor by the merest of margins. One of the details that was to make all the difference may have been his failure to understand thoroughly the terrain upon which the battle was to be fought.

Any ignorance on the duke's part of the nature of the few miles of ground lying between him and his foes was not for want of trying. Monmouth took the trouble to send out a labourer, a local man named Godfrey, to examine the Royalist camp at Westonzoyland and see if they were 'digging in'. The labourer returned with the news that there was no such entrenchment, and nothing in his manner gave the duke reason to believe there was anything else relating to the ground he should know about. Godfrey's information was pivotal in convincing the duke to launch his night march from his base at Bridgwater and attempt a surprise attack.

When the rebel army marched out of Bridgwater that Sunday evening, they easily crossed the Black Rhine, the first of the ditches across their path. The Langmoor Rhine proved to be more of an obstacle. Their guide, Godfrey, failed to find the crossing-point – marked by a large boulder called the Langmoor Stone – at the first attempt. We can only imagine the tension among those rebels, their bodies coursing with fear and adrenaline, as they stood around in mist-shrouded darkness while their officers awaited word that the crossing had been located. Before it could be found, of course, that pistol shot rang out. In the midst of the subsequent mêlée the crossing was found and the cavalry clattered across, desperately trying to reach the king's camp before the soldiers could be alerted.

But still another obstacle awaited them – and it was this, the third of the ditches, the Bussex Rhine, that finally proved to be the rebels' undoing. While the cavalry galloped left and right in search of the crossing-points, and while the infantry stubbornly refused to splash across, the king's soldiers were able to pull themselves together and establish the order that would carry the battle.

Much of the drama of that night, then, revolves around – or rather stumbles around – the Rhines. The Bussex and Langmoor Rhines were filled in many years ago as part of the continuing process of land management. The Black Rhine was later absorbed by a more substantial drainage system, built between 1797 and 1798 and fittingly named as King's Sedgemoor Drain. By the time the first edition of the Ordnance Survey map of this area was produced in 1809, 124 years after the battle, all traces of the Bussex Rhine had disappeared. The 1809 map is characterized by square and rectangular fields and straight drainage ditches with no sign whatsoever of the meandering course of the Bussex Rhine.

Even though the Bussex Rhine has long since disappeared on the ground, thanks to a special kind of aerial photograph we can in places see its meandering course clearly. Using infra-red film, the camera picks up differences in temperature and so the sections of the former drainage ditch that are still wet, and therefore colder than the surrounding ground, show up in a darker colour on the photograph. Even on photographs using standard film we have been able to see the route of the ditch as it arcs around the northern edge of Westonzoyland, because sections of the Rhine survive as very subtle topographic features that cast shadows when the sun is low in the sky. If you visit Mortimer's Field, for instance, across the track from the battlefield monument, you can make out a definite depression running from one corner to another. These features

showed up most clearly on a wartime photograph taken in 1944.

Our first step in locating the ditch on the ground was to mark out its most likely course, using the information we had gleaned from the photographs and maps, and a series of flags, which created quite a dramatic line cutting across the landscape. From the wavy line we had seen on the photographs it now seemed likely that from the Rhine had begun its life as a natural watercourse rather than a man-made drain, even if that was the function it came to serve.

The next stage was to cut a slice through the lines to try to see exactly what sort of obstacle the rebels faced. For this operation we chose a section of the Rhine as it passed through King's Field, at a point quite close to where we suspected the Lower Plungeon had been. Under the keen eye of Paul Duffy, a JCB was brought in to scrape a trench across the Rhine's course. To our relief the weather had been dry for a while and so even though the ground was still moist, as it always is, we didn't risk losing our machine to the muddy depths! With the trench dug we began cleaning up the section face, which would allow us to examine the various deposits and, we hoped, find the bottom and sides of the ditch.

A number of soil horizons were present, most of which were formed from very sticky clay and silt. We were relieved to see that we had been digging in the right place – the edges of the Rhine were visible in the section, and the sides of the ditch sloped down gently from both ends of our trench. Although we had hit

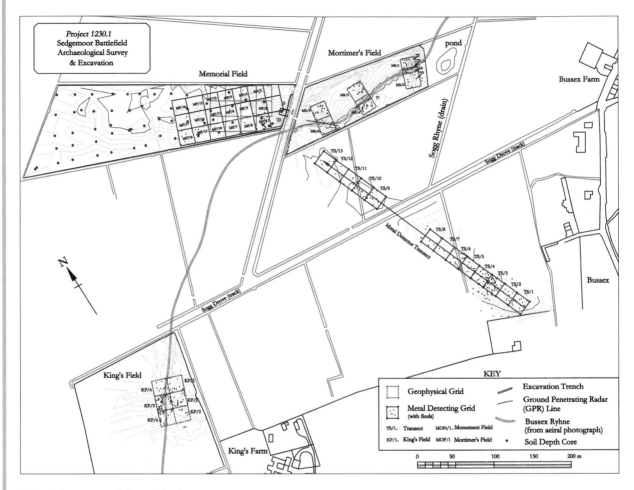

Project 1230.1
Sedgemoor Battlefield
Archaeological Survey
& Excavation

Memorial Field

Mortimer's Field

pond

Bussex Farm

Sogg Rhyne (drain)

Sogg Drove (track)

Bussex

Metal Detector Transect

Sogg Drove (track)

King's Field

King's Farm

KEY

Geophysical Grid

Metal Detecting Grid
(with finds)

TS/1. Transect   MON/1. Monument Field
KF/1. King's Field   MOF/1 Mortimer's Field

Excavation Trench

Ground Penetrating Radar
(GPR) Line

Bussex Ryhne
(from aerial photograph)

Soil Depth Core

0   50   100   150   200 m

Metal-detector grids and finds

water before we could reveal the bottom of the Rhine, we could tell from the angle of the banks that it wasn't especially deep, probably less than a metre. In our mind's eye we had seen the Rhine as an imposing feature, but this wasn't what reality presented us with. What the Rhine lacked in depth, though, it made up for in width. From bank to bank the Rhine, at least at the point where we had cut our trench, was eight and a half metres wide. Its width would have made the Rhine appear quite daunting to anyone encountering it for the first time and the presence of any water at all would have added to the effect, especially in the dark. Even if it was only ankle deep it would have been impossible to tell without

risking life and limb and stepping into it. We can't blame the rebels for not surging across the Rhine and equally we have to admire the royal army for positioning itself behind such a misleading feature. Having been by the Rhine in daylight, the king's men had been able to find out how shallow it was, and when the order came to charge at the rebels they stepped across it without hesitation.

Casting our net wider, we excavated a number of trenches in Mortimer's Field. Some of these raised more questions than answers. The most straightforward of the trenches, cut like the first one straight across the Rhine, revealed the ditch to be equally wide but even shallower than in the first trench, the maximum depth at this point being about thirty centimetres, but again with even a small amount of standing water it would have appeared to be a potential death trap. It is likely that Godfrey, Monmouth's guide, was aware of the shallow nature of the Rhine but to him it may have seemed too inconsequential to merit mention.

Many of the accounts of the battle mention the Lower and Upper Plungeons, which were fords or crossing-points on the Rhine. Even though it would have been possible for men on foot to step across the Rhine at various points, if they didn't mind getting their feet wet, cavalry would probably have had more difficulty; and at the time of the battle the Plungeons were considered important tactical locations. We were obviously keen to try to find one of the Plungeons and we had reason to be hopeful as far as the Upper Plungeon was concerned.

In the aerial photographs we had noticed three sets of parallel lines crossing the line of the Rhine as it passes through Mortimer's Field. Could these represent crossing-points? Close observation on the ground had revealed telltale linear depressions leading up to the Rhine on both sides at points corresponding to the aerial anomalies. We checked these out with a geophysical survey, and sure enough a series of strong areas of high resistance showed up. We decided to place a trench over the most easterly example.

At this point things started to get a bit complicated, and our initial trench turned into no less than four as we attempted to understand what we had uncovered. What we found were a pair of clay banks crossing over the Rhine, each of which was about a couple of metres wide. These would certainly have allowed a man on horseback

to cross the Rhine dry shod, and in fact we found a horseshoe embedded in the surface of one of the banks. What puzzled us was the fact that there were two parallel banks here, and apparently two more sets within the same field. If these were crossing-points, there seemed to be rather a lot of them, and they appeared to be dual carriageways! It was also obvious that the banks would act as dams, blocking the water of the Rhine on either side, which seemed strange if it served as a drain.

Scratching our heads, we went back to the aerial photographs. When we looked at them a little more closely we noticed that parallel lines appeared all over the place, not just at the three points crossing the Rhine. A number of them crossed King's Field, near where we suspected the Lower Plungeon had been. More importantly the lines crossed fields some distance away from the Rhine. We thought for a while that they were trackways, and indeed some of them may have been, but we now think that these strange parallel banks may have been field boundaries, which at some point in the past divided the landscape into a series of fields. These fields are in the area known as the Somerset Levels, which we know – from some of the finest prehistoric timber structures in Britain that have been found there, preserved by the peat – have been occupied for a very long time. At the moment we have no idea how old the banks are, but being man-made they must relate to a period when the Levels were reasonably dry, perhaps during the Iron Age, about 2,000 years ago. They remain a mystery, but we hope to find similar examples in other areas which will help us to understand them better. What is apparent, though, is that at the time of the battle of Sedgemoor these banks could have served as crossing-points, a fact that appears to have been lost on the rebels, who believed that their chances of crossing the Rhine rested on only two of them. But the important point here is that as our banks appear to be the most northerly of those visible on the ground and in the aerial photographs, this crossing-point may well have been that known as the Upper Plungeon.

Metal-detecting the battlefield

We now turned our attention to the details of the battle itself, which in its first phase saw the two sides located on either side of the Bussex Rhine. As Monmouth's army made its way across the moor, the majority of the royal army was at rest in its camp positioned somewhere between the Bussex Rhine and the village of Westonzoyland. Like everywhere else, the village has undergone change in the 300 or so years since the battle. The outskirts have extended, with a large number of houses being built over the past fifty years or so, particularly to the north, in the direction of the battlefield. Although the battlefield itself appears to have survived relatively intact, we were concerned that the site of the royal army camp might have been subsumed beneath these houses. However, it seemed likely that the camp was positioned on the same relatively high ground as the village, the wetter low ground being generally less suitable for the purpose, and there was an area of high ground at the northern edge of the village that had thus far escaped development and was still fields. It was here that we focused our attention.

We set up our first metal-detector survey grids as close to the northern edge of the village as we could, in

a position that placed us comfortably on what remained of the high terrace. We decided that the best tactic would be to lay out a transect or survey corridor starting out on the high ground and leading down across the fields, getting as close to the Bussex Rhine as possible. This would theoretically slice through the camp area and the lower ground where the royal army lined up to face the enemy. The detectors started to buzz, but as ever we would not know what treasures lay beneath our pin-flags until we started digging, and it wouldn't be the first time we had found nothing but junk. We needn't have worried: within minutes of putting the first spade into the ground the right sort of finds started to see the light of day.

The first things to strike us were the buttons, half a dozen or so in the first grid alone. These were circular, in several different sizes, made from a copper alloy and each with an eyelet fastening on the rear side. Some of the largest, about the size of a two-pound coin, had decorations, which were varied and intricate, and this, along with the fact that some were silver-plated, made these more likely to be at home on an officer's frock coat than on a squaddie's tunic. The smaller buttons,

plain and all roughly equal in size, had more of the appearance of fasteners from lower-ranking soldiers' uniforms, possibly from tunics. By the time of the battle of Sedgemoor, the still youthful British army had been issued with regulation uniforms, some of which varied from regiment to regiment. Later on, at least by the time of Culloden in 1746, tunic buttons often displayed distinctive military crests, but at this early period in the army's history tunic buttons were of polished but undecorated metal. Officers, given their gentlemanly status and moneyed backgrounds, displayed more variety in their uniforms.

Thanks to several contemporary accounts from men involved in the battle or close at hand we have some idea of the atmosphere in the camp at the time of the rebel attack. As the attack did not break until about two in the morning, most of the soldiers were asleep when the alarm was sounded. According to Captain Edward Dummer, 'Supineness and preposterous confidence of ourselves, with an understanding of the Rebells that many days before had made us make such tedious marches, had put us into the worst circumstances of surprise.' Though such circumstances might have proved fatal to a less disciplined force, Dummer continues, 'Yet such was the cheerfulness of our Army that [we] were almost as readily drawn up to receive them as a preinformed expectation could have posted them tho' upon so short and dangerous a warning.' A vivid picture of the troops' reactions is painted by Andrew Paschall, Rector of Chedzoy, who interviewed a number of combatants in the days after the battle. 'Now the drums beat, the drummers are running to it, even bare-foot for haste. All fly to arms. All are drawn out of their tents and in five battalions stand in the space between the tents and the ditch, fronting the ditch, not having their clothes or arms all on and ready. Thus were they expecting the enemy.'

The buttons we were finding, we believed, were pulled from their stitches and fell to the ground as the soldiers hurried into their uniforms, and were evidence that the camp was sited here. We also came across buckles, which may have been similarly ripped from clothes in the soldiers' rush to get dressed.

We were quite excited to find a heavy iron tent peg with a curved end, until Andy Robertshaw told us that army tents of the time, which had been only recently issued to the army (before then soldiers were expected to find what shelter they could when they were on campaign, or even sleep out in the open), were probably held in place by wooden rather than metal pegs. But someone was using iron pegs for something and we are keeping an open mind on this one.

We found other debris that may relate to general camp activity. There was an old pewter spoon, which may have been carried in a soldier's personal kit. An interesting set of items were a number of strips of lead, most of which had become bent and twisted over time.

Musket-balls and grapeshot

We had come across similar pieces on English Civil War sites about forty or so years older than Sedgemoor. These lumps of lead, usually folded into neat little parcels, were carried by soldiers and used as raw material to make musket-balls. The Civil War examples, from around Newark, had clearly been pulled from the roofs of buildings or from windows, as many of them had nail holes in them. Those from Sedgemoor were different – in particular they were all the same size and weight. We think that what we found indicates that by this time the army was carrying its own lead, which was transported in handy-sized ingots. Each lead strip would be enough to produce about six musket-balls, and making these is the sort of activity that would take place behind the lines in camp. We found only one musket-ball and a larger lead ball that may have been a piece of grapeshot, both of which appear to have been dropped rather than fired.

The position and patterning of the finds on the ground was another clue that told us we were in the camp. There was a distinct cluster of camp-related finds in the southern part of the survey transect, closest to the village, and this fell off sharply as we moved north. Almost as soon as we stepped off the slightly higher terrace we made very few finds, which suggested that we had moved out of the camp and passed into the dead ground between the edge of the camp and the Bussex Rhine, over which the king's troops hastened towards the enemy. Captain Mackintosh of the Royal Scots Regiment had been so sure of the imminent arrival of the rebels that he had had guide ropes strung out from the tents down to the forming-up area. Such preparedness suggests that although the rebels' arrival was something of a surprise they appeared from the direction they were expected, a factor that seriously reduced any tactical advantage.

On the low, level ground behind the Bussex Rhine we hoped to find the location of the king's troops as they lined up to face their enemy. After a few grids with few or no finds, the detectors started buzzing again, the flags reappeared – and here, all of a sudden, were musket-balls. Many appeared to have missed their targets, as they had retained their spherical shape and showed no evidence of crushing or distorting on impact. Some may have been dropped by the king's soldiers as they loaded their muskets in the dark, but they are more likely to be rebel munitions. As Monmouth's men blasted away across the Rhine, for almost two hours, it is likely that many shots fell harmlessly behind their targets after being fired over the heads of the king's men. As James II notes in his own account of the battle, it is natural for poorly trained or newly recruited troops to fire high, and there was no greener army in the land than Monmouth's collection of rebels.

But the rebel fire was not wholly ineffective and it is

Metalwork from the stock of a musket

a testimony to the discipline and commitment of the royal troops that they stood motionless in the face of this hail of lead. Although fire was returned, this appears to have been limited until light provided clear targets. The right of the royal line was formed by soldiers of the Royal Scots Regiment, among them those of the ever-ready Captain Mackintosh, and it was they who took the severest pounding. Monmouth's three field guns were trained on this regiment, with case-shot as well as musketry brought to bear – a fusillade which left all but four of the Scots officers here wounded or dead (we do not know the fate of Mackintosh) and probably caused most of the twenty-five to thirty fatalities among the enlisted men. Among the musket-balls we found larger balls, which may well be pieces of grapeshot or case-shot launched from Monmouth's guns.

In an effort to get an idea of the extent and position of the royal line, we metal-detected an area covering most of Mortimer's Field, where we had excavated sections across the Rhine, just to the north-east of our long transect. If the line continued into that field we expected to find further evidence of fighting, largely in the form of musket-balls. To our surprise, however, we found not much in the way of battle-related artefacts in this field. This absence of finds may indicate that the right of the royal line ended not far away from the northern end of our survey transect, and this would tie in with finds of grapeshot previously mentioned.

It is just as possible, however, that the royal line was positioned further back from the Rhine, which kinks back as it passes through Mortimer's Field. If this was the case, we would expect to find little evidence of overshoots in the narrow swathe of Mortimer's Field that sits on the southern (royal) side of the Rhine and we would need to look further to the south, in another part of the same field through the corner of which our transect passed. We must always be aware that we have subjected only a relatively small area to investigation and our interpretations must be tempered by this limitation. On our more confident days we may call battlefield archaeology 'the key to unlocking the past' but really it never fully opens the door; at best all we can hope for is a peep through the keyhole that permits a limited view of the room beyond.

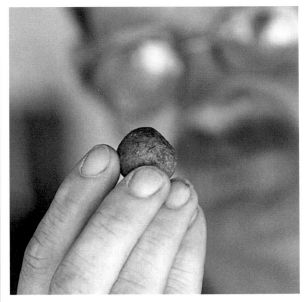

A musket-ball

Thus far we had concentrated our efforts on the Royalist side of the Bussex Rhine. It was now time to try our luck on the opposite side from which the rebel army advanced. It was the cavalry who had been first into action, racing ahead of the slower infantry almost as if it had been a starting pistol that had cracked out into the night back at the Langmore Rhine. The only hope for the rebel horse was to create havoc in the royal camp before the troops had a chance to form up, but Lord Grey's horsemen lost valuable time as they searched for a crossing over the Bussex Rhine. Finding the crossing held by a group of royal cavalry under Compton, they became embroiled in a fast but furious firefight, after which Grey's men turned away from the crossing and passed from right to left along the entire line of the Royalist army, which by now had formed up on the other side of the Rhine. For a time the men in the line appear to have mistaken the rebel horse for royal troopers, but eventually they fired on the moving target. Spurring their mounts back into the moor the rebels raced away from the Rhine as fast as they had not long before galloped towards it. Their troubles were far from over, though, as a number of riders were unseated by fire from their own oncoming infantry, who had in the darkness mistaken them as the enemy.

Metal-detecting revealed no evidence of the cavalry action in the vicinity of the Upper Plungeon, but we only detected in Mortimer's Field, which includes only very narrow areas on either side of the Rhine. An extension of this survey into the field to the north may identify the scene of this initial cavalry engagement. We had more success when we detected on both sides of the Rhine close to where the Lower Plungeon is thought to be, in an area that coincided with our excavation across the Rhine in King's Field. Once again our detectorists came up with the goods. Numerous musket-balls were pulled from the ground on both sides of the Rhine, and some other balls, whose small size suggests that they came from cavalry carbines or pistols. The fact that these balls were recovered from both sides of the Rhine is intriguing, as we have no accounts of a cavalry engagement this far down the Rhine, which must be close to the far left of the royal line. Contemporary accounts tell us that Royalist horse passed on to the moor from both the Upper and Lower Plungeons in order to contain both flanks of the rebel army, before charging into them at the close of the battle. As it is unlikely that royal cavalry fired back across the Rhine, where their own line was positioned, it seems logical to interpret these balls as coming from the rebels. The rebel horse may have fired back into the royal line as they belted across its front; or it is possible that a cavalry-on-cavalry engagement similar to that recorded at the Upper Plungeon took place at the Lower Plungeon.

We also made here perhaps the most evocative find of all – a broken or cut-down scythe blade, which must surely be one of those carried by one of Monmouth's unfortunate scythemen. Who knows the fate of this poor soul? Did he fall in the hail of musket-balls, or was he cut down by the king's cavalry in the rout, having thrown down his weapon? We can only hope that he was one of the fortunate ones who escaped retribution or trial and returned home to his family to live out the rest of his life in peace. But the scythe blade is not just a moving reminder of the battle: its location, close to the edge of the Rhine, tells us that the rebel right may have been close to achieving their goal of crossing over and engaging in combat with the royal army.

A rather different story is told, however, by the distribution of musket-balls in Monument Field, which revealed important evidence of the disposition of the opposing forces. We found very few musket-balls in the west end of the field, which is close to the bend in the Rhine and where the monument to the battle is located. More musket-balls were located further to the north-west, at a distance of about fifty metres from the Rhine, and if these fell anywhere near the rebel line this pattern suggests that the rebel infantry came to a halt some distance from the Rhine before they opened fire. This possibility is supported by Wade's account, in which he says, 'I advanced within thirty or forty paces of the ditch . . . and was there forced to make a full stop.'

For the most part, Feversham's men were protected either by distance, darkness or the inexperience of the enemy musketry – or all three – and the rebel bombardment and musket fire were ultimately failures. By failing to cross the Bussex Rhine and penetrate the royal camp, the rebels surrendered any hope of victory.

Mass graves

Oh Lord, where is my husband now –
Where once he stood beside me?
His body lies at Sedgemoor
In grave of oak and ivy.

Folk song, c. 1692

The corpses of the rebels who were cut down on the battlefield during the fighting, and in scattered groups across the countryside as they were routed and fled, were strewn across a wide area. Historical accounts reveal that some lay undiscovered where they fell until the following harvest, but the majority were given a burial, however cursory.

Whenever we investigate a battle, we are always mindful of the possibility that our excavations might unearth human remains, and Sedgemoor was no different. As is the case with many battlefields, local tradition holds that the dead were buried in large collective pits on or close to the seat of the fighting. There is no shortage of grim clues either: annotations on maps drawn by Andrew Paschall, Rector of Chedzoy, refer to '42 killed' and 'in one pit, 95'; a soldier serving with one of the Royalist militia regiments saw 174 bodies heaped into a mass grave and said that the local folk summoned to bury the battle dead later confirmed that they had accounted for 1,384. Then there are the lurid stories of wounded rebels buried alive among

the dead by Royalist soldiers, and special work gangs being called in to heap extra sand on to one shallow mass grave in the hope of keeping the stench of rotting flesh at bay. There are also recent reports of discoveries of human remains on the battlefield. In 1982, a colleague of ours, Keith Speller, came across a human bone protruding from a drainage ditch while he was conducting archaeological work close to the battlefield.

We were determined to do our best to pinpoint at least one of the locations of the graves. This was not about ghoulishness, or because we wanted to desecrate the graves of war dead. We want to find precise information about historical events in order to improve our understanding of them and enable the management of landscapes to become better informed. If we could locate a mass grave relating to the battle of Sedgemoor, it could be accurately marked, for one thing, and so taken into account in any future developments that may impinge upon the site. On-site examination of any human remains might also reveal information about how the victims had lived as well as how they died.

We figured that our best lead was a fascinating photograph of the nineteenth-century excavation of a mass grave. The field known variously as Monument Field or the Grave Field is generally accepted as the location of one or more of the mass graves and we were persuaded that it was here that the photograph had been taken. We enlisted the help of our surveyor, John Arthur, who cast his topographical eye over the image. He agreed with us that there was a reasonable likelihood that the church spire seen in the distance on the photograph was Chedzoy. Using the image as a guide, we carefully positioned ourselves in Monument Field so

TO · THE · GLORY · OF · GOD
AND · IN · MEMORY · OF · ALL · THOSE · WHO
DOING · THE · RIGHT · AS · THEY · GAVE · IT
FELL · IN · THE · BATTLE · OF · SEDGEMOOR
6ᵀᴴ JVLY 1685
AND · LIE · BVRIED · IN · THIS · FIELD
OR · WHO · FOR · THEIR · SHARE · IN · THE · FIGHT
SVFFERED · DEATH
PVNISHMENT · OR · TRANSPORTATION
PRO · PATRIA

The monument to the fallen

that Chedzoy church spire appeared on the horizon as it does in the photograph. We were all too well aware, however, that pacing about a field armed only with a photocopy of a nineteenth-century photograph was hardly what we could call a scientific approach. So we looked to geophysical survey in the hope of getting some corroborating evidence.

On a cursory walk over the field, we noticed a couple of spots where slight depressions were visible on the surface. These aroused our suspicions. We had read rebel sympathizer William Stradling's 1839 description of a visible mass grave in Monument Field comprising a 'circular dike'. Stradling also mentions the site being disturbed on at least two occasions, on one of which an 'immense number' of human bones had been found. We were increasingly of the opinion that one of these depressions might be the site in our photograph. A hole dug and then refilled will often settle and sink slightly as time passes and if it was a mass grave the steady decomposition of bodies beneath the soil would also have caused a slight depression.

Banksie submitted sections of the field to resistivity and magnetometer survey, paying particularly close attention to the two visible depressions. A concentration of nettles growing in one of these was interesting to us because these plants like to take root in disturbed, and therefore well-aerated, ground, and they thrive in soil that is rich in phosphates. They could be a vital clue, as decayed soft tissue would provide phosphates, while disturbance of the ground by excavations would have loosened the soil. Banksie's geophysical survey also pointed the finger towards at least one of the depressions. There was a suggestion of a rectangular-shaped anomaly beneath the surface. So we called in our mechanical digger to have a proper look.

The possibility of unearthing the bones of dead soldiers is always slightly unnerving. We read and study avidly the experiences of men who fall in such circumstances and have come to have great respect for those ready to lay down their lives for a cause. It is with no small hesitation, then, that we contemplate the prospect of coming face to face with such men, even in death. And so, confident as we had ever been that we were digging in the right place to reveal a mass grave, we were suitably subdued as the digger began to strip back the turf. We looked on quietly as the powerful yellow arm of the JCB went on to remove the dark brown plough soil beneath – and revealed undisturbed

bluish grey clay. It was as clean as could be and had clearly never been interfered with. It had never had a mass grave cut through it – nor any sort of hole for that matter. We could hardly believe it. We even went so far as to ask the machine operator to strip off the clay to reveal the ancient and similarly undisturbed peat beneath.

It was to be the same story in the two other trenches we opened up in Monument Field – one over the other visible depression and the other over yet another of Banksie's geophysical anomalies. Nothing. In each case the machine removed dark plough soil to reveal clean, undisturbed clay. Dogged as ever, Banksie turned to another technique. Arming himself with an auger – a giant corkscrew that penetrates deep into the soil, enabling its operator to remove (with great effort) a soil sample without digging a hole – he embarked upon a soil sampling survey. By this method we hoped to pinpoint an area where there was plough soil either beneath or mixed in with the bluish grey clay, which would be evidence of disturbance: an inversion of the natural stratigraphy. But we worked our way right across that field and found nothing worth investigating. Every sample we took showed undisturbed, clearly stratified layers of soil, clay and peat. It seemed that Monument Field, or at least the part we had time to investigate, was devoid of human remains or of the kind of hole that such remains might have been buried in. Again, despite our careful and methodical investigation of a combination of historical, anecdotal, topographical, geophysical and photographic evidence, there seemed to be no truth to the belief that hundreds of bodies had been buried in a mass grave in this field. And once again we asked ourselves: how can this be? It is worth pointing

An iron horse bit

out that even a relatively small hole, perhaps just a few metres wide and deep, can contain the remains of a surprisingly large number of people. It is therefore possible that graves may exist in the gaps between our auger survey in Monument Field.

However, there is another possibility. We have looked for human remains on many battlefields in Britain and elsewhere in the world. Always we have based our searches on evidence of one kind or another – map references, descriptions in contemporary or near-contemporary accounts of the battle's aftermath, geophysical anomalies. In almost every case, apart from a few human bones we recovered during rescue excavations of a couple of eroding burial cairns on the South African battlefield of Isandlwana (1879) and the

suggestion of burial pits revealed by ground-penetrating radar at Culloden (1746), every so-called 'mass grave' has drawn a complete blank.

We are sure enough of our abilities to say that this can not simply be put down to our failure as archaeologists or the failure of our equipment. We are methodical and rational in our sampling strategies and rigorous in our investigation of all possible leads. The explanation must be that we are looking in the wrong places. And that, we believe, is because of a fundamental misunderstanding of the way in which much of the killing occurred in historical battles.

Time and again, tradition places mass graves of hundreds or even thousands of bodies right there on the battlefield itself; the impression to be had is of huge, regular graves being dug right where the fighting took place and of a wholesale collection of the dead for interment therein. We suspect, though, that the fact of the matter is that bodies are buried where they are found. They are not collected for mass burial but disposed of where they fell. And we believe that the majority of the dead in historical battles fall not on the battlefield during the fighting but across acres of countryside, once one side accepts that all is lost and flees the field. Once the rout is under way, the worst of the killing often begins. Men alone, in pairs or in groups, are pursued over hundreds of metres or even over a few miles. Killed wherever they are overcome, they are then buried close to that spot by whoever is detailed to conduct a general clear-up of the area. Certainly that is suggested about Sedgemoor, in the accounts of some men fleeing into fields, being cut down among the crops and their remains not being found until the following harvest.

If we accept this more realistic picture, it makes sense to suppose that, far from lying in heaps on the battlefield, the dead of a typical battle are scattered across wide tracts of countryside and buried in ones and twos and threes in inconspicuous, unmarked graves. Rather than looking for great holes containing hundreds of dead, then, we should search for dozens or hundreds of small holes containing just one or two corpses. The accounts tell us that 1,500 rebels and about 30 Royalist troops died fighting at Sedgemoor. No doubt some of them are buried in the vicinity of the site now known as Monument Field. We suspect, however, that the remains of most of the slain are scattered across the countryside in this way and are most likely to be discovered by chance, if at all.

The Somerset Levels – an archaeological treasure house

Battles take place over minutes, hours and sometimes days. Our challenge is always to catch glimpses of what are really nothing more than momentary blips on the oscilloscope of human history. We should never forget, however, that the sites of most battles have witnessed human history over many thousands of years, with the battle coming and going within the mere blink of an eye. Sometimes we are made aware of this fact by the objects we find, and at Sedgemoor we were especially rewarded. During the metal-detector survey of the camp area, we discovered a small bronze socketed axe. This related not to the camp or the battle but to the human occupation of this landscape several thousand years ago. The axe is broken, and perhaps was discarded because of this, and damage on the blade suggests that it saw heavy use. You can just make out the remains of a loop which helped to bind the axe head to its wooden shaft below the fracture on its butt. Such axes generally date to the middle to late Bronze Age, which makes it 3,500–4,000 years old.

Despite its small size, the axe was probably used for cutting timber – a function especially relevant to the Somerset Levels. The area is low-lying, and, being closer to sea level than the surrounding hills, has been rather marshy for much of its history, but these wet conditions did not put people off living on the Levels – far from it. There is an amazing wealth of evidence from the area around Sedgemoor that shows how prehistoric people adapted to this environment. The intricately built timber trackways that have been preserved in the waterlogged conditions which prevail on the Levels make the area a unique archaeological treasure house.

A Bronze Age axe head

During the Bronze Age the timber for the trackways would have been hewn and shaped using an axe like the one we found; in the preceding period, the Neolithic, stone axes would have been used. The timber trackways were set up on posts, which raised them above the level of marshy ground, and they probably linked settlements across expanses of the low-lying terrain. The most famous example is probably the Sweet Track, located six miles to the north-east of the battlefield. Excavation has established that this 6,000-year-old causeway runs for over a mile and is a feat of Neolithic craftsmanship. As time passed the water levels rose over it but it was preserved, first in swampy water, then in peat. Smaller stretches of trackway have been found in the immediate neighbourhood of the battlefield. The prehistoric field systems for which we believe we have found evidence in the form of the parallel banks are probably later than the preserved trackways and relate to a time when drainage had done much to alleviate the need for causeways.

Conclusion

The Monmouth Rebellion came to a decisive and bloody conclusion at Sedgemoor. But was Monmouth's cause lost from the start? Was it nothing more than a fool's errand, fired by misguided ambition and false hope?

There can be no doubting the loyalty and determination of the Duke of Monmouth's followers, as many of them paid with their lives for a belief in his cause. Perhaps those who fell on the field at Sedgemoor were the lucky ones, for many more were to die afterwards as the Bloody Assizes earned their name; nor should we underestimate the cruel reality of transportation to the colonies at that time, an act of exile that brought suffering and premature death, through disease or harsh treatment, to many of those

men, who were separated from their homes and families by oceans. All that determination and commitment, though, was not enough to carry the field. The rebellion may not have been quite a fool's errand, but at the end of the day – or rather the beginning of the day, as the battle was fought at dawn – the military inexperience of the rebel army and its lack of training and discipline lost it the battle. It is to Monmouth's credit that he recognized these shortcomings and tried to even the odds by surprising the royal army with a night attack, but from the moment the rebel approach was spotted the battle was surely lost.

Much has been written about the Bussex Rhine and the fact that it provided an impossible obstacle to the rebels. The assumption is often made that if the rebels had been able to cross it they could have fought the troops on equal terms. But our investigations have shown that the Rhine was not impassable, as was in any case demonstrated by the fact that the royal army passed over it when they advanced. In reality the Rhine may have looked like a daunting ditch with water of unknown depth in its bottom but in fact been more of a psychological barrier than a real one. What really stopped the rebels in their tracks were the ranks of disciplined troops that faced them; and it was the frightening prospect of coming to grips with them that prompted the rebel troops to open fire prematurely, apparently to no great effect. We have also established that the rebels had to face volley fire from the royal line. Musket-ball finds on the rebel side of the Rhine dispel any idea that the rebels were entirely unmolested by enemy musketry – and we can be certain that the royal fire would have been far more accurate than that offered by the rebels. Certainly, the rebels came very close to their foe, as demonstrated by our finds in King's Field, which included a scythe blade found near the Rhine, but with the element of surprise gone they didn't stand a chance. And so it was that the Monmouth Rebellion came to a decisive and bloody conclusion at Sedgemoor.

Sedgemoor is often described as the last pitched battle on English soil, as opposed to a skirmish such as Clifton in 1745. This accolade suggests that the battle was followed by a long peace, but nothing could be further from the truth, which is that the battles continued, but away from England.

James II may have succeeded in crushing the Monmouth Rebellion, but he was not to remain on the

English throne for long. His Catholicism made him increasingly unpopular among the predominantly Protestant populace and when, in 1688, he had a son it was feared that the birth marked the foundation of a Catholic royal dynasty. Things came to such a pass that Parliament invited James's son-in-law, William of Orange and his wife Mary, to take the English throne, under new constitutional controls which would limit the power of the monarch. William may have been Dutch, but he was also a staunch Protestant, and in the eyes of many of James's subjects that was all that mattered. In November 1688 William landed with an army at Torbay and proceeded to march on London. In the face of such overwhelming dissent, James chose flight rather than fight, seeking sanctuary in France and leaving the vacant throne to be occupied jointly by William III and Mary II.

William succeeded where Monmouth had failed for two main reasons. First, William had real, widespread support in the face of an increasingly unpopular monarch, while Monmouth never really achieved anything but blind faith among a few thousand otherwise peaceful inhabitants of the south-west of England. To put it another way, William was invited to the party, whereas Monmouth was really nothing more than a gatecrasher. Even if he had won the battle at Sedgemoor, Monmouth may well have failed to take and keep the Crown. Second, and perhaps just as important, William brought with him an impressive fighting force: an army 15,000 strong which included some of the most experienced troops in Europe. The final straw for James, though, came when both these factors combined and the king's army, now under the command of John Churchill, who had served James at Sedgemoor, sided with William. The lack of bloodshed in these dramatic events led to them becoming known as the Glorious or Bloodless Revolution.

But it wasn't long before the blood began to flow. James, while in exile, was not totally without loyal support, especially among the Catholics of Scotland and Ireland; his cause also suited the ambitions of the French king, Louis XIV, who was no friend of William. The first of the Scottish Jacobite uprisings against William (the word 'Jacobite' simply means 'a supporter of James') was part-led by John Graham, Earl of Claverhouse and Viscount Dundee, in 1689 and climaxed with the battle of Killicrankie, in which Dundee was killed. For the next fifty years or so Scotland was to be periodically riven by Jacobite attempts to put James or his descendants on the throne, but the Jacobite cause was lost for good on the field at Culloden in 1746. Ireland was also to suffer. At the same time as the Scottish uprising, James, with strong support from France, besieged Derry, but the Irish Jacobite cause suffered resounding defeat at the hand of William at the battle of the Boyne in 1690. The repercussions of this Catholic-versus-Protestant conflict are still felt in Ireland to this day.

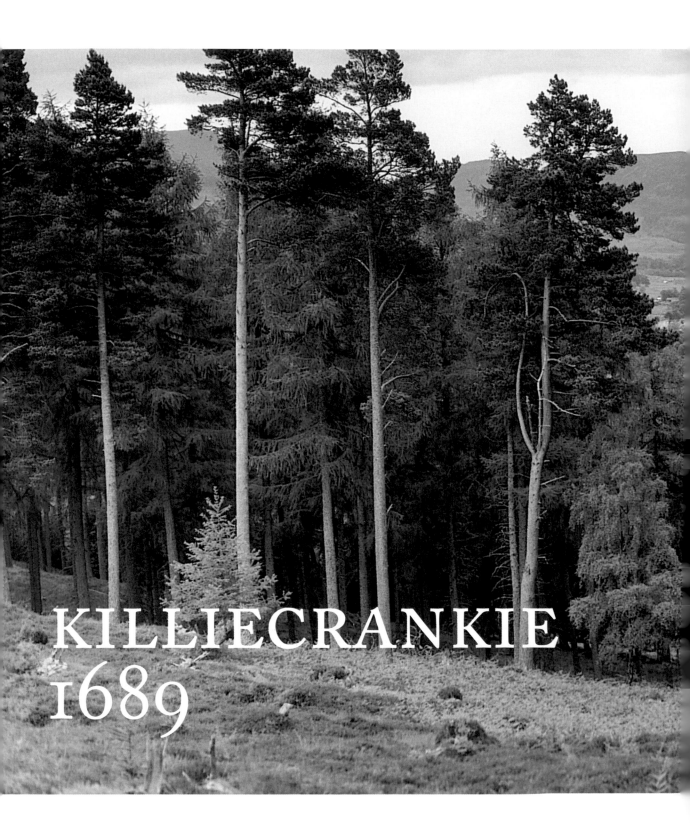

KILLIECRANKIE
1689

KILLIECRANKIE

1689

LORD JOHN GRAHAM OF CLAVERHOUSE AND
VISCOUNT DUNDEE, BETTER KNOWN BY HIS
AFFECTIONATE ALIAS 'BONNIE DUNDEE',
SHARED MORE THAN GOOD LOOKS AND A
CHARISMATIC PERSONALITY WITH THE ILL-
FATED DUKE OF MONMOUTH. HE TOO WAS
THE LEADER OF A REBELLION AT THE END
OF THE SEVENTEENTH CENTURY, IN HIS
CASE THE FIRST JACOBITE UPRISING OF
1689 IN SCOTLAND.

His aim was to restore the ousted Catholic king James II and in doing so remove the Dutch interloper William, formerly Prince of Orange and now William III. As with Monmouth four years before, the rebellion would cost Dundee his life – not, though, under the executioner's axe but in the heat of battle. And in death, too, they had something in common. Just as rumours started to circulate that Monmouth had survived his execution and was ready to lead the faithful once again, so a panoply of stories grew up around the death of Dundee, telling of his possible survival, at least for a short while, after being shot.

By the time of the first Jacobite rebellion Dundee was an experienced military commander. He'd served on the Continent, for part of the time in Holland as a junior officer in a Scots regiment in the French army under the command of the Duke of Monmouth. In one of those quirks of fate so beloved of history books, at the battle of Senneffe in 1674 he saved the life of William, Prince of Orange. Then, back home in Scotland, he played a prominent role in the effort to suppress the resurgence of the Presbyterian Covenanters – a campaign that, with its reprisals and executions, earned him a rather less than bonnie reputation and the *nom de guerre* of 'Bloody Clavers'. It was said by his enemies that it would take a silver bullet to kill him. In the seventeenth century such hyperbole from your foes meant that you really had arrived as a military commander – the same was said of Cromwell, after he sold his soul to the devil outside Worcester.

But it was undoubtedly that universal leveller the plain old lead ball – and not, as one story goes, a silver button tugged from a government officer's tunic and fired from a musket – that did for Dundee in 1689 as he took part in the cavalry charge at the battle of Killiecrankie. There are other stories, of course, many of which provide contrasting reports about where on the battlefield he was shot. The version accepted by most modern historians has him charging down the hill at the centre of the field and shot from his horse as he cleared the smoke of the government musketeers in front of him, although some mystery still revolves around his abandonment by most of his men, who apparently swerved to the left behind him, thus leaving him to his fate.

Another story has him shot not by government musketeers in the line but by a marksman holed up in Urrard House behind it, whose musket ball, fired from a second-floor bedroom window, might have been the shot that was said to have killed him near a mound known as Tomb Clavers. It certainly couldn't have been the same shot that felled him while he was down on the river terrace, where the Jacobites, the battle

Opposite John Graham of Claverhouse (Bonnie Dundee)

Dundee takes the fatal shot at Killiecrankie

The Claverhouse Stone, one of the supposed sites of Dundee's death. Urrard House can be seen in the trees on the high ground

won, were busy looting the government baggage train – the spot today memorialized by a standing stone locally known as the Claverhouse Stone. None of the stories specify whether the skeleton later found in the garret of Urrard House, and said to be the remains of a government soldier, was the aforementioned marksman.

It's already apparent that if you were a detective investigating Dundee's death all these conflicting accounts would make for a pretty difficult case. But if it isn't confusing enough already, there's more. Another batch of stories claim that, having survived the shot on the battlefield, Dundee dictated a letter to James, in which he reported his victory and the belief that his wound was not fatal. Whether he composed this as he lay bleeding on the field or, as another tale has it, from a bed in Blair Castle is uncertain. One of the few known facts is that three days after the battle Dundee was buried in St Bride's kirk at Old Blair, near the castle.

But according to another story Dundee was not laid to rest for long. This account has him exhumed and his body moved to the burial ground at Old Deer, in Aberdeenshire. Then, finally, there is the one about the ransacking of the grave at Old Blair and the removal of the armoured breastplate and helmet in which he was buried. These artefacts were sold to tinkers but later recovered and put on display in Blair Castle. At last some hard evidence – but all is not as it seems. The breastplate has a neat round hole straight through its middle, supposedly made by the bullet that killed him – but it doesn't take a forensics expert to see that the impact came from the back rather than the front. This hole was in fact created by a carpenter using a punch on the orders of one of the Dukes of Atholl (owners of Blair Castle), the desired effect being to make the object seem more 'authentic'. A ragged tear under the left arm, which would have been an obvious weak point in the armour, is more convincing as the place where he was wounded, and this ties in with the account that Dundee turned right across the front of the government line just before he was shot.

Dundee was just one man among thousands at the battle of Killiecrankie. So many men, so many stories. One of the things we hope battlefield archaeology can do is tease fact from fiction. On the basis of the above Killiecrankie seems a more than suitable case for treatment.

All these conflicting accounts make for a pretty difficult case. One of the things battlefield archaeology can do is tease fact from fiction

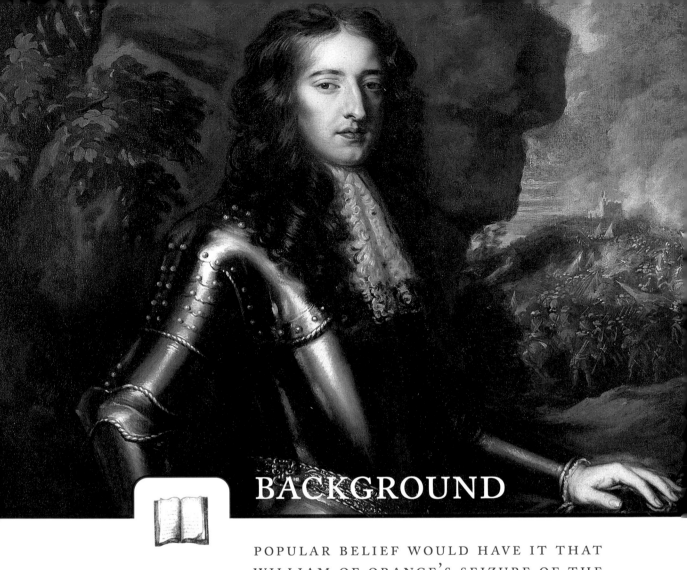

BACKGROUND

POPULAR BELIEF WOULD HAVE IT THAT
WILLIAM OF ORANGE'S SEIZURE OF THE
BRITISH THRONE IN 1688 WAS PEACEFUL,
AND THAT THE FIRST JACOBITE REBELLION
HAPPENED IN 1715. THE FIRST BELIEF IS
ECONOMICAL WITH THE TRUTH; THE
SECOND IS PLAIN WRONG. THE VERSION OF
EVENTS FEATURING IN MANY GENERAL
HISTORY BOOKS DRAWS A VEIL OVER A
SHORT BUT BITTERSWEET STORY SHOT
THROUGH WITH DRAMA AND INTRIGUE,
LOYALTY AND BETRAYAL, STRUGGLE AND
BLOODY SLAUGHTER.

And most fascinating of all, closer attention to what happened in Scotland between the autumn of 1688 and the summer of 1689 reveals events were shaped not just by the hands of men but by Lady Luck as well.

The middle years of the seventeenth century were violent and turbulent for Scotland. In 1637 Charles I had tried to force a new prayer book upon the Scots – a move that led circuitously to civil war in England. Once that disease took hold south of the border, her northern neighbour endured the symptoms too, with the Covenanters – signatories of the National Covenant against the king's meddling with their religious life – taking up arms. The Earl of Montrose successfully fought the rebels in 1644–5 before the king finally called him off and he fled to the Continent. Charles's fortunes, meanwhile, went from bad to worse to terminal. While his staunch supporter languished in temporary exile, the king surrendered to his foes in 1646, escaped captivity to fight again with a Scots army, was defeated and recaptured at Preston, and was finally executed in 1649. Montrose returned to fight for the right of the Stuarts, but was defeated and in 1650 sent the way of his late monarch via hanging, drawing and quartering. In 1651 Charles I's son, later Charles II, had himself crowned at Scone, in Perthshire, and invaded England with a would-be avenging army that was crushed and humiliated at Worcester by Oliver Cromwell's Roundheads. Thereafter Scotland suffered Cromwell's cruel attentions until his death in 1658. Charles II was eventually restored to the thrones of England and Scotland in 1660 and north of the border things returned to some semblance of normality.

When Charles II died in 1685, he was succeeded by his brother James, Duke of York. James II was a Catholic in a Protestant land and, to make matters worse, cheerfully declared that he would be tolerant towards both religions. Soon Catholics were being promoted to high office and resentment of what was seen as a general and insidious advancement of the forces of Popery under the indulgent eyes of the king grew steadily. James was not a young man, and his opponents consoled themselves with the thought they had only to wait for him to die. Then, they hoped, he would be replaced on the throne by one of his Protestant daughters by his first wife, Mary or Anne. But the distinctive crack of a camel's back breaking under the weight of a final straw was heard when James's second wife, the Catholic Mary of Modena, produced a Catholic son and heir. Facing the prospect of a Catholic dynasty, which they could see only as a cancer that would lead

Opposite **William, Prince of Orange and later William III of England**

**Dunkeld in the seventeenth
century**

1689

inexorably to their spiritual strangulation and death, the king's
Protestant critics – and they were many and powerful – took matters
into their own hands. They invited the Protestant Dutch Prince William
of Orange, James's son-in-law courtesy of marriage to his daughter
Mary, to invade England and replace the Catholic king and his heir.

By October 1688, with the threat of invasion looming, a Scots army
was marching south to support those Englishmen still loyal to James.
After William arrived in November, accompanied by a force of 13,000
men, James's opponents in Scotland took advantage of the Scot's army's
absence and elbowed the old king's supporters aside.

The Scots army that had crossed the border in support of James
included a cavalry force led by Viscount Dundee, Lord John Graham of
Claverhouse. Because of his tireless suppression of religious unrest, on
the king's behalf, in south-west Scotland, Dundee enjoyed the patronage
of the house of Stuart. He counted James as a personal friend.

Dundee felt keenly the indignation of many Scots at the removal of
the rightful, Stuart monarch and his replacement by an upstart
Dutchman. Such indignation seems to have been sadly lacking, however,
in the heart of the king himself. Rather than immediately go to war to

reclaim his God-given birthright, James fled to France. He harboured hopes of return, however, and apparently sent Dundee back to Scotland to await his call to arms. Dundee duly made his way home but was without any real proof of the trust placed in him by the king – or the means to do much about it. He was a gentleman by birth, certainly, but not of the rank that would expect to shoulder responsibility for the rights of a dispossessed king. Just what was he to do?

Dundee was among the Convention of Estates of the Realm that met in Edinburgh in March of the following year to decide whom they would support – James or William. Dundee's loyalty to his friend never faltered, and he wasn't afraid to say so, but the majority of opinion went against him and the Convention agreed to offer the throne of Scotland to William and Mary. While those with more wealth and social position to lose – men such as the Marquis of Atholl – preferred to prevaricate, Dundee stood firmly by the side of James. Public loyalty to the exiled king was therefore left conspicuously to Dundee. He had unexpectedly caught a rugby ball thrown clear of a scrum. Unless he started moving quickly, he would be in danger of being pounded into the pitch by the opposition. Justifiably fearing for his life, he left the Convention and returned to his family home at Dudhope Castle, on the lower slopes of Dundee Law, the eminence looming in the background of the city. His enemies were quick to move against him, and in his absence from the Convention he was denounced as a fugitive and a rebel and had a price placed on his head.

In the second week of April, Dundee set out to raise James's standard on Dundee Law, having taken it upon himself to lead the first Jacobite Rebellion.

Back in Edinburgh, the Convention delegates heard the news of Dundee's intentions with not inconsiderable alarm. A force under Major-General Hugh Mackay, commander of William's Scottish army, was sent north to nip the revolt in the bud. Hopes were high that the whole thing would end with the speedy arrest of Dundee.

As before, so again: when the Scots nobility had to jump one way or the other, most picked the path of conspicuous indecision. Fearing for their lands and titles, the great names of Scotland, who owed their stations in life to the ruling monarch, generally stayed away from James's banner in droves. A handful of gentlemen of conscience rallied to Dundee, along with some of their tenants. An educated man, who had spent much of his adult life politicking, Dundee would have understood

The battle of the Boyne

that the rising's fate now rested with the will of the Highland clans, traditional supporters of the house of Stuart. Desperate to find men and supplies, Dundee and his few supporters headed at first towards the north and east and then to the west. Much to his relief, word soon reached him that many in the Highlands were rising in support of James – and they wanted him, a Lowlander, for their leader.

Perhaps success seemed attainable in those early days. Having pulled himself together after the initial shock of exile, James now had an army in Ireland, which was striving to subdue his opponents there before using the island as a springboard for operations in England. (In fact the army would remain in Ireland, tied up in the Siege of Derry, until final defeat by William's men at the battle of the Boyne in 1690.) By 18 May, the clans had gathered at Glenroy, home of the legendary chief, Ewen Cameron of Lochiel. With this army of more than 2,000 men at his command, Dundee had only to establish and maintain a momentum that his king could carry forward to London, to drive the usurping Prince of Orange and his Dutchmen back to where they'd come from. Given time, Dundee hoped more clansmen would surely join the rebellion and that no government force would have the strength or the will to stand before it.

Throughout April, May, June and most of July, Dundee and his Jacobites avoided pitched battle with Mackay's government forces – but the months were not without clashes. On 29 May the Jacobites laid siege to Ruthven Castle, held for William by one Captain Forbes and about a hundred men. They surrendered to the Jacobites on 1 June, Forbes having realized that his position was hopeless, and the victors razed the castle to the ground.

Any delay was to Dundee's advantage. Both Dundee and Mackay found the time for much letter writing during this period – with Dundee in particular using all his political skills to try to secure support for his cause while simultaneously justifying his actions. He was on home turf, biding his time and allowing his support to grow. In stark contrast Mackay, though a Highlander by birth, had become a stranger to the place, having lived his adult life on the Continent. And as well as having the psychological difficulties of leading men in a hostile environment ruled by customs and practices that were alien to him, Mackay was at the end of an overstretched supply line and every day that passed put his resources under yet more strain. His priority must have been to try to quell Dundee and his Highlanders as soon as possible, before the rebellion could gather any more support.

Dundee and his gradually swelling army remained at large, however, until late July. Both commanders understood the importance of Blair Atholl, about twenty miles north-west of Perth, situated on the only viable route linking the Highlands and the Lowlands of Scotland. Mackay needed to control it in order to curtail his enemy's passage up and down the country and Dundee required control over it so as to maintain freedom of movement for his men. By the last week of the month, both forces were bent upon control of the strategic points at Blair Atholl, Blair Castle and the nearby Pass of Killiecrankie.

Mackay was at Dunkeld, ten miles away, on 26 July 1689 with his army of about 4,000 men when news reached him that Dundee and his force of 2,500 Jacobites had reached the target first. By now it would have been clear to the men of both armies that matters were shortly to come to a head.

Ewen Cameron of Lochiel

Given time, Dundee hoped more clansmen would surely join the rebellion

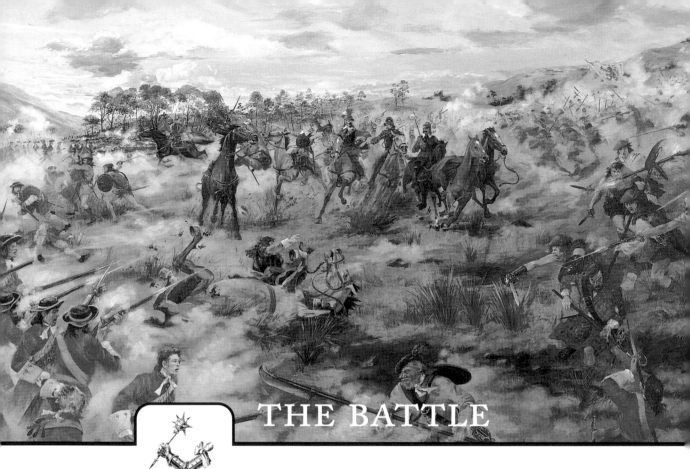

THE BATTLE

MACKAY'S ARMY SET OUT FROM DUNKELD ON THE MORNING OF 27 JULY. IT WAS WARM AND SUNNY BUT THE BEAUTY OF THE LANDSCAPE MUST HAVE BEEN SCANT COMFORT TO THOSE RED-COATED SOLDIERS AS THEY TROOPED NORTH, WEIGHED DOWN WITH KIT AND TROUBLED BY THOUGHTS OF A HIGHLAND HOST CONCEALED IN THE HILLS AHEAD OF THEM. THEY WERE ALLOWED A COUPLE OF HOURS' REST AT PITLOCHRY BEFORE MARCHING ON IN GOOD ORDER TOWARDS THE ENTRANCE TO THE NARROW GORGE CUT BY THE RIVER GARRY. THE DAY BEFORE, MACKAY HAD SENT A SMALL ADVANCE FORCE TO RECONNOITRE THIS PASS AND TO REPORT THE PRESENCE OF ANY ENEMY SOLDIERS.

Opposite The battle of
Killiecrankie. Dundee tumbles
from his horse in the centre
Left The Pass of Killiecrankie with
the river Garry

As the main body of the government army arrived, Mackay sent a
further 200 or so men of the Earl of Leven's regiment to carry out a
further check. When they reported that the way ahead was clear, the rest
of the redcoats began their steady advance into the pass, regiment by
regiment. Balfour's, Ramsay's and Kenmore's men went first, followed
by Belhaven's troop of horse, then Leven's regiment, a baggage train of
about 1,200 animals, the Earl of Annandale's troop of horse and finally
Hastings' regiment, supervising the baggage. Mackay would have had
good reason for being in buoyant mood for he was confident in his
numerical superiority and secure in the knowledge that his men were
better equipped and armed. He no doubt expected to drive the Jacobite
rabble before him, clear out any diehards in Blair Castle and then
commence a mopping-up operation to obliterate the revolt once and for
all. Having secured the pass, he arrived on the level ground that
stretched from the river on his left to the foot of a steep ridge on his
right, atop which sat Urrard House. Here, in a cornfield, he unsaddled
and waited for the rest of his army to close up.

Dundee, meanwhile, was doing his damnedest to put himself in a
position to take the wind out of Mackay's sails. At a council of war at
Blair Castle, he had taken pains to hear the views of all the clan leaders,
upon whom his success depended. The Lowlanders had sounded a note
of caution – the men were tired, they said, and dangerously

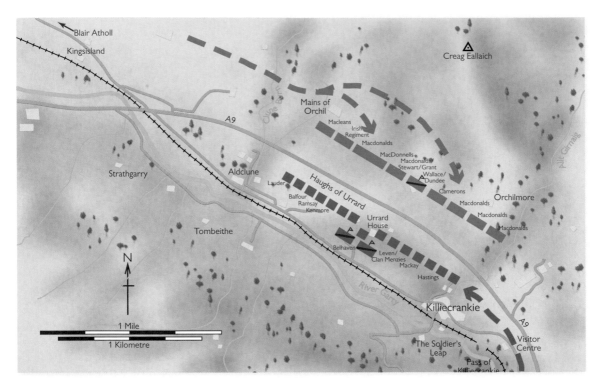

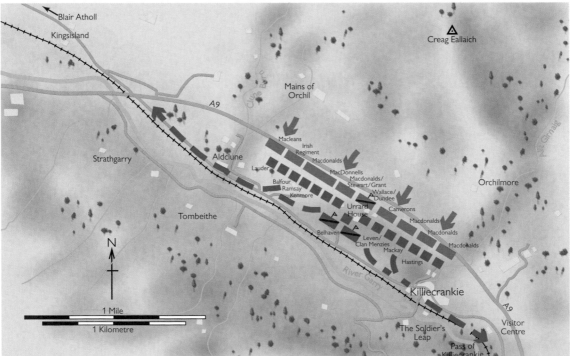

Movement of troops during the battle of Killiecrankie superimposed on to a modern map

Dundee resolved then to march out and meet Mackay face to face

outnumbered. Would it not be better to embark on something more akin to a guerrilla campaign, drawing pockets of the government army into skirmishes but holding the worst of it at arm's length until more Jacobite support came? James's army would soon arrive, they said, in numbers more able to deal with Mackay in open battle. But it was to be the voice of the Highlands that proved decisive in determining the way ahead – in particular, that of Cameron of Lochiel. The clans were ready to fight, here and now, he said: 'Our men are in heart; they are so far from being afraid of their enemy, that they are eager and keen to engage them, lest they escape their hands, as they have so often done. Though we have few men, they are good, and I can venture to assure your Lordship that not one of them will fail now.'

Dundee resolved then to march out and meet Mackay face to face. But rather than march straight out of Blair Castle and down the main road towards his foe, he led his army across the river Tilt and east around the back of the Hill of Lude. There they were out of sight of the enemy and, by skirting round Loch Moraig and following the line of the Clune burn, they were able to emerge on to the lower slopes of the mountain of Craig Eallaich before Mackay's men had even detected their presence in the area.

From there the Jacobites stepped out on to a ridge above Urrard House, wearing shirts of saffron yellow and tartan plaids and bearing targes to defy musket-ball and bayonet, broadswords and dirks for artful butchery. Worst of all were their war cries: like the baying of wild animals the Highlanders' howling swept through and around the red-coated ranks and bounced off the rocks on the other side of the valley, surrounding them with the promise of their imminent demise. Lowlander he was, but Dundee had spent time enough with Highlanders to know that he would do well to keep them in their clan groups. The unbreakable ties of kith and kin would drive forward each mass of men formed up behind their chief. What hope for the sulking levies of Mackay's army, driven forward only by fear of their officers, in the face of men bonded brother to brother, father to son?

Surely Mackay's confidence must have dipped when he heard a shouted alarm and looked up to see that his foe had appeared from nowhere, in the worst possible location, from his point of view – high above him? But he responded like the experienced fighting man he was. He ordered his infantry to turn to their right – a manoeuvre known by military men of the day as 'a *quart de conversion*' – and to advance in their battalions uphill towards the enemy. This was crucial: Mackay instantly understood that his numerical advantage would be dangerously imperilled without the advantage of high ground. Up they marched, through trees and thick undergrowth, on to a level terrace. But they were too late. Strung out above them further up the slope was the whole Jacobite army, still ready, still howling. As Mackay later described the situation in his memoirs, his army had 'got a ground fair enough to receive the enemy, but not to attack them'. Still Mackay kept his head and, in order to avoid being outflanked and to enable his men to perform the tactic of platoon firing upon which he placed all of his hopes of victory, he had them form up three ranks deep along a front perhaps half a mile across.

Dundee gave orders that each clan should attack a specific regiment in the government line. This would maximize the horrifying impact of what forces he had. He hoped the slaughter meted out to government soldiers singled out for attack would persuade the remaining redcoats to take themselves far away.

The extreme right of the Jacobite army was made up of Macleans, facing Balfour's regiment on the government left. Next were Colonel Alexander Cannon's Irishmen, who had recently arrived from the Jacobite army in Ireland, facing Ramsay's regiment; then the Clanranald

**The battle of Drumclog, 1679, a
Covenanters' battle in which
Dundee fought**

Macdonalds, facing Kenmore's; then Glengarry glowering down at
Leven's – and so on down the line. Past the centre of the Jacobite line
were Lochiel's Camerons, then a body of mixed clans and finally at the
extreme left the Macdonalds of Sleat.

Then came an uneasy stand-off. Perhaps Dundee wanted to wait
until the sun, beating into the faces of the Highlanders all afternoon and
blinding them, had set. In any case, he held them back. Mackay's
gunners let fly with their three light leather guns – until the hastily
assembled carriages they perched upon gave way after just a few rounds
apiece, much to the amusement of the Jacobites. Highland marksmen,
taking cover in a building above the government right, passed the time
by taking pot-shots at the Major-General every time he came into range.
Mackay records:

> The ennemy having a full view of our forces, by reason of the height they
> possess above us, discerned presently the General, which drew their shot
> into all places where he stood or walked, whereby severals of our men were
> wounded before the engagement; and to have the so much nearer aim, they

possest themselves of some houses upon the ascent of the height whereupon they stood which the General not willing to suffer, least the ennemy should be emboldned thereby, ordered his brother, commanding his own regiment, before whose front the houses were, to detach a captain with some fire-locks to dislodge them; judging withal that the skirmish might draw on a general engagement, which he earnestly longed for before the night approached.

Mackay recorded that several Jacobites were killed in the engagement, but still Dundee held back his men. Perhaps the government soldiers began to think it was too late in the day now for any engagement. But at about eight o'clock, with the sun beginning to set, Dundee gave the signal to attack. The cry of 'Claymore' rang up and down the line and every one of those redcoats understood that the moment had come.

Down rushed the howling Highlanders, gathering speed and casting aside their plaids in favour of running almost naked into the serried ranks of wide-eyed government soldiers below them. Those who had muskets or pistols let fly with a single round and cast them aside – the better to wield those basket-hilted broadswords. The Highland way of killing was face to face – close enough to smell the sickening sweat of fear upon a man before cleaving him in two. As the avalanche of men descended, Mackay's infantry let fly. Platoon by platoon they fired and a pulse of lead rippled out from the government line, cutting down five, six, seven hundred of the Jacobites. 'Keep to the drill,' those redcoats must have thought as they turned to the business of reloading, their hands trembling with adrenalin overload. Perhaps some officers realized that reloading again, for the second or third time, wasn't an option, and called out to their men to 'Screw in your daggers!' – to jam plug bayonets into musket barrels ready to fend off the attackers. But the government troops could achieve little in those brief seconds as the Jacobites came on. An account by Donald MacBane, a government soldier, tells us, 'At last they cast away their muskets, drew their broadswords, and advanced furiously upon us, and were in the middle of us before we could fire three shots apiece . . .'

As the Jacobites closed the distance, men fumbling with powder and ramrods were the most impotent of all, cut down like reeds by the Jacobites unleashing the stored power of a downhill charge edged with well-aimed steel. Mackay's left took the worst of it; and Lauder's, Balfour's and Ramsay's men either fell where they stood or turned to run, according to Mackay, without having fired a shot. But Mackay, out

The Highland way of killing was face to face

**The Jacobite charge at the battle
of Killiecrankie**

on the right, stood firm with Leven's and Hastings' regiments, the musketeers tearing great gaps in the Jacobite left, which had fallen into disarray. Cameron of Lochiel's men in the Jacobite centre didn't charge straight down the hill but swerved to the left in their eagerness to join in the attack on Mackay's hard-pressed regiment (under the command of his brother, Hastings). It cost them dear when they took heavy fire in the flank from Leven's regiment as they passed across its front. Sensing an opportunity, Mackay ordered his horse in the centre to take the fight to the enemy. Belhaven's mounted men briefly advanced towards the foe, and made a few metres, but in the face of the Jacobite cavalry charge turned to run, riding through Kenmore's foot, who chose that moment to join the mounted men in their flight. A general rout had begun.

But then Lady Luck reached out a hand. At the council of war, the clan chiefs had begged Dundee to keep out of the line of fire so that the rebellion could continue under its leader, regardless of one fight's

1689

outcome. He understood and admired the Highland way too much, though: he knew that chiefs commanded respect, in part, because they put themselves at the front of any fight, and that they had most to gain from victory and, accordingly, risked most to attain it. No, he would not hang back in safety – he would lead from the front, as befitted a man commanding Highlanders. So it was that he was to the fore of a cavalry charge towards Mackay's own regiment, commanded by the young Sir William Wallace, when confusion or some other misfortune caused the bulk of it to veer to the left. Oblivious, Dundee and a handful of others continued forward and a well-placed shot passed under Dundee's upraised arm and into his chest. His mount, fatally wounded, fell under him and Dundee, dead or dying, tumbled to earth. At the moment of victory, then, Lady Luck plucked the leader away.

Out on the right, Mackay was losing the battle but, thanks to disciplined firing from Leven's, he was able to withdraw his survivors in good order while the bulk of the Jacobites fell to looting the government baggage train to the rear. He briefly considered retreat to a large walled garden to the government rear – probably that of Urrard House – but dismissed the thought on the grounds that once there he and his surviving men would have been trapped like fish in a barrel. Cool-headed to the end, Mackay continued his withdrawal. Soundly beaten though his army was, it was Mackay who had ended the day in possession of the field of battle.

Of more than 4,000 government troops, between a half and two thirds were killed in the fight or in the rout that followed. The Jacobite loss had been cruel too – as well as Dundee, perhaps as many as half of the 2,500 or so souls who took the field had been cut down.

Dundee to the fore of the cavalry charge

THE AFTERMATH

ONCE ALL WAS LOST, MANY OF THE
GOVERNMENT SOLDIERS TURNED TAIL AND
FLED, PURSUED BY BROADSWORD-WIELDING
JACOBITES. ONE OF THESE WAS THE
GOVERNMENT SOLDIER DONALD MACBANE,
WHO EARNED HIMSELF A PLACE IN LEGEND
BY JUMPING SIX METRES ACROSS THE RIVER
GARRY TO ESCAPE HIS WOULD-BE KILLERS.
THE SPOT IS COMMEMORATED TO THIS DAY
AS THE SOLDIER'S LEAP. OTHERS,
HOWEVER, WERE NOT SO LUCKY.

Bonnie Dundee, who had been shot, was found by the Earl of Leven's men. Their advance stalled by stout resistance from Hastings' foot – one of the few government regiments that stood its ground – they were drawing back when they happened upon their leader. It is not clear whether he was alive and mortally wounded or dead – but he was certainly taken to Blair Castle. There, three days after the battle, he was buried in the crypt of St Bride's kirk, Old Blair.

A letter purporting to have been dictated by Dundee in the hours after the battle reads:

Dundee is found, dead or dying, by his men

> To King James, Killiecrankie, 27 July, 1689
>
> Sir, It has pleased God to give your forces a great victory over the rebels, in which 3-4ths of them are fallen under the weight of our swords. I might say much of the action if I had not the honour to command in it; but of 5000 men which was the best computation I could make of the rebels it is certain there cannot have escaped above 1200 men; we have not lost full out of 900 . . .
>
> My wounds forbid me to enlarge to your Majesty at this time, though they tell me they are not mortal. However Sir I beseech your Majesty to believe that whether I live or die I am entirely yours.

While the writing style tallies with Dundee's, sceptics have dismissed it as a much later fake or as propaganda released by the Jacobites in a bid to delay news of the catastrophic death of their leader so early in the campaign.

Dundee was among a death toll reputed to have run into thousands. Cameron of Lochiel describes how the following day he forced his troops back on to the battlefield to see what had been done there in the name of King James:

> . . . the dreadful effects of their fury appeared in many horrible figures. The enemy lay in heaps almost in the order they were posted, but so disfigured with wounds, and so hashed and mangled that even the victors could not look upon the amazeing proofs of their own agility and strength without surprise and horrour. Many had their heads divided into two halves by one blow; others had their sculls off above the eares by a back-strock, like a night cap. Their thick buffe-belts were not sufficient to defend their shoulders from such deep gashes as almost disclosed their entrails. Several were cut quite through, and some that had scull-capes had them so beat into their brains that they died upon the spott.

The notorious savagery of the Highland host had been ably demonstrated and their already fearsome reputation was elevated to legendary status. Here were a people to be feared and distrusted. Their frenzy of killing on the slopes of the Pass of Killiecrankie planted the seeds of the ruthlessness demonstrated by the Duke of Cumberland's men after Culloden – the battle that ended Jacobitism once and for all in 1746.

Dundee's death denied the first Jacobite Rebellion any real hope of ultimate triumph. Had he survived, matters might have been otherwise: within days of the battle of Killiecrankie the Jacobite ranks swelled to around 5,000 men and who knows what Dundee might have been able to achieve with such a force. He was succeeded in command by Colonel Alexander Cannon. His first action as leader was to send a raiding party to gather supplies in Perth, but Mackay's men swiftly drove them off. For an army still reeling from the loss of its skilful and charismatic leader, this was another blow to its morale. From then on, the cause seems to have steadily unravelled. It came to grief at Dunkeld on 21 August. A force of 1,200 Camerons holding the town under the command of Lieutenant Colonel William Cleland repulsed Cannon's 5,000 Highlanders after several hours of close-quarter struggle, after which the Jacobites seem to have lost heart completely. Many sloped off home to their crofts and Cannon withdrew with his Irishmen to spend the winter at Lochaber.

There was a half-hearted attempt to revive their cause the following year, but a defeat for those first Jacobites at Cromdale on 1 May brought their story to a close. Soon after Killiecrankie, one Archibald Pitcairn had written of Dundee:

Dundee's body is borne away from the field

> Scotland and thow didst in each other live,
> Thou woudst not her, nor could she thee survive.

This first failure to return the house of Stuart to the throne might well have been the most significant. The great and the good in Scotland turned more and more towards London in search of a bright future for themselves, and the righteous indignation of those Scots with rebellious hearts would never burn so bright again. What had been a just cause at Killiecrankie had become by 1715, 1719, and then again in 1745, an increasingly lost cause. Killiecrankie marked the climax not just of the first, but of the most honest Jacobite Rebellion of them all.

WHO FOUGHT HERE

THE BATTLE OF KILLIECRANKIE WAS
FOUGHT BY TWO VERY DIFFERENT ARMIES,
CONTRASTING IN THEIR EXPERIENCE,
ORGANIZATION, WEAPONRY, TACTICS AND
MOTIVATION. IT WAS THESE DIFFERENCES,
IN CONJUNCTION WITH THE TERRAIN OVER
WHICH THE BATTLE WAS FOUGHT, THAT
HELPED BRING ABOUT VICTORY FOR THE
JACOBITES AND DEFEAT FOR THE
GOVERNMENT ARMY.

THE LEADERS

At forty-nine years of age, Hugh Mackay of Scourie was eight years older than Dundee at the time of Killiecrankie. Though a Highlander by birth, he despised the traditions and culture of the folk who rose in support of the first Jacobite Rebellion. He had fancied the life of the soldier since childhood and enlisted with a Royal Regiment of Foot soon after the Restoration. As was common for young British men committed to a military career, he earned his spurs on the Continent, fighting first on the side of the French. He seems to have fully embraced life on the Continent, and when he inherited the family pile in 1668 he failed to return and claim it. In 1672 he fell in love with a young Dutchwoman, Clara de Bie. Her family liked him, but could not countenance the thought of her marrying a man in the service of the French. Such was the depth of Mackay's feeling for Clara that he transferred his allegiance to William of Orange and was married soon after. Starting out as a captain in the Dutch army, he was steadily promoted to the rank of colonel in a regiment of that army's Anglo-Scots Brigade. Such was his loyalty to his new master that when King James recalled the regiment to Britain in 1688, Mackay stayed behind at William's side. He went on to command an English and Scots division during William's invasion of England and, once the invasion was complete, became Major-General and commander of William's Scots forces.

Mackay survived Killiecrankie and went on to bring the rebellion to a successful conclusion. But like Dundee he was to die in battle. Still doing faithful service for William, he fell while leading his men against the French at the battle of Steinkirk, Belgium, in 1692.

There is no definite date of birth recorded for John Graham of Claverhouse, but we know that he was born in the late summer of 1648. Eldest son of the Claverhouse family, he grew up in turbulent times. War had been raging north and south of the border for years – and for the Claverhouse family, hard times were made harder still by the death of the father when young John was four years old. A graduate of St Andrews University, he joined a Scottish regiment of foot as a lieutenant when he was in his twenties. Like Mackay, he learned the art of war by fighting on the Continent, first for the French and later for the Dutch. It was while in the Dutch service that he distinguished himself by saving the life of the young Prince William of Orange. He expected promotion as his reward, but was passed over (in one version of events, the promotion he coveted went to one Hugh Mackay of Scourie). Incensed at the snub, he returned to Scotland where, from late 1678 onwards, he put

The battle of Killiecrankie was fought by two very different armies

John Graham of Claverhouse
and his wife

1689

his military training to use by serving as a kind of religious policeman on behalf of the house of Stuart. His harsh repression of all forms of religious unrest – legend has it that he was out chasing Covenanters even on the morning of his wedding in 1684 – brought him the nickname 'Bloody Clavers'. It also earned Claverhouse the patronage – and even the friendship – of the house of Stuart, along with improved social status and a family home at Dudhope Castle, outside Dundee. Finally, in 1688, King James created him Viscount Dundee, Lord John Graham of Claverhouse.

THE ARMIES

The government force, led by Major-General Hugh Mackay, was part of a professional, regular army – the martial legacy of Cromwell's New Model Army, which was subsequently broken down and rebuilt by Charles II.

Although many of the 4,000 troops under Mackay's command had never seen action before, several units, notably those composed of Anglo-Dutch troops, had taken part in fighting on the Continent. These troops were part of the army of 13,000 men William of Orange, now William III of England, had brought with him from Holland in 1688. They joined a force of 34,000 troops, which represented – for want of a more suitable term – the British army (at the time, though, the forces of

England, Scotland and Ireland, although loyal to the Crown, were separate entities). The rest of Mackay's force was composed of inexperienced levies, many of them from Lowland Scotland, but all of them paid soldiers.

The Jacobite army under the command of Viscount Dundee was a different animal entirely. This was not a modern, professional force but a body of men drawn together in clans by ties of blood, fealty and obligation. In that regard it was almost medieval in character, for a clan chief held feudal authority over his people, and clan territory was held by immediate relatives, wealthy tenants and tacksmen, who in turn rented lands to commoners and their sub-tenants – the lowest members of the clan, who led a serf-like existence.

The general population of the Highlands practised subsistence agriculture, with most landholdings focused on a farmstead or farmtoun,

1689

had been used by the Dutch: it was introduced into Britain via the troops accompanying William of Orange on his arrival from Holland. Platoon firing evolved from numerous systems for giving fire developed by various armies during the seventeenth century, notably those of the Swedes and the Dutch. In these earlier systems fire had been delivered by ranks six deep. The older Dutch practice was for the first rank to fire before wheeling behind the rear ranks to allow the second rank to fire, with each successive rank repeating the process. A technique favoured among the Swedes, introduced by Gustavus Adolphus, was for the six ranks to close up to create three much denser ranks, with the front rank kneeling, the second rank standing behind them and the third rank staggered to the rear, levelling their muskets between gaps in the second rank – and for all three ranks to fire simultaneously. This technique delivered a single devastating salvo, but the obvious drawback was that since all the musketeers discharged their weapons at the same time no one was left to provide cover while they reloaded. Accordingly, this technique was generally used just before coming hand to hand with the enemy. Having fired, the musketeers then charged forward, wielding their fired weapons like clubs.

The platoon firing system allowed continuous fire, as some platoons reloaded while others fired. The companies of each battalion were sub-divided – twelve companies usually breaking down into sixteen platoons, with two more provided by the grenadiers on the wings. The platoons were then organized into three or more firings, with the front rank of each platoon kneeling and the second and third ranks standing behind, as in the Swedish system. All the platoons of the first firing discharged at the same time, followed by the platoons of the second firing and then of the third, by which time the platoons of the first firing were reloaded and ready to go again. The platoons of each firing were distributed as evenly as possible along the line, to achieve concentrated fire along its entire length. Platoons were not necessarily bound to concentrate fire immediately to their own front, and sometimes they might have been ordered to fire to the left or right of their position, thus providing direct fire support to neighbouring reloading platoons if required. The reduction from six ranks to three, following the Swedish practice, and the general adoption of the scarlet tunic or coat as standard uniform for the British infantry combined to create the legendary thin red line.

The main advantage of platoon firing over previous systems was its capacity to offer continuous fire without the need to move men to the rear of the line to reload, a procedure which could delay fire from the next rank. A positive knock-on effect of this system was the reduction in the amount of black powder smoke produced when muskets were fired, thick clouds of which belching across the front obscured visibility and could be an advantage to the enemy. Platoon firing also allowed smoke to clear while the platoon responsible for creating it reloaded and waited for its turn to fire again. A drawback of the platoon system was its complexity: great precision was required in the formation and organization of the line and rigorous drill essential if each platoon was to know its position within the overall firing sequence and stick to its timings within it. Mackay was fully aware of these requirements and appears to have spent much of his time during the hours between his army's arrival on the field and the Jacobite charge putting his men into line, and making sure that the battalions were positioned to best effect and the companies and platoons within them correctly placed.

Mackay was later criticized for thinning his line from six to three ranks and so overstretching it: the move was blamed for his inability to hold back the shock of the Jacobite charge. Although Mackay did this because he was rightly worried about being outflanked, largely because

Great precision was required in the formation and organization of the line

he had too few cavalry to protect his wings, this deployment was also in keeping with the new practice of platoon firing. Rather than criticizing him for being an over-cautious traditionalist, we should perhaps see Mackay as a progressive commander prepared to use the latest innovations in high-risk situations.

TWO MEN FIRING

While at Killiecrankie we were delighted to have the opportunity to do some target shooting with a musket dating from the time of the battle. Martin Hinchcliffe from the National Army Museum set up a series of targets to stand in for Jacobite soldiers, using blocks of ballistic soap (which is used to replicate the impact of a bullet on the human body), racks of pork ribs, tartan fabric and a Jacobite targe (or shield). By doing some experimental archaeology we hoped to find out how accurate and effective the muskets of the time were, and what sort of effect different targets had on the musket-balls fired at them. In our time we have collected a lot of musket-balls from various battlefields, but we have never been entirely certain whether misshaped balls had hit their target or whether they had missed and hit the ground. We were in for a few surprises.

After loading the musket, with powder ball and wadding, we thought we would be clever and try to hit one of the targets from 100 yards (91.5 metres) away. Needless to say, we all missed and our bullets crashed into the woods behind. But Martin got a ball close enough to show that an experienced marksman could hit a human target from that distance. We moved to the twenty-five-yard (22.8 metres) mark, and from there we hit almost every time. The musket-balls did terrible damage, passing straight through all we put before them – through the targe, through the block of ballistic soap, through a box of straw and then almost through a sandbag on the other side. When we turned the block of soap round, the exit hole was at least twice the size of the entry hole. It made us feel quite ill to think what the ball could do to a human body.

But it wasn't just the musket-balls that caused fatalities. We could see that small fibres of fabric from the tartan material had been pushed into the bullet hole, adhering to its soap walls. Such fibres could have carried bacteria into a wound and caused infection, which in the days before antibiotics and modern medicine would probably have brought about a slow and painful death.

Our greatest surprise came when we collected the musket-balls, cutting most of them out of the sandbags behind the targets. Even after passing through fabric, soap, wood and sand the balls retained their spherical shape; only when you looked carefully could you see a slight compression, making the ball slightly ovoid. Only when we hit a log or a stone did the balls become heavily distorted. This was a real breakthrough – it meant that we could now look at excavated musket-balls and know without doubt whether or not they had hit their targets. We were also stunned to see that a ball fired at tartan fabric picked up the impression of the weave as it passed through the cloth – so now we would be able to say not only whether a musket-ball had hit a man but also whether or not he was wearing a plaid. Unfortunately, though, analysis of our archaeological musket-balls in the light of these discoveries will take time and the results will have to wait for publication in the full report of our investigation.

THE HIGHLAND CHARGE

The Jacobite victory at Killiecrankie owed much to the Highland charge – their headlong rush forward into the ranks of government soldiers. It was this battle that earned this tactic its legendary status and the Highland charge was to serve the Jacobites well over the next fifty-five years or so of intermittent fighting during the various Jacobite Rebellions. The tactic was ideally suited to an irregular army, which lacked formal drill and was more primitively armed than its foe. It wasn't rocket science, but that was one of its benefits. Unlike the government army's battlefield drills, such as platoon firing, it didn't require complex manoeuvres or intense training. It was also the best means of denying

The Jacobite victory at Killiecrankie owed much to the Highland charge

Lochiel's charge at Killiecrankie

the enemy the advantage of its superior firepower, as it closed the distance between the sides as quickly as possible and reduced the amount of time the enemy had to use their muskets – at Killiecrankie the Jacobites' charge left the government soldiers no time to fire more than three shots apiece.

The Highland charge was not, however, suited to all occasions. It relied heavily upon suitable terrain. The chargers ideally needed to be on higher ground than their enemy: a gradient gave the charge added momentum and it was harder for the enemy to fire accurately uphill than it was on the level. In this respect the skill and judgement of the Jacobite commander at Killiecrankie played a vital role. Dundee picked his ground masterfully, including an extra feature of the terrain which we will discuss later. The Jacobite charge at the battle of Culloden in 1746 failed because the ground was fairly level, though, as we discovered during our investigation there, not as level as it may at first seem. But perhaps most importantly for its success the Highland charge relied on gaps in the enemy line, already present due to deployment or created as units took to their heels in the face of the charge. As historian Stuart Reid has pointed out, there isn't a single recorded instance of a Jacobite charge smashing its way headlong through a line which chose to stand and fight. At Killiecrankie, the government troops realized that in order to have any chance they needed to stand their ground in front of the charge – a point that Mackay claimed to have tried to hammer home in his address to his men before Killiecrankie.

The Highland charge was also a bit of a one-trick pony: once launched it could not be recalled or effectively alter its course part-way through an attack. Once a charge was pushed home, Jacobite troops were rarely regrouped and returned to the battle. At Killiecrankie, once the government troops to their immediate front were routed the Jacobites fell to pursuit and looting the baggage train, allowing Mackay and a good number of his men to make an orderly departure from the battlefield. If instead the Jacobites had regrouped and launched a fresh attack on Mackay's remnant force they would have stood every chance of annihilating the government army. This lack of discipline and inability to recall was also a problem with cavalry charges during the English Civil War. Prince Rupert's charge at Edgehill serves as a good example: it was initially very successful but his side lost its opportunity when the troopers fell to looting while the Parliamentarians recovered.

The Jacobites' weapon of choice was the basket-hilted broadsword, introduced as a replacement for the much bigger and rather awe-

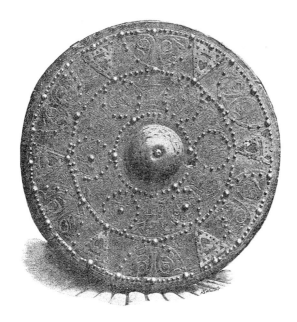

An ornate example of a Highland targe. Note the decorated metal boss in the centre

inspiring two-handed broadsword, which was very much a medieval weapon. Many people argue that the word claymore should apply only to the earlier two-hander and not the later basket-hilted broadsword. But in fact claymore simply means 'great sword', and both would have been regarded as such in their time. The basket-hilted sword appears to have arrived in the Highlands some time in the late sixteenth century or early seventeenth century. The two-handed sword was a specialist weapon, usually reserved for strong men assigned as bodyguards or guardians of the colours, the sword, swung around the head, keeping the enemy at a distance. These impressive weapons gradually fell out of use during the seventeenth century. A few of them might have been carried into battle for the last time at Killiecrankie.

The Jacobites also used firearms – there was a fine tradition of gun manufacture in Scotland by the late seventeenth century. In the classic Highland charge these weapons were generally discharged into the mass of the enemy within reasonable range, perhaps fifteen metres or so, and then dropped to allow use of the broadsword as the charge closed with the enemy. At Killiecrankie, however, we see a more thoughtful use of the musket as a sniping weapon in the opening stages of the battle. Although the accuracy of the musket at distances of over a hundred metres was not great, the massed government troops would have provided a large target area and incoming musket-balls must have had an unnerving effect as soldiers waited for the battle to kick off.

Incoming musket-balls must have had an unnerving effect

the Dig

We had been drawn to the battle of Killiecrankie not just because, being the first of the Jacobite Rebellions, it is an historically important battle, or because it was such a dramatic and stirring story, but because our reconnaissance suggested that its archaeological potential was high – despite the fact that the A9, a main arterial road, was built through the site in the 1970s. That it had potential was partly because Killiecrankie is a relatively little known battle and despite the nearby National Trust for Scotland visitors centre, which is located in the pass, the battlefield itself does not attract many visitors. Every day thousands of people using the A9 drive straight through the middle of the battlefield without even knowing it's there.

Most of the battlefield is now on private farmland, and during our discussions with landowners we learned that the site had apparently escaped the past attentions of metal detectorists. This was great news, as so often

we hear that detectorists have been picking over the ground for years and taking away battle-related artefacts. There were also a number of sites related to the battle which might contain archaeological remains. There was the so-called Grave of the Officers, consisting of an earth mound and a commemorative plaque on a stone plinth. This feature is a focus for small-scale pilgrimage by the White Cockade Society, which exists to keep alive the spirit of the Jacobite Rebellions, and whose members regularly place wreaths in memory of the fallen on both sides. There was also Urrard House, which stood at the time of the battle, and a small house that provided shelter for Jacobite snipers. We were also fortunate to have several eyewitness accounts of the battle by participants, including one by Cameron of Lochiel on the Jacobite side, and another, the fullest, by the government commander, Mackay. One of the things we hoped to do was find out whether or not the

Ian Marshall lifts turfs at Urrard House

archaeology matched Mackay's account, which is an example of history written not by the victor but by the vanquished.

Urrard House

Urrard House sits at the centre of the battlefield, occupying the plateau across which Mackay deployed his men. Sitting just behind the government line it would have provided an ideal spot from which to witness the unfolding battle – there is the story that Dundee was shot by a marksman from one of the upstairs windows. Today, as then, much of the ground on which the battle was fought sits on the Urrard estate; fields for stock grazing, wooded slopes and the gardens around the house all played host to the terrible events of 1689. But the house standing today is not the original building. Our aim was to learn more about the original Urrard House, so as to place it within the landscape of the battle. Thanks to a very useful archive of architect's plans, accounts and old photographs held in a vault by Mr and Mrs Cairns, the present owners of the house, we were able to get an insight into its complicated history.

The first clue was provided by a photograph taken in 1860. It showed a view of the house, which consisted of a long, whitewashed two-storey wing abutting a larger, grander edifice topped by a chimney stack with four pots. A scribbled note accompanying the print told us that the white wing was pulled down not long after the photograph was taken. We had every reason to believe that the white wing was the original Urrard House, which at some time in the first half of the nineteenth century had an impressive stone-built extension added

Location of excavation trenches around Urrard House

to it. It seemed likely that the part of the building with the chimney stack was still standing, forming part of the modern house. Using the photograph as a guide we walked around the house and tried to work out where the demolished wing once stood. We found a chimney stack topped by four pots on the north side of the house, and thought we'd got our location. So certain were we that we set Banksie to work with his geophysics equipment on the lawn outside the house, which according to our observations was where the old part of the house once stood. But the survey drew a total blank. It was only when we looked at the house and photograph again that we realized that there was another similar chimney stack hidden almost out of

sight behind a part of the house built in the 1960s. There was only one word to express our reaction to this discovery – a good old-fashioned, Homer Simpson style 'D'oh!'

At this point two more important documents came to light, shown to us by Victoria Cairns, the lady of the house. These were architect's plans dating to the 1830s, showing the part of the house still standing today and the old wing that was demolished in the 1860s. The plans had been drawn up to show what the new extension would look like and how it would be built on to the original part of the house. We compared the plans to the old photograph and by counting the windows in both found them to be a pretty accurate representation.

Victoria then took us into the house and showed us a stone lintel, which passed across the ceiling in the hallway. On one side of the sill was the inscription 'JS.JS 1681'. This was an exciting architectural detail. This lintel had sat across a doorway in the eastern gable of the old house and when the extension was built in the 1830s it had become an interior feature, over a doorway connecting the new and the old buildings. The initials related to J. Stuart, the owner at the time of the battle of Killiecrankie, and his wife. The date referred either to their wedding or perhaps even the date of construction of the original house. It looked as though Urrard House might have been a relatively new building at the time of the battle.

It was clear that the ground on which the old house had once stood was now under a wing built to replace part of the building which burned down in the 1960s, this fire-gutted wing previously sitting over the site of the original house demolished a hundred years previously. Something shown on the plans but not visible on the photograph, because of the direction from which it was taken, was a small block of rooms which jutted out to the rear. This area is today occupied by the back lawn, and so we were hopeful that some remains might be uncovered by excavation. Further potential came to light when we realized that the old part of the house shown on the architect's plans was actually longer, from gable to gable, than the modern wing. This was exciting, as it meant that further remains of the old house might survive under the small stretch of lawn at the gable end of the standing building, next to the back door.

Banksie carried out a new geophysical survey, and although far from conclusive his results suggested that buried archaeological deposits existed beneath the grass – although it remained to be seen how much damage a modern drain had done to these deposits. Relieved to be able to put a spade confidently into the ground at last, we set to work.

We carefully cut and removed the turf, as we had promised to return the lawn to its former condition once we had finished our investigation. The soil beneath was gravelly and quite hard going, and in the bright sunshine we soon worked up a sweat. The first clue that we were on to something was a layer of mortar which came up in the corner of the trench closest to the back door. Fragments of brick and tile also started to appear, and the presence of ash strongly suggested we had come across the remains of the building that had burned down in the 1960s. But most of the trench was filled with gravelly soil and large water-rolled pebbles – material that we guessed had been imported to create a nice level lawn after the third and final version of the wing had been constructed. We needed to dig deeper.

After several hours of backbreaking mattocking and shovelling, we came across a large square block of stone in the rear face of the trench. This was below the more modern debris but directly in line with the back wall of the standing building. The stone sat in the bottom of a slot cut into the natural subsoil, indicating a foundation trench. This was the giveaway that we were looking at the remains of the back wall of the original house. Unfortunately, though, a massive service trench had been cut through the ground just to the front of this stone with a ceramic drain in its base. This modern disturbance had removed all trace of the original wall line beyond the single stone protruding into the back of the excavation trench. After we had cleaned up the rear face of the trench we could see the sequence of

The small trench in the foreground contains one corner of the original building demolished in 1860

Ian Marshall and Stephen Clancy backfill a trench

construction and destruction which over the past two hundred years made the history of the house so complex. In the upper part of the trench was the demolition layer created when the fire-damaged building was levelled out in preparation for rebuilding. Beneath this rubble was the original wall line, marked out by the stone block in its foundation slot, and even the remains of what looked like a stone-flagged floor on the inside of the building.

If we wanted to see any more of the original house, we would have to leapfrog the modern service trench and open up a new area on the boundary of the lawn and the driveway. Having taken fresh measurements we felt that the effort would be worth it, as there was a chance that we would uncover the remains of the original gable end, which should appear along the edge of the driveway. We were bang on the money. In a small metre-square hole we came across the continuation of the rear wall and the corner where it turned to join the gable end. The wall was well made and quite thick, with a rubble core and inner and outer facing stones. The architect's annotated plan told us that this end of the building was occupied by the kitchen, and this tied in nicely with the numerous fragments of cut animal bone which came out of this small trench. We found only a few artefacts relating to the old house: a collection of rusted nails, which might have held up timber panelling against the inside walls, and part of a very old wine bottle, possibly from the 1700s.

Using the results of our excavation, the architect's

plan and the upstanding house, we could now place the original Urrard House accurately within the landscape of the battle for the first time since its demolition in 1860. Not a bad start at all.

The Grave of the Officers

We are no strangers to battlefields, and we have looked for the graves of the dead on several, including Shrewsbury, Barnet, Flodden and Sedgemoor, while at Culloden we did a geophysical survey over the low mounds that mark the graves of the Jacobites, which showed up pits beneath the mounds. But when we have used excavation in ground long associated with the graves of the war dead, we have always drawn a blank. Despite clues provided by old documents and the handed-down testimony of farmers who came across bones in the nineteenth century, again and again we have failed in our quest. We always seem to have been looking in the wrong place. We hoped that at Killiecrankie an excavation of the square, grass-covered mound topped with a stone plinth said to mark the graves of officers would be more conclusive.

As at other battlefields there are stories of bones being found at Killiecrankie. The Old Statistical Account (which is like a local census, usually compiled by the parish minister) of the 1790s mentions human bones that had recently been dug up by workmen quarrying gravel close to a mound known as Tomb Clavers, and were apparently reburied on the site. The plinth on the mound and its brass plaque is a later addition. Part of the inscription reads: 'The cairn marks the grave of officers of both sides and honours all who on that day died on their duty as became the men of valour and conscience.' But, built by the owners of Urrard House,

Iain Banks takes a break at the Grave of the Officers

this memorial utilizes a site already associated with the victims of war to commemorate also a soldier in a much later conflict: a relative, possibly a son, who died while serving as a soldier during the Malayan insurgency in 1950.

We were very aware of the sensitive nature of the cairn site but felt that a careful and limited excavation would make a valuable contribution to understanding of the treatment of the dead after the battle of Killiecrankie and also answer a number of questions that puzzled us – for instance, how did the creators of the cairn know that only officers were buried in it? The dead were probably stripped of their clothing before burial and it seems unlikely that the bodies of officers would have been distinguishable from common soldiers, especially after decay had set in, which in the case of possibly heavily mutilated bodies in summer temperatures would have occurred very quickly. Nor did the mound appear on the Ordnance Survey map surveyed in 1860, which seemed strange, given that things like old lime kilns, small wells and the Claverhouse Stone were marked. Could this mean that the cairn was a relatively recent feature, perhaps built some time in the late nineteenth century?

A geophysical survey over the mound showed a dark outline of what were probably stones around its upper edge, which emphasized the mound's roughly square shape. In order to minimize our disturbance of the site we decided to position a trench over the back of the mound, behind the plinth. (We intended to return the mound to its former condition once we had finished the excavation.) As we began to cut the turf there could be no denying that we were all rather nervous – it is always a strange sensation to encounter the remains of dead people, and knowing that these people died under the most dreadful, violent circumstances always heightens this sense of trepidation. But we had a job to do and do it we did.

Below the turf we came across a layer of angular stones, just as we would expect to find in a prehistoric burial cairn or tomb. Around the edge of the cairn the stones were laid in a more regular fashion and seemed to form a lip or ledge, as suggested by the geophysical survey. Once we had cleaned the soil from the stones we carefully planned them, then started to remove then, one by one. Someone had obviously gone to some trouble to build the cairn and at first we took this a positive sign that it might indeed contain burials. Beneath the layer of stones we encountered a coarse, gravelly soil, which covered a very sticky clay deposit. As we went deeper the stone ledge turned into a very carefully made drystone wall. The soil deposits continued down for the best part of a metre before we hit the natural stony subsoil, across the surface of which the lowest course of the wall had been laid. We had reached the bottom of the mound without coming across a single human bone. There was no sign of a grave pit cut into the natural soil beneath the mound. We had been here before. We couldn't give up now without taking another bite at the cherry. We decided to open a second trench on the mound, this time in front of the plinth.

It was the same as before: a layer of stones overlying redeposited gravelly soil and clay, sitting on top of the subsoil. There were no bones in the mound – or at least in the two trenches we had excavated, which covered about a quarter of its surface area. What was going on?

It crossed our minds that the soil in the area is fairly acidic, which is obviously not good for the preservation of organic materials such as bone. But if enough bones are buried together they tend to change the chemistry of the soil and make it more alkaline, thus promoting preservation. It seemed likely, then, that if a large number of bodies were buried in the mound at least some bones would survive. After much deliberation, we came to the conclusion that few if any bones were ever interred in the mound.

We think the story goes something like this. In the

late eighteenth century estate workers extracting gravel came across a small number of human bones. These were brought to the attention of the master of Urrard House, on whose land they had been discovered. The owner would have been very aware that just over a hundred years earlier a bloody battle had been fought in his grounds. Assuming that the bones must have been the remains of men killed in the battle, he instructed his workmen to rebury them, and either then or some time later decided that some sort of memorial would be appropriate. Accordingly, the cairn was built. First a drystone enclosure was constructed; then soil was dumped into the area encompassed by the wall. The human bones might have been buried in these soil deposits. The cairn was then capped by a layer of stones placed over the top. In retrospect it seems to us pretty unlikely that such an elaborate grave would have been constructed immediately after the battle, as the priority would have been simply to get rid of the rotting corpses that lay all around, as quickly as possible.

Further landscaping took place around the outside of the mound with the construction of a bank enclosing three sides of the cairn, which given the wet ground conditions might have created a kind of moat around the mound. Thus as well as being a grave and memorial to the dead the mound became a picturesque landscape feature in the grounds, like a folly or a statue. It was a site that could be integrated into garden walks, a place where after dinner guests could be told the story of the battle.

The nineteenth century saw the romantic revival of interest in the Highlands and the Jacobite Rebellions, through – among other things – the writings of Sir Walter Scott, whose novel *Old Mortality*, which featured Dundee as a character, was published in 1816. In addition, the poets Robert Burns and William Wordsworth wrote a song (1789) and a sonnet (1803) respectively about the battle of Killiecrankie. The identification of the grave with officers from both sides was probably a by-product of this process and, too, a reflection of the social context within which the cairn was created. Given his wealth and social standing, the master of the house, having gone to the trouble of building a grave mound on his land, would have been inclined to tell people that officers and gentlemen rather than common soldiers were buried in it. Over the years the origins of the mound were forgotten and its association with officers was adopted as a fact, which was literally set in stone with the casting of the bronze plaque and the raising of the stone plinth in 1950 or not long after.

The dead of Killiecrankie were obviously disposed of somehow – according to historical accounts there were nearly 3,000 bodies littering the relatively small area over which the battle was fought. One story tells of bodies being thrown into the burns or streams which ran into the river Garry at the foot of the glen but at that time had been dammed. When all the bodies had been collected in this fashion the dams were broken down and the bodies flushed away down the river like so much toilet waste. It is indeed possible that some bodies were disposed of in the river, and probably some men drowned in the Garry as they tried to flee from the victorious Jacobites. Some of the dead would undoubtedly have been buried. As we worked away on the mound, local visitors told us that we would find graves in other nearby mounds and we even dug test pits into some of these, but again we found nothing.

A pricker used to clear powder residue from a musket's touch-hole, made from an old strip of copper

Our investigation finished, we left the dead of Killiecrankie to rest in peace, wherever they are.

The snipers' house

The opening shots of the battle were fired by Jacobite snipers. First blood is said to have been drawn by a well-known Atholl hunter called Ian Ban Beg MacRan, who positioned himself in the trees on the opposite bank of the river Garry as the government column made its nervous way through the pass and, using his hunting skills to good effect, fired a bullet that sent a cavalryman tumbling from his saddle. Then when Mackay's troops were deployed along the plateau in front of Urrard House, as both sides faced off, each waiting for the other to make the next move, the Jacobites on the hillslope above tried to make things uncomfortable for the government troops. As Mackay's account describes, a small party moved down the slope

in front of their own lines and, taking cover in a house, began to fire down on the government troops below. Eventually Mackay ordered a counterattack by men from his own regiment, which was positioned directly opposite the snipers' house. A captain led a raiding party up the hill and after a fight sent the Jacobites scuttling back to their own lines, leaving several of their comrades dead in their wake.

Mackay's account provides us with a wonderful little snapshot of the early stages of the battle – but how reliable was it? To check the veracity of this part of his account we set ourselves the challenge of finding the building or buildings used by the Jacobite snipers. Our search began with the 1860 map, which showed some buildings no longer standing today, some of which might have been standing at the time of the battle. Two possibilities presented themselves. The first of these was a small farmstead known as Lagnabuiag, located not far to the north-east of Tomb Clavers. This cluster of buildings had disappeared from the maps by the time of the 1990 edition, and for a while we thought it might have been trashed by the new road in the 1970s. We first visited the site on a very snowy day when we could barely see our hands in front of our faces. But the snow wasn't deep enough to bury the remains of the farmstead, which we were pleased to see had survived. Fighting our way through the snowstorm we stumbled across two rows of tumbled stones sitting along the edge of a terrace cut into the hillside. To our experienced eyes it was obvious that these were the remains of a rectangular building that had once nestled in a tongue of higher ground overlooking the plateau on which the government army was arrayed. The remains of deserted houses are a characteristic feature of the Highland landscape, which was cleared of large parts of its human population during the first half of the nineteenth century. This was the period of the notorious Highland Clearances, when landlords moved people off their land and replaced them with more profitable sheep. Set down-slope from the initial Jacobite position and close enough to the government line to allow accurate musket fire, this was certainly a possible location for the snipers' den. There was one problem, though. Mackay states that the snipers were directly opposite his own regiment, which, under the command of his brother, was positioned towards the right of the line. Lagnabuiag is located well to the west of Urrard House and was therefore – if contemporary accounts of Mackay's deployment are to be relied upon – on the left rather than the right of the government line. Nevertheless we decided to excavate, hopeful that our work would throw up some answers.

Finds recovered from Lagnabuiag. Is this the front-door key?

We opened a trench across the front wall of the building, hoping that we would find government musket-balls fired during the counterattack. Doing this meant that we didn't have to worry about the much thicker pile of rubble at the other end of the building, which itself rang a few alarm bells – but more of this later. Banksie and Dave, along with our volunteers, set to work. With the tummocky turfs out of the way the team began to work their way through the rubble, using their experience to tell which stones could be removed and which should be left in place. As they hefted more stones out of the way, the true shape of the building slowly appeared, as sharp edges came into focus when the blurring rubble was removed.

With the front wall exposed it was obvious we were looking at a well-made building with nicely finished, rubble-filled walls tracing straight lines over the ground. The inside face of the wall still carried traces of plaster, which would not have been out of place in a house but would have been a bit over the top for a barn or byre in which livestock were kept. So far the signs were good – it seemed that we were looking at a house, as described by Mackay – but we needed evidence of the presence of the snipers and of the government counterattack. The house began to open itself up to us. A gap in the middle of the front wall marked the doorway. While cleaning around the threshold, Banksie found a key, which had perhaps been kept under the doorstep. We had a house all right, but was it the snipers' house? We used metal detectors across the front of the building to look for musket-balls, but nothing turned up, apart from the odd nail and piece of iron scrap. The only pottery we found was clearly nineteenth century, including several pieces from an attractive decorated bowl, of a ceramic type known as Spongeware, as the coloured decoration was applied with a sponge. It began to sink in that the finds were telling us that far from being the snipers' house the house was a later building that was not here at the time of the battle.

The floor of the house had at one time been covered with stone flags, bedded on clean sand. There was no trace of an earlier building below this and nothing to suggest any use of the house earlier than the beginning of the nineteenth century. It was then that we were

forced to confront the issue of the large mound of rubble heaped up on the south-western end of the house. It had sounded a few alarm bells but we'd ignored them. We didn't have time to excavate it but we knew enough from seeing similar ruinous buildings to realize that this pile of stone had been created by the collapse of a gable-end chimney. The truth was that formal fireplaces and chimneys did not appear on small rural houses until long after the time of the battle. In the seventeenth century, and in some places well into the nineteenth century, these buildings, usually known as longhouses, had a simple hearth on the floor in the middle of the building and the smoke from the fire was allowed to percolate through the thatched roof, which must have made the atmosphere in the house fairly uncomfortable. All the evidence, then, pointed to a nineteenth-century cottage built on a site which had seen no earlier building activity. We had little choice but to look elsewhere for our snipers' house.

All our hopes now rested on the second possible site, which on the early map was known as Stirkpark, but is today called Croftcarnoch. In 1860 there were two buildings here; now there is just one, a recently built holiday cottage – possibly incorporating stones from the older buildings. We were in two minds about this site. On the one hand its location was more likely to have been opposite the right flank of the government line. But on the other, it seemed from the maps – both old and new – to be a bit too far away from where we first thought the government line was positioned; and we knew from our own experience in firing muskets that hitting a target over a hundred yards away was a very difficult thing to accomplish. But these doubts were lessened when we visited the site. It became apparent that there was an area of flat ground at the base of the slope on the north side of the main road which, if occupied by government troops, might have put them within range of snipers at Stirkpark (the modern road tended to obscure the original topography – it was all too easy to assume that the government line was in all places located to the south of the road). A sniper positioned at Stirkpark would certainly have had a good view down on to this area, and as we levelled our imaginary muskets at the sheep that now grazed there, Stirkpark seemed more plausible as the snipers' house than we had first thought.

We poked around the cottage's garden looking for traces of earlier buildings. The most promising-looking area was to the east of the standing building, where a terrace had been cut into the hillside, the earth face at the rear kept in place by a drystone wall. Studying the map again we were pleased to see that this site corresponded pretty closely to that of one of the earlier buildings, and we'd already learned at Lagnabuiag that houses in this hilly country were sometimes built on small artificial terraces. The area was overgrown with nettles and other weeds and we set to work clearing the vegetation and marking out a metre-wide slot trench. After pulling out a lot of modern rubbish, we were horrified to find further downward progress blocked by a mass of huge boulders. With great difficulty we lifted out a few of these but there seemed to be no end to them. If the remains of an old building were there, they were buried beneath tons of stone. Disappointed, we all agreed that without the aid of a block and tackle to help with lifting we would have to abandon the task.

We closed down the trench and after we'd taken photographs we reluctantly started to backfill. It looked as though we would have to give up our search for the snipers' house. Our last hope rested with a metal-detector survey of the cottage's garden, in the hope that a scatter of musket-balls might at least provide evidence of fighting. The survey of the garden came up with nothing more than modern pieces of junk, but then our luck changed. When a detectorist strayed out of the garden on his lunch break he made a startling discovery. He was just messing around not far to the west of Croftcarnoch and a little further down the slope, when his machine came up with a strong signal. Even though he was outside our survey area we gave him permission

Above and below **Olivia plans the remains of the house at Lagnabuiag**

to dig it up. We couldn't believe it when he pulled out a curved strip of brass – a trigger guard from a musket.

This was more like it. We called in Olivia to set up a series of survey grids around the find spot. The rest of the detectorists were drafted in and the new area swept. Then Olivia's experience in Scottish landscape archaeology paid dividends. As she wandered about the hillside checking progress she came across telltale lumps and bumps – the heavily eroded remains of buildings that didn't appear on any of our maps. Low, grass-covered mounds marked out the walls of at least two buildings, one of them roughly square and the other rectangular in plan. A circular depression might have marked the location of a corn-drying kiln. There was even a hollow way – an old track coming down the side of the hill into the cluster of buildings. The discovery of this and the trigger guard near by was exciting enough,

but when a slightly distorted pistol-ball was pulled from one of the wall mounds, we couldn't have been happier if we'd found buried treasure. The buildings and the finds, with one or two more musket-balls added to them, could mean only one thing: we had found the snipers' house.

Home from home: our tent near Urrard House

The cluster of buildings had been built on a natural terrace, almost halfway down the hill, closer to the flat ground below than Croftcarnoch. Snipers here would have had an excellent view of the enemy below. The position was correct for the right flank of the government line, and the trigger guard and musket- and pistol-balls provided evidence of fighting on the spot. The musket-balls might have been fired from a distance, but the pistol-ball lodged in the wall was clear evidence of close-quarter fighting. We imagined what might have happened here: a small group of government troops making their way up the slope after the snipers' initial fire and storming the building; shots being exchanged and the Jacobites being forced on to the back foot; the government officer leading the counterattack firing his pistol but hitting the wall; then a Jacobite's trigger guard breaking loose during a hand-to-hand struggle as he tried to escape back to his own lines. Capturing fleeting moments such as this is the essence of what battlefield archaeology is all about.

Metal-detecting the battle

Believing that no one had ever metal-detected at Killiecrankie, we held out high hopes for this part of the project. And our optimism was rewarded.

Our main objective in metal-detecting was to define the extent of the battlefield and the character of the various events that had taken place on it. To do this, we planned to survey three transects across the battlefield, starting up on the hill which the Jacobites charged down and running out on to the flat ground on which the government troops were positioned. One of these slices across the field was to be in the centre, just to the west of Urrard House; the other two to the east and the west of this position. We would have to line up our grids on either side of the modern road as best we could. A fourth area to be detected was the level area below the plateau from where Mackay had first seen the Jacobites and where he left behind the 1,200 packhorses of the baggage train when he led his men up the slope. This flat ground down by the river was described by Mackay as a cornfield, and today some of the fields here are still used for growing crops. The baggage train offered rich pickings for the victorious Jacobites and we hoped to find the detritus created by their frenzied activity when they looted it.

The slope on the north side of the modern road is divided today into various fields, enclosed by fences and drystone walls, but the ground was open and free from obstruction at the time of the battle when Dundee's men charged down it towards Mackay's line, desperate to close the distance between themselves and the enemy as quickly as possible. Mackay's best chance of victory was to break the Jacobite charge with massed and disciplined musketry before the Jacobites could come to handstrokes, using the newly introduced platoon firing system. In the central of our three transects on the slope we encountered plenty of evidence of government fire, in the form of musket-balls scattered across the hillside. Some were heavily distorted, as though they had hit bone or stone, while others were just slightly misshapen, and we knew from our firing experiments that these had probably passed through one side of a Jacobite's body and out through the other.

We also found masses of round metal buttons, of various sizes – far more than at any other site we have looked at. Many of these were plain, but some carried ornate crests and other designs. Close to the road we found a silvered button decorated with a human figure holding a key in one hand and a dagger or sword in the other. It was only later when we visited the chapel and burial ground at Old Blair and saw this design on a memorial stone that we recognized it as the Atholl crest. Although some Atholl men took part in the battle, we

In memory of Bonnie Dundee at Old Blair

think this button might have been more recent, perhaps falling from the tunic of one of the Duke of Atholl's militiamen while on manoeuvres during the nineteenth century. There was other evidence for later military activity in the form of heavy-calibre bullets, probably from an Enfield rifle dating to the 1850s or '60s. It is well known that the Jacobites divested themselves of their plaids before they charged downhill, but other buttons suggested that many of them were far from naked, wearing shirts and waistcoats or even tunics with buttons on them. Mackay's account supports this, mentioning them wearing surcoats (waistcoats) over their shirts. Buttons would have been torn from clothes as men were hit by musket-balls and fell to the ground, and during hand-to-hand fighting. Others might have been loosely attached and simply fallen off in the stress and strain of the charge, with men perhaps buffeting against one another as they ran. This second mechanism of deposition might account for the large number of buttons in the western transect, where they far outnumbered musket-balls. This distinctive pattern appears to back up Mackay's claim that the troops on the left flank of the government line were so panicked by the oncoming Jacobites that they barely fired a shot before turning to flee.

One piece of evidence in the western transect on the southern side of the road suggested that the Jacobites didn't get it all their own way here. We found a highly decorated piece of copper alloy, of which there was enough to tell us that we were looking at a part of a finely worked circular fitting about eight centimetres across. There was also a small broken rivet still sitting in a hole on its outer edge. Having seen a number of targes, most recently those on display in Blair Castle, we were convinced that this concave creation was the boss from the centre of one of these distinctive shields. Given the fine workmanship and high level of decoration it was obviously from a wealthy man's shield, belonging to a Jacobite officer rather than a lowly foot-soldier. We

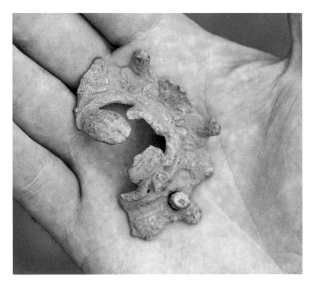

An ornate boss from the centre of a targe

knew from our experiments with the musket that the targe, no matter how expensive, provided little protection from a well-placed musket-ball. Jacobite officers led from the front, not only to encourage their men but also because they tended to be among the best-armed troops, and many of them must have fallen in the face of government fire. There didn't appear to have been much in the way of fire here on the government left. However, the boss's heavily fragmented state strongly suggests that not all the government troops on this end of the line showed the Jacobites their heels and that the shield was broken during vicious hand-to-hand fighting.

Among the government musket-balls in the central transect there were a number of smaller balls, too big for a pistol but too small for a standard government musket. These may be musket-balls from smaller Jacobite muskets, which presumably they fired as they approached the enemy line, before discarding them and going in with the sword. Or they may be carbine balls, from weapons carried by the mounted men on both sides. This possibility is certainly in keeping with the government and Jacobite horse being positioned close to the centre of the line. The Jacobite horse charged down the middle before veering to the left, perhaps to support the Macdonalds who were suffering at the hands of the most disciplined of Mackay's regiments. It was at this point that most accounts say that Dundee was shot down, as he crossed the front of the government line. Who knows – one of the musket-balls recovered from this central transect might be the very ball that killed Dundee!

The pattern of fairly heavy government musket fire continued in our eastern transect, back towards the

An axehead, possibly used as a weapon

pass, where buttons and balls were scattered across the slope. It wasn't, though, until we crossed the road that some of the most incredible metal-detector results came to light. Just below the road, in a couple of fields to the east of the walled garden of Urrard House, we found a concentrated scatter of musket-balls. About a dozen were spread out across a natural terrace, which dropped down like a step on to another flat shelf before the ground gave way to the steep tree-covered ridge, which dropped down towards the lowest of the terraces and the river. These musket-balls were so close to the government position that we knew they were the last volley fired by the right hand of the government line before the Jacobites closed. The distance between the musket-balls and the edge of the tree-covered ridge was no more than thirty or forty metres, which means – since the fighting took place in the open space – that the gap between the government line and the Jacobites when this volley was fired must have been somewhat less than that. This closeness suggests a high degree of discipline among those in this part of the government line, which again ties in with Mackay's account. Some of these balls might have been incoming fire from the Jacobites, perhaps even from the snipers, but their position told another story – and one which helps to explain the general success of the Jacobite charge in the battle.

We spent a lot of time walking up and down the hill over which the Jacobites charged. As we familiarized ourselves with the terrain it became apparent that the hill was not an even slope, but in most places took the form of natural terraces which dropped down the gradient like a huge flight of stairs. There were places where the topography was not so pronounced but in general terracing was the dominant feature of the slope – but not one that would necessarily be apparent to a casual observer looking up the slope. What struck us about this terracing was that a man moving down the hill would at times be out of the sight of someone looking up from the bottom; he would come into view

234 | two men in a trench II

only as he stepped on to the edge of the terrace and for as long as he moved down the slope on to the terrace below, at which point he would disappear from view again before appearing once more at the lip of that terrace.

The terracing might therefore have shielded the Jacobite charge from government musketry at various points as it moved down the hill. This 'now you see them now you don't' effect might have been one reason why, according to MacBane's account, the government troops managed to fire only about three rounds apiece before the Jacobites were among them – though we shouldn't underestimate the speed of the charge as a factor. The evidence of the musket-balls from the terrace described above matches this picture exactly. We tried an experiment. One of us took up a position where we thought the government line had been. Marked by a couple of musket-balls and a pistol-ball, this was on the lower terrace, at the top of the steep ridge. The other one went to the back of the higher terrace, where we'd found the dramatic scatter of musket-balls. To begin with this 'Jacobite' was totally out of sight, but as he moved forward towards the edge of the terrace he came into view, head then shoulders. Just at the point where he provided the 'government soldier' with a good torso shot he walked into the musket-ball scatter. Probably most of these balls hit their targets, passing through bodies before dropping to the ground. Balls that missed their targets continued their flight and probably came to rest higher up the hill. If we are right, each of the musket-balls on the terrace lay just behind where a Jacobite soldier had fallen. It was one of the eeriest encounters we'd ever had with our subject matter.

One more find from the battlefield deserves special

mention. The central transect skipped over the main road to continue through the field in which we had pitched our tent, a paddock where the Cairns family kept a small herd of Highland cattle. At the top of the gently sloping field was the tongue of slightly higher ground and the remains of the nineteenth-century farmstead of Lagnabuiag. At the bottom, just across the driveway up to the house, was the edge of the plateau, giving way to the steep, tree-covered slope that dropped down to the river terrace beyond. We found more musket-balls here, and even an iron axe head, possibly from a Jacobite weapon. We also found a pretty unassuming fragment of iron, which looked as though it had broken away from a hollow sphere about twice the size of a cricket ball. It was only when we showed it to Andy Robertshaw that we learned the amazing truth about this object. He weighed it in his hand, studied its shape and thickness and rubbed his thumb over the casting seam before delivering his verdict. It wasn't, as someone had jokingly suggested, a piece of the ballcock from a toilet cistern, but a fragment from an exploded hand grenade. These weapons were similar to those used during English Civil War sieges and were later adopted as the specialist weapon of the grenadiers.

Although by the time of Killiecrankie grenadiers were part of every infantry battalion, none of the accounts makes any reference to them using grenades during the battle (nor is mention made of the role of the pikemen who also took part). The discovery of an exploded grenade on the plateau, at the point where the Jacobites came into contact with the government line, points to the last-minute throwing of grenades, in a desperate attempt to break up the charge before it crashed home. The attempt obviously failed, and might

The baggage train

When the Jacobite charge hit home, most of the government line turned and ran back towards the river Garry, down the steep ridge which they had climbed a few hours previously. Many of these unfortunate souls must have been cut down by their pursuers as they stumbled through the trees on to the broad river terrace at the bottom of the ridge. The presence there of the baggage train awaiting the return of the army probably saved many a government soldier's skin, as the Jacobites proceeded to loot the baggage four ways from Sunday.

Most of the troops guarding the train surely turned and ran as, having already heard the dreadful clamour of battle, they now saw their panicstricken comrades come screaming out of the trees with sword-wielding Jacobites hot on their heels. Stuff must have been scattered everywhere as the looters ripped packs from the 1,200 packhorses' backs, either to get at the contents or to take the horses. To the victor the spoils, and what spoils there must have been! All manner of things were there for the taking – muskets, powder and ball, swords and other weapons, crockery, cutlery, flour, salt, biscuits, bread, beef on the hoof, bottles of wine, kegs of spirits, pots and pans, clothing, footwear, tents, farriers' gear, tools, saddlery, money and all manner of personal possessions. At the time it wasn't unusual for officers to take some very incongruous domestic luxuries on campaign with them, including fine furniture, carpets and even paintings. A victorious regular army would have found good use for all these arms and supplies, but the Jacobite host was far from a regular army. Once satisfied with their individual loot most men began to stream away from the field, setting out for home.

Fragment of a grenade

even have caused death and injury among government troops as well as Jacobites – throwing a ball-shaped grenade up a slope could not have been recommended practice. Since grenadier units had become part of the British army as recently as 1677 it seems highly likely that our grenade fragment represents the first ever use of this weapon in battle by these troops, at least on British soil – they certainly do not appear to have been used at Sedgemoor, three years earlier.

As we walked across the buttercup-strewn field in the summer sunshine, it was hard to picture the slaughter and looting that took place here. But our detectorists' finds soon helped us to focus our imaginations. Again there were plenty of buttons, but even more evocative of flight and pursuit were a couple of shoe buckles, which would easily have been ripped away from the feet of running men, especially if this field had corn in it, as suggested by Mackay's account. There was the odd coin, perhaps dropped in the fracas that surely must have developed around any box or bag containing hard currency – and there must have been a lot of money with the baggage, as the army needed to be paid. Silver-plated tea spoons, knives and forks gave us some idea of the luxury in which the officer class were used to keeping themselves – these certainly weren't the eating implements of the enlisted men, which probably consisted of a knife, possibly even a bayonet, and a wooden spoon. We also found part of the pewter rim of a small wooden bucket or pitcher,

The Jacobites charged down the hill in the background

with a loop for a carrying handle. The metal was twisted and broken, but several metres away we found another piece from the same object.

When we showed Andy Robertshaw the finds from here he singled out a small rectangle of lead and told us that when bent double it would have been used to secure a flint in the hammer of a musket. As it would have required regular replacement, there must have been hundreds or thousands of spare parts such as these in the baggage. Tellingly, we found only one or two musket-balls – evidence that down here what fighting there was must have been a bloody hand-to-hand affair.

Just across from where we were detecting is the standing stone known as the Claverhouse Stone, which some stories would have you believe marks the place where Dundee breathed his last. Don't believe any of it – it is most likely a megalith from the Bronze Age that has been standing on that site for about 3,000–4,000 years.

Battlefields and the Heritage Industry

The British Isles are littered with battlefields. On Ordnance Survey maps, a crossed-swords symbol and a date mark the supposed location of scores of bloody interludes in our history. Take a look at a few OS maps, start counting up the crossed swords, and it's easy to get a sense of the headache our battlefields pose to those who look after our heritage. It would be impossible to preserve them all and protect them against road building and urban expansion without unhelpfully fossilizing our landscape. But we argue that it's vital to guard against unnecessary destruction of such historic sites.

Unlike buildings and monuments, battlefields do not enjoy the protection of specific legislation. It is often down to the diligence of individual archaeologists, employed by local authorities, to make sure that a red flag is raised when sites in their areas come under threat. Even when a threat to a battlefield is identified, there is no guarantee that steps will be taken to avoid or even minimize damage to the site. The battlefield of Killiecrankie has remained remarkably undisturbed – but only because much of it has remained in the hands of private individuals who have prevented any interference with the site.

The Battlefields Trust, a charitable organization set up in 1993, works hard to raise awareness of battlefields and campaigns vigorously for their preservation. English Heritage has also made a significant contribution by compiling a Battlefields Register that pinpoints locations and provides useful information to would-be visitors. But the simple fact of the matter is that there is as yet no unified, nationwide approach to the care of these important places.

There are visitors centres at the sites of the battles of Killiecrankie, Culloden and Bannockburn in Scotland, Hastings and Bosworth in England and the Boyne in Ireland; but in the case of most other battlefields, the visitor is largely dependent on OS maps and helpful staff in local museums. During the course of our work, it has been made clear to us that local communities and visitors are fascinated by battlefields and the stories surrounding them. It is likely that richer sources of information about the battles which were so often pivotal in our history would be welcomed by many.

The situation has, in the past, been complicated by uncertainty surrounding the location of many battlefields. Even when battlefields are marked on the maps, traditionally it is historians rather than archaeologists who have pinpointed their locations. With the best will in the world, by working only with second-hand information – eyewitness accounts written hundreds of years ago, often by biased authors, and other documentary sources – historians cannot always be relied upon as accurate. When the A9 was being built through the Pass of Killiecrankie in the 1970s, the engineers simply consulted the OS map, noted the location of the crossed swords marking the traditional site of the fighting, and plotted a course that avoided that particular spot. Given an absence of accurate, archaeological information about the site, there was little more that the road builders could have done. It is hard to make a case for the protection of an area when its status as a battlefield is based on little more than tradition.

We hope that our work over the past five years has gone some way towards beginning to redress this balance. Only battlefield archaeology, after all, can unearth the physical evidence of warfare and thereby help prove beyond doubt the location of a battle. By taking the work of historians that last crucial step forward into the realms of forensic evidence, battlefield archaeology can clarify what are often confused and incomplete stories. Supposed locations can be examined and either ratified as genuine or rejected in favour of ones supported by the archaeological evidence. Once a battlefield has been accurately located, the archaeological and historical evidence together can be used to inform the visitor about what went on there. Equally importantly, the combined data can be used by planning authorities and others making decisions about development.

Battlefield archaeology is a new kid on the block, but it is already making an important contribution to our understanding of the landscape in which we live.

Conclusion

No matter how many battlefields we go on to investigate, our time at Killiecrankie will always be special, not just because of the glorious weather, the stunning scenery and the good company, but because it proved what an archaeological approach can achieve on a battlefield. Excavation uncovered the partial remains of Urrard House, allowing us to place the building in the landscape for the first time. It also revealed the Grave of the Officers to be a much later monument, which at one time might have contained a few stray bones. This feature was fascinating for the insight it provided into the way that historic battlefields become incorporated into later landscapes and coloured by the society of the time.

Perhaps the most exciting discovery was the snipers' house, the location of which matches pretty accurately the description given by Mackay in his account of the battle. We didn't have time to excavate the buildings visible as lumps and bumps, but we'd certainly like to at some point. Overall Mackay's memoir comes out fairly

well as a reasonable account when matched to the sample of the battlefield we investigated. As well as telling us where the snipers' house was he claimed that the left of his line folded without firing a shot, and sure enough, although there was evidence of fighting there, we recovered very few musket-balls.

What struck us most of all was the quality of the metal-detector finds. The concentration of musket-balls on the ridge to the right of the government line provided us with an amazing insight into what happened during the battle, bringing us as close to the battle and the people who fought it as we could ever hope to get. Killiecrankie showed what might be left behind several hundred years after a battle before metal detectorists start to remove objects. Metal detectorists and archaeologists should learn from this, and work together to ensure that battlefields are protected from unauthorized detecting which makes no attempt to record the location of finds or make them available for the public to learn from.

HORNCHURCH 1940

**Flight mechanics at Hornchurch:
Dave Davis is at the back, third
from left**

Gardens is named after Edgar Ryder, who was shot down over France
and spent four years as a prisoner of war; Bouchier Walk for Air Vice-
Marshal Sir Cecil 'Boy' Bouchier, who commanded RAF Hornchurch
during the battle of Britain.

The list goes on: Lock Close, named after the legendary ace Eric Lock,
who notched up twenty-six victories before being shot down and killed
somewhere over France; Gray Gardens, for New Zealander Colin Gray,
who saw action over Dunkirk and who, with twenty-seven kills, became

the highest-scoring pilot from his country and was awarded the DFC and two bars; Malan Square, for Adolf 'Sailor' Malan, a South African pilot who notched up thirty-two kills, one of the highest scores of the war, and wrote *10 Rules of Air Fighting*, which was to become a bible for RAF pilots. Tuck Road is for Robert Stanford Tuck, an ace shot down over France and treated to dinner by Luftwaffe ace Adolf Galland. Taken prisoner, he escaped his captors in 1945 and made it to the Russian lines before being repatriated.

Archaeology is about landscapes and the people who shape them and leave their marks upon them. Battlefield archaeology is about the impact left upon landscapes by the business of war and the men and women who make it and endured it. The men who are remembered as the 'few' made their marks in the sky, which has no memory and bears no traces. At Hornchurch, *aides-mémoires* left by those determined that the heritage of the place should not be forgotten helped inspire us to investigate what marks those people and the conflict of which they were part left on the ground below.

BACKGROUND

THE ROYAL AIR FORCE WAS FORMED IN THE
SPRING OF 1918 BY THE UNIFICATION OF
TWO EARLIER GROUPS OF FLIERS, THE
ROYAL FLYING CORPS AND THE ROYAL
NAVAL AIR SERVICE. WHILE THE RAF
WOULD IN TIME ESTABLISH ITS OWN
LEGENDS, THERE WAS ALREADY A
TRADITION OF DERRING-DO AMONG THOSE
MAGNIFICENT MEN IN THEIR FLYING
MACHINES. ONE SUCH ACTION OCCURRED
ON 2 SEPTEMBER 1916, ON A HELLISH
NIGHT OF LOW CLOUD AND DRIVING RAIN,

when a 21-year-old lieutenant of the RFC named William Leefe Robinson climbed into the cockpit of his BE2 biplane to face a terror that had been looming over London for months: giant Zeppelin airships, which had been attacking the capital since May, causing several deaths and mounting fear and alarm among the civilian population.

That night the Germans had massed their largest raid of the First World War. A total of twelve Zeppelins – like a pod of malevolent whales in a dark sea of sky – were attacking the capital that night and eyewitness accounts said that the young pilot had to fly through a heavy bombardment aimed at the airships from the ground. As Leefe Robinson came within range of his prey, the Schutte-Lanz SLII, he fired a Very light (flare) to tell the ground troops to hold their fire. As thousands of Londoners looked on, hanging out of windows and gathering on street corners to gaze skywards at the spectacle, Leefe Robinson emptied an entire drum of ammunition into the Zeppelin's bloated belly. Nothing. Again he turned to the attack and pumped a second drum into the giant craft: still no effect. Turning around for a third time, he targeted a specific point on the Zeppelin's hull with more of his incendiary rounds – and was at last rewarded with the sight of a red glow building up inside the monster's skin. All at once, the Zeppelin burst into flames and fell slowly towards the ground, at Cuffley, Hertfordshire, amid the cheers of onlookers. Leefe Robinson was an instant hero – and an instant celebrity. He was awarded the Victoria Cross for his efforts and his fame was assured. Sadly, he was shot down over France in 1917 and taken prisoner. Weakened by his harsh imprisonment, he died of influenza on the last day of 1919.

William Leefe Robinson had taken off, that famous night, from an aerodrome known as Sutton's Farm, in quiet countryside at Hornchurch in Essex. The burgeoning threat of the Zeppelins had created the need for a protective ring around London, and the small team of RFC personnel that set up camp in 1915, on land farmed by Mr Tom Crawford, initially shared the defence of the capital with eight other aerodromes dotted around the counties of the south-east. It is hard to imagine just how primitive these early aerodromes were. To say that pilots flew from them on a wing and a prayer is quite apposite. Illustrating just how basic things were for the aviators at Sutton's Farm is the fact that night flights were made possible only by lines of petrol-tin flares marking the landing strips across the grass.

Leefe Robinson was the first RFC pilot from Sutton's Farm to notch up a kill against the German airship fleet, but not the last. Three weeks

Opposite **Winston Churchill watches a Mark I Stirling, 1940**

A German fighter just before it crashes into the sea

later, two more pilots took off from there against another Zeppelin raid. Flight Lieutenants Brandon and Sowrey brought down one apiece. These successes brought to an end the terror of the airships, but not the threat of attacks on London from the air. The Germans' next tactic was bombing raids by twin-engined Gotha G.II aircraft. To counter these, the coverage from aerodromes such as Sutton's Farm was beefed up. By the end of the war, Sutton's Farm was part of the London Air Defence Area and the place had taken on a more permanent feel – with timber buildings in place of the canvas hangars that had been thrown up in 1915. Within a year or so of peace being declared, however, the wisdom of the time suggested that the need for aerodromes to defend London had passed. In the months following the end of the war the Air Ministry significantly downsized the fledgling RAF. It returned the Sutton's Farm land to Mr Crawford, after first demolishing most of the so-recently completed buildings and digging up the newly laid roads and drains.

Military intelligence being what it is, however, by 1922 the men from the Ministry had concluded that the same land should be reacquired for a permanent aerodrome. Mr Crawford was somewhat less than thrilled and initially attempted to keep the land he had just got back. However, with its compulsory purchasing powers the Ministry was not to be thwarted, and by the summer of 1923 Sutton's Farm had been designated a role in the defence of London once more.

By 1928, the RAF had stationed 111 Squadron at the newly completed aerodrome – which in January 1929 was renamed RAF Hornchurch. The significance of the place – and of the RAF in general – grew and the following year a second squadron, 54 Squadron, was stationed there. In an age when the skies are seldom without the track of one or more planes, it is difficult to imagine today the novelty presented to the general population of the 1930s by the presence of aerodromes on their doorsteps. Places like RAF Hornchurch became popular with day trippers keen to see aircraft taking off and landing; they enjoyed events such as air displays and 'Empire Air Days', which also served to boost the skills and experience of the pilots. There were no runways, as such, at Hornchurch. Spitfires required about 150 metres to get up into the sky and the grass of the aerodrome provided runs that were more than adequate.

By 1936, Hornchurch had been assimilated into No. 11 Group, overseen by Fighter Command. In 1938 the station, by now a sector headquarters, took part in the home defence exercises designed to test, among other things, the efficacy of the recently constructed radar shield

A flight of Supermarine Spitfires take off from Hornchurch

provided by stations constructed along the south and south-east coastlines. Now Hornchurch had the atmosphere of a place with a job to do – and it was populated by people ready and able to do it. By 1934 111 Squadron had been relocated, and 54, 65 and 74 Squadrons now occupied the station. (They were subsequently joined by other squadrons.) In August 1939, when Hitler's behaviour in Continental Europe was making it harder and harder for Britain to turn a blind eye, orders were issued at Hornchurch, as elsewhere, for all buildings to be camouflaged. By the time Britain and France jointly declared war on Germany on 3 September, the operations room at the station was already being manned round the clock.

Spitfires – a squadron of twelve planes each from 54 and 74 Squadrons – flew the first offensive patrol out of RAF Hornchurch on 21 May 1940, but landed again without incident. The following day, Spitfires shot down a Junkers 88 over Flushing. The station's perimeter was now protected by pillboxes and barbed wire. Accommodation blocks were home to the necessary personnel. Soldiers manned strategic points on the ground in case of enemy attack, a searchlight cut the night sky in search of enemy bombers and Bofors guns were trained in readiness. There was oil and fuel aplenty and one and a half million rounds of 0.303 ammunition. RAF Hornchurch was at war.

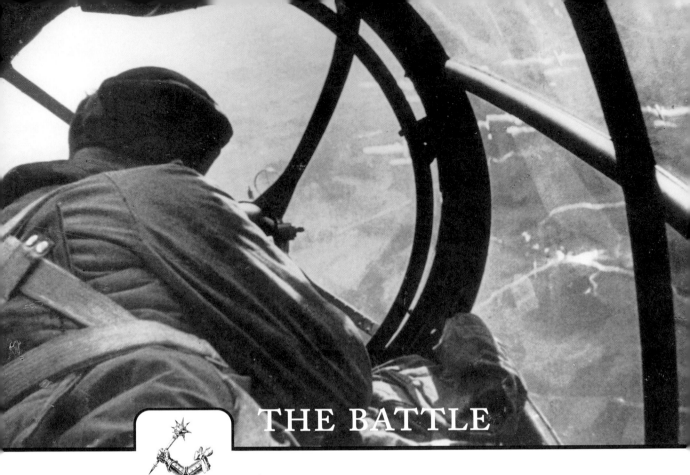

THE BATTLE

'THERE WAS NO SOUND NOR FURY – ONLY A
PATTERN OF WHITE VAPOUR TRAILS,
LEISURELY CHANGING FORM AND SHAPE,
TRACED BY A NUMBER OF TINY SPECKS
SCINTILLATING LIKE DIAMONDS IN THE
SPLENDID SUNLIGHT.'

Air Ministry account of the battle of Britain

RAF HORNCHURCH'S BATTLE WAS THE
STUFF NOT OF HOURS BUT OF DAYS AND
WEEKS AND MONTHS. THE AIRFIELD AND
ITS PERSONNEL FOUGHT AS ONE SOLDIER,
UNITING WITH THE OTHER SOLDIERS –
THE OTHER AIRFIELDS IN THE SOUTH AND
SOUTH-EAST OF ENGLAND – IN THE
SUMMER OF 1940 TO CREATE THE GREAT
STORY THAT IS THE LEGEND OF THE
BATTLE OF BRITAIN.

Opposite View from the bomb-
aimer's position in the nose of a
Heinkel III
Left Scramble: RAF pilots run to
their Hurricanes as the alarm
sounds

What was at stake, the risks taken to defend it and the victory seized
despite the odds need no hackneyed description. The truth of what was
achieved by those few pilots has been made hard to see by the proud
telling and retelling of a thousand interconnected stories. Undoubtedly
there were many reasons, apart from the doughty defence put up by the
RAF, why the proposed German invasion of Britain was cancelled. Allied
victory in the battle of Britain is not the whole story – no one battle ever
is. Perhaps it is enough to say that the defiance of those pilots in the face
of the Luftwaffe played its part in turning a tide so that other, finally
decisive, events could take place elsewhere. Nevertheless, plain
description of a little of all that happened during the battle of Britain is
enough to beggar the plot of many a novel written since.

During the crucial months of July, August and September 1940,
Hornchurch was home to squadrons of Blenheims, Defiants and
Spitfires. As part of No. 11 Group, covering the south-east, its aircraft
and pilots worked with the squadrons of No. 10 (south-west), No. 12
(eastern counties and the Midlands) and No. 13 (north England, Scotland
and Northern Ireland) to create a shield defending Britain against
airborne attack. Hornchurch and the rest of the squadrons making up
No. 11 Group – Biggin Hill, Kenley, Middle Wallop, Northolt, North
Weald and Tangmere – bore much of the brunt.

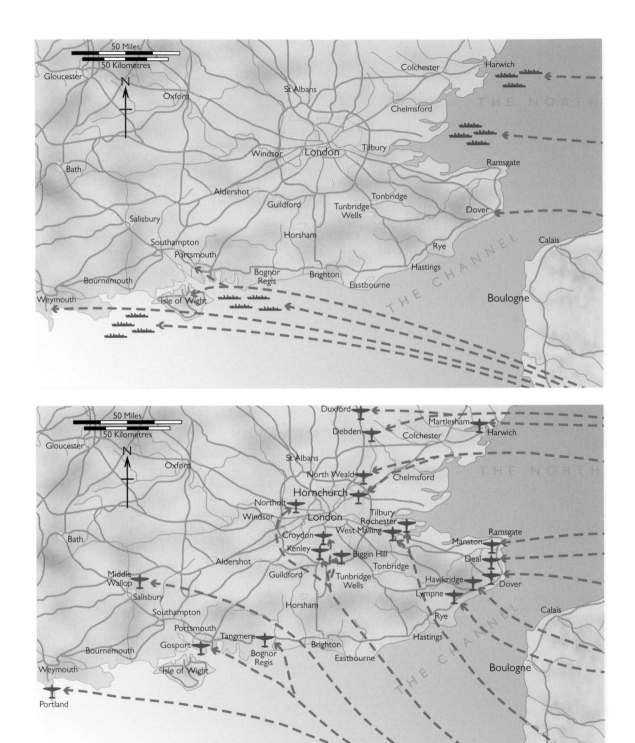

Top Phase I of the battle of Britain, ports and convoys targeted by Luftwaffe (July–August)

Bottom Phase II and III, attention switches to airfields (August–September)

The Luftwaffe had been attacking British targets under cover of darkness for most of June, but the battle of Britain proper began on 10 July when the mainland suffered its first daylight bombing raids. From that day on, at Hornchurch, as at every other airfield, the order to get airborne was just a breath away and pilots went about with at least one ear cocked for the only word that could bring relief from the simmering tension: 'Scramble!' Anything's better, after all, than endlessly crouching in the blocks waiting for the sound of the starter's pistol.

Squadron Leader Ronald Adam recalls the atmosphere in the Hornchurch operations room at the time in the following account:

> We all knew how limited our resources were and we . . . could not understand why the enemy did not come for us at once . . . We held our breath . . . and then the radar plots began to show the enemy assembling . . . There he was milling around as one formation after another joined up, and we went to our loudspeakers when our Group Headquarters gave the order telling the squadron to take off . . . 'Scramble' we would say and Spitfires would tear into the sky . . . We would sit there on the ground and watch the plots . . . We would pass information to the pilots, telling them all the changes in the enemy's direction, how he was splitting up into different formations, what height he was flying at and guiding our fighters to the most advantageous position up in the eye of the sun, ready to attack. The battle of Britain is summarized for me in one snatch on the radio-telephone from a famous New Zealand fighter . . . I heard his voice in my ear as he sighted the enemy: 'Christ Almighty tally ho! Whole bloody hordes of them.'

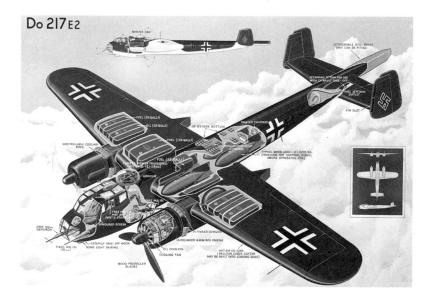

Plan drawing of a Dornier 217, nicknamed the 'flying pencil' because of its slim profile

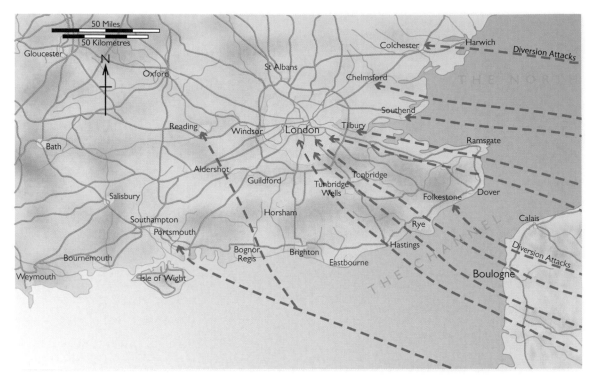

**Phase IV of the battle of
Britain, the Blitz**

In his famous panegyric Churchill described the pilots tasked with fighting off the Luftwaffe as the 'few'. The paucity of trained men was a problem snapping at the heels of Fighter Command for the duration of the battle of Britain. By midsummer 1940, production of aircraft to replace those shot down in combat had been steadily increased to a point where losses of metal could be sustained indefinitely. Able pilots were a different matter, however, and those at Hornchurch and elsewhere were an endangered species, facing extinction if matters in the air could not soon be brought to a close.

In early to mid-August, the RAF had fewer than 800 fighters to throw against more than 1,000 single- and twin-engined fighters on the enemy side, although on both sides the complement was never fully serviceable. The Luftwaffe had a further 1,500 or more bombers and other aircraft – any and all of which might have to be marked by a defender. Add to that the fact that each fighter needed about a quarter of an hour to reach the altitude from which an effective attack could be launched and it's not hard to see how big a headache Fighter Command was enduring from day to day. Every thought was turned towards finding ways of making the best use of pilots.

**RAF observers watch for enemy
aircraft at Hornchurch**

Part of the key to maximizing the outnumbered British resources was radar. A web of recently constructed radar stations along the south and south-east of England supported by visual sightings from members of the Observer Corps were to give early warning and location of imminent attack, anything up to 100 miles distant. This ability proved to be crucial to the successful defence of these islands, ensuring that the comparatively slight resources of Fighter Command could be efficiently targeted. The web was briefly compromised on 12 August, when a raid damaged or destroyed several radar stations. Enemy aircraft swarmed in, hoping to neutralize the defending airfields while the defenders were temporarily blinded – but fighters from Hornchurch and the rest of No. 11 Group were able to intercept almost every formation and fight them off before any irreparable damage was caused.

As well as taking the fight to the enemy countless times, Hornchurch was on the receiving end on more than one occasion. A score of bombing raids targeted Hornchurch during the battle of Britain, killing and injuring personnel, damaging and destroying aircraft and buildings, and threatening the operation of the airfield. Through it all, though, the

Above **A German bomber over England**
Right **A Junkers 87 begins its recovery from a diving attack, as the bomb falls away**

station remained operational, still sending its pilots into action whenever the enemy loomed into view on the radar screens.

The most serious attack hit Hornchurch at about lunchtime on 31 August, when a huge formation of German bombers dropped some sixty or more explosives in a wide swathe across the airfield. Apart from hundreds of broken windows, little effective damage was caused and the grass of much of the airfield, though badly impaired, remained serviceable. For some of the pilots and their aircraft it was a slightly different story. Scrambled just as the first bombs began to fall, part of the squadron made it into the sky, and comparative safety, with seconds to spare. Those slower off the mark or further back in the queue, however, were still on the ground when the first shattering blasts came. Planes just taking off or still earthbound were instantly wrecked – but to the grateful astonishment of all concerned, no one was badly hurt.

One Sergeant Davis was in mid take-off, undercarriage just parting company with terra firma, when an explosion tossed his craft aside like an autumn leaf in a gale. Plane and pilot came to rest together two fields away and upside down on the far side of the river Ingrebourne, and Davis walked away from the wreckage with scarcely a scratch. Elsewhere another pilot, Flight Lieutenant Deere, similarly nearly slipped the surly bonds of earth. Going hell for leather as bombs fell all around him and as he saw one pal's craft after another crumpled and thrown aside by blast, perhaps he felt he was going to get away with it – but then an explosion almost right underneath him brushed away wing and propeller

Flight Lieutenant A.C. Deere (right)

like so much tissue paper. Flung into the sky the remains of the craft then flipped over and plummeted earthwards. He recalled afterwards:

I seemed to be flung miles into the air, then my machine flicked on to its back and crashed on to the aerodrome to career upside down for some 250 yards. My head was scraping along the ground and slowly but surely I was being squeezed into a ball in the cockpit. At last the aircraft stopped. Everything was pitch black. The earth shook with the explosion of bombs. My mouth was full of blood and grit; my head rested in a pool of petrol from the burst tank.

It was frightening, balancing there on my head, realizing that with one spark I would be enveloped in flaming petrol. Then a voice called, 'Are you all right, Al?' Spitting out mouthfuls of earth, I bawled, 'Yes, but for hell's sake get me out of here.' A rending and tearing from the outside broke open the cockpit door, through which, after releasing my harness and parachute, I managed to crawl. My rescuer was my Section Number Two, Pilot Officer Edsall. Supporting each other (Edsall was injured too), we made a dash for the shelter of the hangars. Our bright yellow 'Mae Wests' had attracted the attention of a Hun fighter pilot who was diving down to machine gun us. Somehow we managed to reach the safety of the hangars just in time to miss a stream of hot lead, which spattered on the iron girders.

Afterwards I had a good look at my machine and wondered: 'How did I get out of that alive?' The engine had been blown off – this explains the absence of fire – the port wing was nowhere to be seen, and the complete tail unit rested in a huge bomb crater, which marked the spot at which I had been hit.

While the pilots who had so narrowly cheated death dusted themselves down ready for business as usual next morning, their colleagues in the air were dishing out medicine of their own. Flyers from 603 Squadron, hailing originally from Edinburgh, accounted for the destruction of fourteen enemy aircraft, losing only one pilot and two Spitfires themselves. Around dinnertime the same day a second formation of bombers tried its luck against Hornchurch. Though they were harried by fighters and anti-aircraft fire, the German flyers managed to drop their deadly payloads close enough to destroy two Spitfires on the ground and kill one airman. Damage to the airfield was relatively slight, however.

Hitler had expected his Luftwaffe to sweep aside the RAF within days, or a few weeks at the most. The hammerblow was scheduled for 13 August – *Adlertag* or Eagle Day – when close to 1,500 sorties were sent across the Channel. The RAF more than held its own, though – as it did again two days later, when an even greater force was flung at them. Every time the Luftwaffe attempted to invade the skies over southern England, Fighter Command found just enough pilots and aircraft to repel the worst of them. As August gave way to September, still the outnumbered defenders held on. Now Hitler planned to destroy the RAF once and for all by 11 September, so as to clear the way for the long-awaited, and now delayed, Operation Sealion – the invasion of Britain. The Luftwaffe turned their attention to London, the German commanders hoping that raids on the capital and its civilian population would simultaneously crush the defenders' morale and provoke the RAF into a final showdown that it surely could not win.

The battle of Britain is usually discussed in terms of four or five distinct phases. The first lasted from early July to early August, when the Luftwaffe concentrated on Channel convoys and ports. The second and third phases, lasting from 8 August to 23 August and from 24 August to 6 September respectively, saw Fighter Command airfields and other ground targets increasingly hard hit as the Luftwaffe went all out to pound the RAF into extinction.

From 7 September onwards, the battle entered its fourth phase, 'the Blitz', when raids day and night pounded the city (Londoners would have to endure these until the spring of 1941). All the while that targets were being hit on the ground the battle raged in the air, and on 15

A destroyed Spitfire upside down on the airfield at Hornchurch after the raid of 31 August (E-pens can be seen in the background on the left above the wing)

September the battle reached its climax – 162 German bombers targeted London, many of them flying several sorties, while more planes bombed Portland and other targets, including the Supermarine factory at Woolston. Through the course of the day every available single-engined German fighter, numbering some 620 serviceable Me 109s, was committed to the battle and confronted by determined RAF fighters, of which by the afternoon 31 squadrons were committed. On the morning of that day Churchill was in No. 11 Group's underground operations room at Uxbridge. With RAF fighters engaged in deadly combat with the numerically superior opposition, he asked Air Vice-Marshal Park, commander of No. 11 Group, to describe the reserve force. He was informed that there was no reserve – everything the RAF could muster was already in the air.

The true extent of the losses on both sides that day has been the subject of some controversy. British Air Ministry accounts of the time claim that RAF fighters shot down 177 enemy raiders (124 bombers and 53 fighters), and that an additional 41 aircraft were probably destroyed and 25 damaged (although these numbers vary slightly depending on

The battle of Britain, August to October 1940

which book you happen to be reading). However, examination of German Luftwaffe records after the war suggests that Luftwaffe losses were not as great, with a figure of 60 being most commonly quoted.

As for RAF losses, the initial Air Ministry account claimed that 30 fighters were lost, although this was later reduced to 25 (some books say 26); 12 pilots were reported killed. The German accounts of Allied kills were not as accurate as those made for their own losses, reporting 79 RAF planes destroyed. Over-inflation of their kill rates throughout the conflict was one reason the Germans were so stunned at the effectiveness of the RAF's defence on 15 September, for it led them to believe that the RAF had barely any aircraft left – but this was not the case. Though the figures claimed for enemy losses by both sides were roughly three times the reality, the coarse ratio of 3:1, with roughly just less than three German aircraft lost for a single RAF fighter, holds true for 15 September and for the battle as a whole. Steady attrition of the Luftwaffe was beginning to take a heavy toll and this was the day the

A crashed Dornier 17

pendulum swung in favour of the RAF: the Luftwaffe would never have things its own way again. But the battle wasn't yet over, and the Luftwaffe didn't throw in the towel until late October. During the final phase the Germans lost 325 planes, while the RAF lost 100 fighter pilots.

During the battle of Britain, between early July and late October 1940, more than 1,700 German planes were shot down. The price exacted for that triumph was a heavy one: nearly 500 Allied airmen, from 14 different countries, had lost their lives and over 400 more had been wounded.

The battle of Britain is remembered as a close-run thing. Just how close remains open to debate, but there can be no denying the bravery and sacrifice of those men from both sides who took part in it. Long before the battle was won Churchill ensured that the debt owed to RAF Fighter Command would never be forgotten, when in his famous speech to the House of Commons on 20 August he said, 'Never in the field of human conflict was so much owed by so many to so few.'

WHO FOUGHT HERE

THE SPITFIRE

THINK OF THE BATTLE OF BRITAIN AND IT
IS PROBABLY THE SPITFIRE THAT FIRST
FLIES PAST YOUR MIND'S EYE, ITS MERLIN
ENGINE ROARING. UNLIKE ANY OTHER
WEAPON FROM THE SECOND WORLD WAR,
THE SPITFIRE HAS COME TO OCCUPY AN
ALMOST MYTHICAL STATUS IN THE
POPULAR IMAGINATION; IT IS REGARDED AS
MUCH AS AN AESTHETIC IDEAL AS A
DEADLY AIRBORNE WEAPON. THE PLANE'S
WINGS TRACE AN AERONAUTICAL GOLDEN
MEAN IN THEIR GRACEFUL CURVES, EACH
OF THEM SHROUDING FOUR BROWNING
0.303 MACHINE-GUNS BEHIND THEIR
LEADING EDGES. THE SPITFIRE IS A
TERRIBLE BEAUTY INDEED.

Opposite **A Spitfire with a
mechanic at Hornchurch**

When we talked to people who flew Spitfires during the battle of Britain
or modern pilots who fly them today, they spoke of these machines as
though they were alive, almost human. It is not unusual to hear an old
Spitfire pilot talk about falling in love with his plane the moment he sat
in the cockpit for the first time. Alan Deere said of the plane, 'A Spitfire
is the most beautiful and easy aircraft to fly and has no tricks and
peculiarities normally attributed to high-speed fighters.' When we
climbed inside the cockpit of the only flying example of a Spitfire to
have seen action in the battle of Britain, which incidentally was based at
Hornchurch, we too became infected with this passion.

   To understand the high regard in which this little plane is held we
need only look at its war record. The Spitfire, along with the Hurricane,
provided the backbone of the RAF fighter force upon which the defence
of the British Isles in 1940 almost entirely depended. With the removal
of the British Expeditionary Force from Dunkirk, the only buffer
between the aggressive might of the German Reich and the shores of
Britain had been removed; and with the German occupation of France,
invasion was surely inevitable. But it could not be achieved without the
Luftwaffe dominating the air. Reich Marshal Hermann Goering had
promised Hitler that his planes would crush the RAF, but by mid to late
September 1940, after over three months of fighting, it was obvious that
Germany had lost the battle of Britain.

   The Spitfire and the Hurricane were designed in the 1930s, when as
aircraft technology developed they became successful responses to the
need for a monoplane aircraft capable of providing a fast and stable gun

Heinkel 111 bombers on a raid

platform. It was calculated that with the increasing speeds of aircraft, particularly bombers, at least a two-second burst of machine-gunfire would be required if there was to be any chance of downing the enemy plane. In order to achieve this, eight wing-mounted machine-guns (four in each wing) were seen as the most efficient fire-delivery system. Vickers-Armstrong's Supermarine division won a contract to build its proposed new fighter in 1934, and the prototype successfully completed its flight trials in 1936; it was when the Spitfire made a fly-past at the Hendon air show that the British public's love affair with the Spitfire began. The plane's design, by R. J. Mitchell, was based on the celebrated Supermarine racing seaplanes, which won the coveted Schneider Trophy on four occasions between 1922 and 1931. The first Spitfires were powered by Mark II or III Rolls-Royce Merlin engines, which gave the plane an impressive top speed of 364 mph, a clear indication of its racing pedigree. The first of the Mk I Spitfires rolled off the production line in 1938, and the rest, as they say, is history.

But what of the Spitfire's main purpose – to kill other aircraft? Each of the Spitfire's eight 0.303 machine-guns was provided with 300 rounds of belt-fed ammunition, which meant that each plane carried a total of

2,400 rounds when fully loaded. This may sound a lot, but when the gun button was pressed all eight guns fired in unison and it took only about fifteen seconds for the entire payload to be discharged. A proportion of the bullets were tipped in phosphorus: these were known as tracers as they produced a visible, luminous trail as they flew through the air, thus allowing pilots to see where their bullets were going. The main drawback of the Mk I Spitfires was that they only carried relatively small-calibre machine-guns, which fired the same bullets as the British infantry rifle. There are stories of German bombers being hit by hundreds of bullets and still managing to limp home. Unless the engine, the pilot or other essential control mechanisms were hit, it was no easy task to down an enemy aircraft. This problem was partially overcome by turning the guns slightly inwards, so that the bullets fired by all eight guns converged at the apex of a triangle, over a relatively small area. The firepower of the Mk IIB Spitfire was increased by the replacement of the inboard 0.303 on each wing by a pair of Hispano 20mm guns (also known as cannon), which fired much larger-calibre armour-piercing and explosive ammunition.

Before Spitfire production ceased in 1948 (the plane was withdrawn from RAF service in 1951), twenty-two different marks of Spitfire were produced, with at least forty-eight variants; weight increased from 6,800lb to 11,000lb and top speed from 365 mph to 452 mph. The equally important role of the slightly less glamorous Hawker Hurricane cannot be forgotten, but as Hornchurch was primarily a Spitfire station the latter is obviously of primary interest here. The Hurricanes, with their distinctive humped backs, were the most numerous of the RAF's fighters, and although slightly slower than the Spitfires, were similarly armed and renowned for their reliability and sureness in flight and fight. The only other fighter to see widespread action with the RAF during the battle of Britain was the Boulton Paul Defiant, a largely forgotten aircraft. This was a two-seater with four machine-guns mounted in a revolving turret positioned behind the cockpit. It suffered badly at the hands of the enemy and was finally withdrawn from service as a day fighter and along with the Beaufighter and Blenheim was confined to night-fighter duties.

THE MESSERSCHMITT 109
The Spitfire's worthy German counterpart was the Me 109 – not as pretty to look at perhaps, but just as deadly in combat. The Messerschmitt was the main German fighter of the Second World War, and was produced in

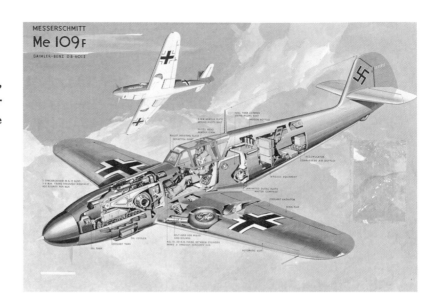

Plan drawing of the Me 109, backbone of the Luftwaffe's war against the Spitfire

greater numbers than any other war-plane of the period: 33,000 were produced between 1936 and 1945 (at least 10,000 more than the Spitfire over its entire period of manufacture between 1938 and 1948). It first saw service in the Spanish Civil War, which was an important testing ground for Hitler's war machine. During the battle of Britain it was accompanied by the twin-engined Me 110 fighter and, less successfully, by the Stuka fighter-bomber. It was later to be joined by the Fokker-Wolfe 190 and in the war's final months by the prototype jet fighter, the Me 262. The Me 109E went into service in early 1939, powered by a 960 hp Daimler-Benz engine, which gave it a top speed of 359 mph. The plane was regarded as fairly equally matched against the Spitfire, but Alan Deere, who met plenty of them in combat, reckoned that the Spitfire had the edge, especially in its speed of turn, even though the Me 109 had a faster initial climb rate and dive speed.

Where the Me 109 may have had the edge is in its armament, which differed dramatically in its arrangement from the wing-mounted guns of the Spitfire and Hurricane. A pair of 7.9mm machine-guns were mounted in the cowling to the front of the cockpit, and fired between the propeller blades as they rotated (a synchronization system that had been pioneered on First World War biplane fighters). In addition, one 7.9mm machine-gun was mounted in each wing. But where the Messerschmitt really packed a punch was in the 20mm cannon mounted in the hollow shaft of the propeller: this effectively made the Me 109 a 'point and shoot' weapon, as the cannon shells came straight out of the front of the plane. However, having most of the firepower centred in the nose was perhaps not the great idea it first seems. The arrangement needed a pilot of considerable skill and confidence to place such tightly focused munitions in the place required and, as the German ace Adolf Galland put it, the Me 109 was like a rifle, whereas the Spitfire, with its widely spaced guns, was more like a shotgun.

If length of service can be taken as a testimony of reliability, the Me 109 wins hands down, as it has the longest service history by far of any of the Second World War fighters. The plane first went on active service in 1936 during the Spanish Civil War and stayed in service with the Spanish air force until 1967, for a total of thirty-one years, as opposed to the Spitfire's twelve years of active service with the RAF.

Major-General Adolf Galland, the most successful German fighter pilot

THE PILOTS

Incredible and even beautiful as the aircraft are, we should not get too carried away with them. After all, a plane is only a machine, and a machine is only as good as the person who operates it. The battle of Britain could not have been fought without the pilots who flew the aircraft.

The Spitfire may have been an entirely British invention, but the men who flew them came from all four corners of the globe. The RAF of 1940 was a diverse force that included pilots and aircrews from Britain, Ireland, Canada, New Zealand, Jamaica, Australia, South Africa, Rhodesia, Palestine, Czechoslovakia, France, Belgium and Poland. Many of these men came from Britain's overseas dominions and saw it as their duty to serve their mother country; others had escaped from places invaded by the Germans and so were eager to free their homelands and exact revenge. But such was the romance of aerial combat that a small but determined number of Americans also came to England to risk life and limb against the Luftwaffe, two years before the United States entered the war – the first American Eagle squadron was formed in September 1940 and earned a fearsome reputation.

In most battles the men who did the fighting are anonymous; only the names of the generals pass down into the history books. But aerial combat is unique in the annals of warfare as it almost harks back to the medieval ideal of single combat. Compared to other arms of the services involved in other fields of combat, there were relatively small numbers of pilots involved in the battle of Britain, which is one reason that we still remember the names of individual combatants today – just 3,080

**Confident young Luftwaffe pilots
prepare for combat**

1940

RAF pilots took part at some point in the battle. But there is more to it than that. When a fighter pilot took to the skies he was entirely alone; even though he had his mates to cover his back, he had to think for himself, react to any situation independently and be entirely responsible for his own survival. It is no coincidence that fighter pilots tended to be men of strong, independent spirit, and that is why we remember them as individuals.

Among the pilots in the RAF, the aces are the best known: those who shot down at least five enemy aircraft, so proving their skill in aerial combat. We should not forget, though, the other pilots, who were in the majority after all. Even if a pilot went through the entire war without achieving a single confirmed kill, he had still served a vital function, by defending the members of his flight and squadron and by causing damage and disruption to enemy aircraft – a shot-up enemy bomber might have made it back to France but it probably carried dead and injured crewmen and was so badly damaged that considerable time and effort were needed to make it airworthy again. But there can be no denying that the aces served an important role, not only in the air but also on the ground – at a time when the country needed heroes they became instant celebrities and helped maintain morale on the home front. The names of these aces have entered folklore and sixty years after the battle some are still household names. There was Wing Commander James 'Johnnie' Johnson, the top RAF ace of the entire war, with thirty-eight kills to his name; Pilot Officer 'Sailor' Malan, of 74 Squadron, Hornchurch; and Pilot Officer Eric Lock, stationed at Hornchurch with 603 (City of Edinburgh) Squadron, who with twenty-six kills was the most effective RAF fighter pilot during the battle of Britain. And there was Douglas 'Tin Legs' Bader.

Perhaps the most famous of all the battle of Britain aces, Wing Commander Douglas Bader was a Hurricane and Spitfire pilot, perhaps best known for flying in combat despite having two artificial legs. A larger-than-life character, Bader was regarded by his peers as perhaps a little arrogant. He was undoubtedly a man of strong will, with a total lack of fear which was responsible for the loss of his legs in the first place. In 1931, aged twenty-one, Bader was flying a Bristol Bulldog biplane on a training exercise, and was coming in to land when he attempted a roll. A wing tip hit the ground and the plane cartwheeled across the airfield. His attempt at showmanship almost killed him, but he survived, having both legs amputated. Not a man to be written off, he had two artificial legs fitted and learned to walk again. Bader's new legs

**Wing Commander Douglas
Bader climbs into a Spitfire, 17
September 1945**

were made from aluminium alloy, the same metal used to build aircraft such as the Spitfire – he had become part plane. When the war began Bader was readmitted to the RAF and won the right to fly again – testimony to his skill as a pilot. During the battle of Britain he flew Hurricanes and went on to command a Canadian squadron. Miraculously he was to survive further crashes.

On the first occasion he misjudged a take-off, and his plane went through a hedge and once again ended up cartwheeling across a field. This crash was caused by Bader forgetting to flick a switch which changed the propeller from coarse to fine pitch for take-off – a common problem for pilots after the introduction of the de Havilland two-pitch propeller, which shortened the aircraft's take-off distance. The plane was a write-off, but Bader survived without a scratch. The second crash, in August 1941, was potentially much worse. This time flying a Spitfire, he had a mid-air collision with a Messerschmitt 109 over France. Bader managed to get out of his plane and deploy his parachute, despite having to leave his tin legs in the cockpit, where they had become trapped. He was captured and put in a military hospital. Not a man to admit defeat, he attempted an escape, using tied-together bed sheets to shimmy out of a window. Without his legs, he was soon recaptured and put in the notorious prison for recaptured escapees – Colditz castle. It is here that Hornchurch enters the story. On 19 August, during a sortie over France in which six German planes were shot down, a Spitfire flying from Hornchurch dropped a pair of replacement legs, and with the assistance of Luftwaffe pilots, who held their indomitable foe in great respect, the new legs were delivered to Bader at Colditz, where he served out the rest of the war. By the time of his removal from combat, Bader had twenty-two and a half confirmed kills to his credit.

Bader may be the most famous fighter pilot of the battle of Britain – largely because his exploits were immortalized in a best-selling book called *Reach for the Sky* by Paul Brickhill, which was later made into an even better-known movie starring Kenneth More – but he was only one of the 'few'. The exploits of another of these men, New Zealander Alan Deere, were also recorded in literature, in his autobiography *Nine Lives* – its title an allusion to the luck every pilot needed in order to survive. Deere was shot down no fewer than seven times. He not only survived the war but also continued to serve in the RAF until 1977, when he retired as an air commodore. Unfortunately most pilots did not share in his good fortune: 800 of the RAF pilots who survived the battle of Britain unscathed died in combat later in the war.

Deere saw action before the battle of Britain in the skies over France, where he took part in the defensive action at Dunkirk. During that fight, in May 1940, he shot down three Me 109s and three Me 110s over a period of four days. For this achievement he was awarded the Distinguished Flying Cross, which was presented to him by King George VI at RAF Hornchurch. During the battle of Britain Deere flew out of Hornchurch with 54 Squadron and claimed seven fighters and a bomber, going on to finish the war with twenty-two confirmed and ten probable kills. He was awarded a bar to his DFC for his actions in the battle of Britain, and later awarded the Croix de Guerre by the Free French.

The Luftwaffe's most distinguished fighter pilot was undoubtedly Major-General Adolf Galland, who had no fewer than 103 kills to his name by the time the war ended. He was the moustached, cigar-smoking epitome of the glamorous fighter ace – even his surname is almost a play

A Luftwaffe bomber pilot

Flight Lieutenant A. C. Deere

on words of his image as a gallant knight of the air. Galland began his career in 1932 as an airline pilot with the newly founded German national airline Lufthansa. Unlike most of his counterparts in the RAF, Galland was already a veteran by the time of the battle of Britain, having flown 300 missions with the Condor Legion during the Spanish Civil War – the legion that gained infamy when its bombers dropped their deadly cargo on the Spanish town of Guernica in 1938.

During the battle of Britain, Galland flew Me 109s with the renowned Jagdgeschwader 26. Unlike the German High Command, he maintained a healthy respect for the capabilities of the RAF, to the extent that when asked by Goering what would improve Germany's chances in the battle

**A German bomber crew makes
ready for combat**

of Britain he is supposed to have replied 'a squadron of Spitfires'. He displayed more of the fighter pilot's independent spirit in his criticism of Goering's deployment of the Luftwaffe's fighters. He strongly believed that they should be used as an offensive weapon against RAF fighters, rather than simply as bomber escorts – that fighters, with their speed and power, should be used creatively as championship boxers, rather than function reactively as past-their-best bodyguards. Galland blamed this perceived misuse of fighters by Goering for the Luftwaffe's defeat in the battle of Britain.

Despite these tactical limitations, during the battle of Britain Galland managed to shoot down at least ten Spitfires and eleven Hurricanes, along with fourteen other aircraft. On 21 August 1940 alone he downed two Spitfires and a Hurricane – a toll that made him, along with pilots such as Werner Molders and Helmut Wick, more than a formidable foe. His sky path crossed with the men of RAF Hornchurch on several

Neil and Tony in flying formation

occasions. He engaged in combat with Alan Deere on 14 August 1940, both of them surviving the encounter. On 24 August 1940 Galland shot down a Defiant flying out of Hornchurch, helping to hammer the last nail in the coffin of these second-rate fighters, which were never again used as day fighters. He was also in the vicinity when Bader suffered his last crash over France in August 1941. At the end of the day it was Galland's longevity that allowed him to earn so many kills, many British pilots having been taken out of service – either because, like Bader, they spent the rest of the war in prison, or because they were killed in action.

Galland's long run came to an end when his Me 262 jet fighter was shot down by an American Mustang just two weeks before the end of the war. He survived, though, and even went on to become friends with Bader in the post-war years. When Galland died in 1996, Bader's sons attended his funeral. What stronger symbol could there be of the mutual respect in which these enemies held one another?

OUR VETERANS

One of the high points of our work at Hornchurch was the privilege of meeting three veterans of the battle of Britain, all of whom had served at RAF Hornchurch in 1940. It was one thing to read about the events of the battle of Britain and accounts written by people who had taken part in them, but quite another to talk to some of them in person. It was all the more of a privilege as opportunities to talk to people who were in their late teens or early twenties at the time are diminishing, as these people move into their eighties and beyond. Despite their age, we found

**Members of 222 Natal Squadron
take time to relax**

1940

all our veterans to be full of energy and life, entertaining and happy to tell us about their experiences. For people who had gone through so much, or perhaps because they had gone through and survived so much, they each appeared much younger than their years – age has certainly not withered them. These people have more reason than most to know the meaning and importance of life, and we have much to learn from them. Our conversations with them provided us with some important insights into the site we were investigating; but perhaps more

Heading off to take a pilot's-eye view

importantly our time with them proved to be a genuinely moving experience.

Peter Brown, sensing that trouble was brewing, learned to fly in 1938 and by the time of the battle of Britain he had twelve months' experience of Spitfires. He was a squadron leader with 41 Squadron, stationed at Hornchurch. During the battle he shot down three Me 109s. He explained what it was like to fly in combat.

The image of the fighter pilot is a romantic one – of a man who drove a sports car, had a dog and spent his off-duty time chatting up barmaids at the local pub; who lounged about in armchairs, reading newspapers or playing chess as he waited for the order to scramble. Compared to the lives of those who suffered the mud and blood of infantry combat or the abject cold and tomb-like conditions of naval warfare, the fighter pilot's life appears to have been privileged. When he was flying, he was free, like a bird; and when he was in combat he was like a knight of the air, respecting his enemy and looking after his mates.

What we learned from Peter somewhat dispelled this image. The reality of sitting around waiting to scramble was that most of the time you were asleep. At the height of the battle pilots suffered badly from exhaustion, which was one reason that squadrons rotated between stations: those in the south regularly moved north, where there was less

Awaiting a call to scramble

action and pilots could recoup before returning to what had become the front line. Peter talked of the fleeting nature of aerial combat – about it all being over in a flash and about barely having time to think. Planes at speed travelled about one mile every ten seconds. One second the sky would be completely empty and the next it would be full of aircraft spitting bullets; then just as quickly the sky would be empty again. Peter told us that when firing at the enemy you had to shoot ahead of them so that they flew into the bullets. Pilots were encouraged to take up rough shooting, using shotguns to shoot pheasants and other birds, as this trained them to lead and helped develop a killer instinct. Everyone's nightmare was to be 'bounced' – that is, taken by surprise by an enemy aircraft diving down on you from above. We were shocked to hear that pilots were not always as chivalrous and knight-like as we had imagined. Peter told us that he had seen bailed-out pilots shot as they hung in their parachutes. We'd heard such stories and thought them to be nothing more than propaganda designed to show the enemy in the worst possible light. But war is war, Peter reminded us.

When we raised the issue of death and what it was like to face it every day, he explained that attitudes to death were different then, and necessarily so. The loss of a friend or a near miss had to be shrugged off, put to the back of the mind; a 'stiff upper lip' had to be adopted. There was no such thing as post-traumatic stress disorder, or at least its existence was not admitted; there was no counselling service to help people overcome their stress and grief. To illustrate the necessity for uncomplaining stoicism Peter recalled a young, inexperienced pilot who had gone up in a brand-new Spitfire and survived being bounced, although his plane was peppered with bullet holes. On landing he walked up to his superior, expecting sympathy and praise for surviving this scrape. After inspecting the gashes and holes in the plane's fuselage, however, the officer gave the young pilot a stiff dressing-down for bringing the aircraft back in such a shocking state, when he had been given specific orders to look after it. The pilot apologized and promised it wouldn't happen again. Peter explained that the officer acted that way so as to draw the pilot's attention from his near miss and make him focus on something else. If he had been allowed to think too hard about how close to death he had been, there would have been a possibility that he would crack up and not be able to go up again – which he would have to do, again and again and again.

Just as the warplanes could not fly without pilots, so neither planes nor pilots could take to the skies without the skills, bravery and

Armourers reload a 20-millimetre cannon in the wing of a Mark V Spitfire

Members of the WAAF

accurately girls, as she was only eighteen years old at the time of the battle of Britain. Joy was in the Women's Auxiliary Air Force (WAAF) and she worked at Hornchurch in the signals and operations room, which was the station's nerve centre. One of Joy's duties was to call in casualties at 17.00 hours every day – which made her the first on the station to know who hadn't made it back from the day's sorties.

Even on the ground Hornchurch was a dangerous place, sometimes even more so than in the air. In the bombing raids the station suffered during the battle, Joy had a couple of close shaves. On one occasion she was walking across to the NAAFI when she heard the drone of unfamiliar engines. She looked up to see a low-flying German Dornier bomber, which had strayed off course and decided to take an opportunistic crack at the station. The pilot took a bead on Joy and sprayed bullets across the parade ground. With lightning reactions she dived through the nearest door and on her stomach slid across the polished wooden floor to a bunk as the bullets ripped into the wall behind her. It was only as Joy dragged herself from under the bunk that she realized that she was in the men's quarters, which, prior to her impromptu arrival, had been full of sleeping men. According to Joy, the awakened men were more surprised at finding a woman in their midst than by the fact that their building had just been strafed by an enemy plane.

During one raid, the Germans, or 'the Jerries' as Joy called them,

New deliveries for the Luftwaffe – bombs are carefully handled to be made ready for the next attack on England

dropped a parachute mine which became tangled on the roof of one of the station buildings, leaving the explosive dangling precariously in mid-air. The bomb squad arrived and cut down the mine before making it harmless. With the job finished, the crew sat down with Joy for a well-earned cup of tea, chatting and joking together. Later that day Joy was stunned to learn that every member of the bomb squad had been killed when, during their next job, a bomb had gone off as they attempted to defuse it.

Although Joy was well aware of the tragedy and danger that war brought, she spoke of her time at RAF Hornchurch as one of the happiest and most exciting episodes of her life. With her sense of fun still very much in evidence, she told us about the hole in the fence which she used to sneak in and out of the station when she wasn't on duty to visit her mother down the road. Everyone knew of Joy's comings and goings, which were against the regulations, but nonetheless chose to turn a blind eye – she seems to have had that effect on people.

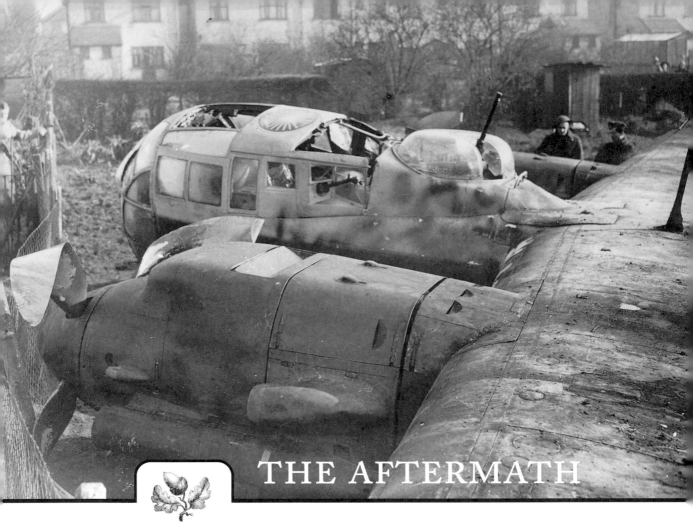

THE AFTERMATH

WITH AIR SUPREMACY DECIDED BY THE RAF'S VICTORY ON 15 SEPTEMBER 1940, THERE WAS GRADUALLY LESS ACTION FOR THE SQUADRONS AT HORNCHURCH. MINES WERE DROPPED ON THE AIRFIELD ON 20 SEPTEMBER, PUTTING LIVES AT RISK ON THE GROUND, BUT THEY WERE SUCCESSFULLY DEFUSED. IN OCTOBER THE OPS ROOM WAS MOVED TO ROMFORD, THE SHIFT MARKING A CHANGE IN ATMOSPHERE AT HORNCHURCH.

Opposite and left **Germany pays the price: crashed German bombers in south-east England**

After October 1940, things never felt quite so close-run again – but there was still a clearly defined job to do. From then on, although the Blitz continued until 1941, after all those desperate weeks and months when Britain was ever on the back foot, it was time to take the fight to the Germans. There was a new kind of success to boast about: Spitfires from 41, 64 and 611 Squadrons, for example, acted as escorts for Hornchurch's fleet of Blenheim bombers on a successful raid against the Luftwaffe in France, on 7 January 1941.

The airfield's time in the spotlight was undoubtedly passing. But although it was no longer in the thick of things, squadrons still came and went. Pilots from all over Europe and the Commonwealth put in time at RAF Hornchurch and the tally of victories continued to grow. Throughout 1942 and 1943, with the Germans still to be repulsed and the build-up for an Allied invasion of Europe in progress, there continued to be work to be done by the pilots based there.

By the end of 1943, however, the focus of the war against Germany and her allies had moved elsewhere and the door was closed on the ops room for the last time. Like birds leaving the nest, the remaining squadrons flew off to face action from other stations. Hornchurch had done its job.

the **Dig**

It is something of a wonder that anything remains of the RAF station at Hornchurch. At first sight there is not much to tell the visitor that in relatively recent times anything other than trees, footpaths, children's play areas and expanses of wetland occupied the area of Hornchurch Country Park. The eastern outskirts of the park, across which winds the river Inglebourne, are a haven for ducks, swans, geese and other wildfowl, which enjoy the luxury of one of the largest expanses of marshland in the Greater London area. The country park, opened in the 1980s, is the result of careful landscaping and manicuring in the wake of gravel extraction followed by the dumping of rubbish in the huge hole left by the quarry. All this has happened since the late 1960s, when the redundant airfield, which was finally abandoned by the RAF in 1962, was sold to the London Quarry Company, which wanted to exploit the river gravels beneath the airfield.

Long before these gravels had provided a nice free-draining area of flat ground for an airfield, they had made good agricultural land, worked by farmers for centuries before. As the London Quarry Company started work and the topsoil was stripped away to reveal the gravel beneath, a stunning archaeological find was made. The circular traces of prehistoric houses were clearly visible, along with the remains of field boundaries and even plough marks. The vestiges of a late Bronze Age landscape, about 3,000–3,500 years old, had been exposed. In the 1970s archaeologists spent months excavating the site before quarrying operations began, digging against the clock to record as much as possible as the giant earth-eating machines advanced across the site.

But it was the archaeological remains of a much more recent period that we were interested in. Over the years, the quarrying ate away all of the area once

Olivia planning the Tett turret interior

covered by RAF Hornchurch's grass airstrips, but fortunately for us the edges of the airfield, particularly to the east, were left untouched. Today, a footpath used by dog-walkers, joggers and people out for a leisurely stroll skirts this part of the country park. If you walk along here and keep your eyes peeled, you will see some obvious and less obvious reminders of the old airfield. The car park at the northern end of the park is the first landmark. It is located in the airfield's only surviving fighter pen: dog-walkers' cars are now parked on tarmac that in 1940 served a similar function for a pair of Spitfires. Steeply sloping earth banks surround the rectangular car park on three sides.

With the car park behind you it won't be long before you stumble, almost literally, across the next clue that not all is as it may first appear. Embedded in the footpath is a ring of concrete, about four metres in diameter, which disappears under the edge of the playground. We didn't excavate this enigmatic remnant, but later a local expert told us that the pole upon which the airfield's windsock had been suspended once stood in the centre of this ring. The windsock served the vital function of indicating which direction the wind was blowing. Small planes such as the Spitfire always took off into the wind, as it provided lift and prevented the plane from being bowled over by crosswinds – which is why most airfields had runways oriented in four directions.

The next clue is a dead giveaway: a concrete pillbox that sits on the edge of the marsh, its harsh lines pleasantly blurred by the reeds in which it stands. This small, fortified bunker protected the eastern approach

A pillbox almost lost in the reeds

Tony in a Tett turret

to the airfield against ground attack. The back wall, which faces the footpath, accommodates a doorway, while the other walls in the hexagonal building are punctuated by small window-like holes, through which guns would have protruded. This is one of three pillboxes on the site, of which we investigated one, largely because it displayed some unusual features not shared by the other two.

But first, to continue our walk. Not far beyond the first pillbox is a small group of strange structures, again built from concrete, sitting close to the ground. What look like cut-off concrete cones sit on top of concrete slabs. These appear to cover chambers accessed through the tops of the cones. Like the pillboxes, these are also defensive structures, of a type known as Tett turrets.

Off again, down past the second of the pillboxes on the left, and then you will see on the right a high tree-covered bank, which looks suspiciously man-made. There is a small wood here, with bushes encroaching on the footpath, and if you look carefully into the undergrowth you will see another Tett turret, entirely overgrown and

almost buried. Just as the path comes out of the other side of the wood, on the right, there is the last of the three pillboxes, sitting much lower to the ground than the others, and strangely lacking a doorway or other obvious means of access.

Leaving the trees behind us, our walk finishes by a large pool, around which fishermen hunch over their rods waiting for those ever elusive bites – a pretty, peaceful spot and an ideal place to pitch our tent before getting down to work.

The gun emplacement

Our walk through the country park had convinced us that the site had good potential to satisfy our archaeological curiosity. But as well as the remains of the old airfield that could still be seen – the fighter pen, the pillboxes and Tett turrets – we were interested in any invisible remains that had survived: we wanted to find out if there were any and if so what they might tell us about the life of the airfield and its wartime experiences. The country park occupied what had been

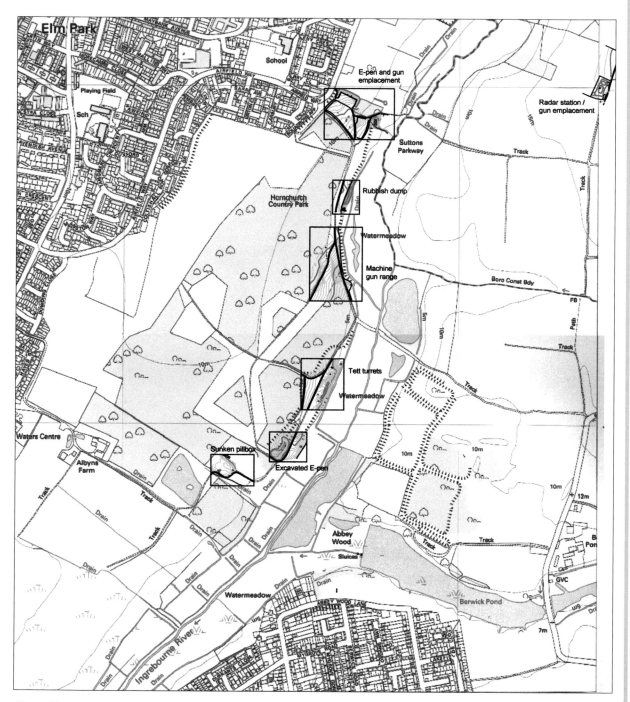

Map of Hornchurch showing areas we investigated

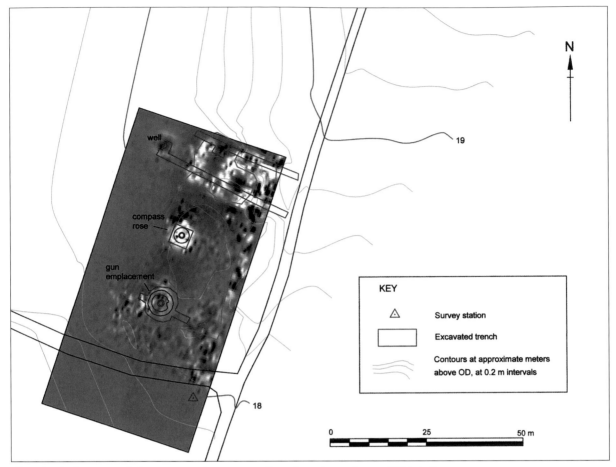

Geophysical survey of the gun emplacement – first thought to be an RDF station

the main part of the airfield: the landing strips at the core, surrounded by the fighter pens, hangars, support buildings and accommodation, and the outer perimeter defended by fortifications such as the pillboxes and Tett turrets. But we had reason to believe that there was more to the place than that. We got wind of something interesting up on a ridge to the east, in a farmer's field way out beyond the boundary of the park. A quick visit confirmed the rumours we'd heard. In the corner of a ploughed field, where two tracks meet, was a rectangular area of rough ground that had escaped the plough. We walked over the grass-covered lumps and bumps with our eyes glued to the ground and found what we were looking for. Towards the centre of the

rough patch, part of a concrete slab protruded from beneath the turf. But this wasn't any old concrete. Fastened into it, equally, spaced around the outer edge of the slab, were a series of brass numbers – 90, 180, 270 – just like those you see on the front door of a house. With a little more turf removal the slab proved to be circular. Being the men of the world we are, we guessed that the numbers represented the degree points on a compass, although what function this huge compass face might have served we did not know.

Excited by what we had seen, we set about consulting old maps, documents and a small collection of aerial photographs. We also spoke to Joy, one of our veterans, who remembered taking fish and chips from the airfield up to the boys who were stationed in an RDF shack on the ridge. RDF means radio direction-finder. Although related to radar, radio direction-finding was different from radar in that it didn't detect enemy aircraft but allowed a friendly aircraft to find its own location. Radio signals were sent from the plane to masts at the RDF station, which, through triangulation with other stations, told the ground controllers exactly where the plane was and allowed them to set it on the correct course to intercept the enemy, which had been located using radar. The compass points, Joy's memory of the RDF station on the ridge – it all added up. Our documents, on the other hand, didn't have much to add to the picture. The site did not appear on any of our pre-war and wartime maps of the airfield. It was on a late 1940s aerial photograph, but it was so small that we couldn't make out much detail. We hoped that geophysics would be able to shed some light.

Iain Banks took his box of tricks up on to the ridge and set to work. After a hard day's labour he transferred the data into his laptop and started to process his results. Even to us non-geophysicists what eventually popped up on the computer screen was spectacular. Our compass circle showed up clearly – even the below-ground parts we had not been able to see. And, to our surprise, two other circles showed up, as well as the regular outlines of what must have been buildings. The site had become more intriguing than ever – what were these other circles? Excavation would, we hoped, provide the answer.

We got the JCB up on the ridge and with Banksie's geophysical printout as our guide we set it to work opening trenches. We placed one trench on the farthest edge of the rectangle, so that we could look for what we

Compass face: the airfield is on the lower ground beyond the trees

thought from the printout was a building. The machine bucket pulled up the turf and topsoil, exposing concrete and timber, which Helen, Olivia and the team set about cleaning. Wasting no time, we moved the machine on to our compass circle and, very carefully, so as not to damage the numbers, we removed the soil overburden. With hand cleaning we exposed a circle about five metres in diameter with numbers extending all the way around its outer edge. In places, though, the numbers had some time ago been prised away, leaving only indentations to show where they had been – could it be

Mounting for the 4.5-inch gun – view across to London in the north-west

that the missing numbers had found their way on to people's front doors? Our belief that the numbers represented degree gradations was confirmed when we found that the highest number, 360, corresponded exactly with north on our own compass. The numerals were spaced around a wide iron disc, like a huge washer, which was also set into the concrete. Evenly spaced holes in the concrete suggested that the disc was some sort of mounting or connection point.

Next, we went for the second of the circles, to the north of the compass face. The topsoil here was deep, and things didn't look too promising. We were expecting another concrete circle like the first, but there was nothing to be seen other than the odd loose brick and some iron scrap. Iain was disappointed, and didn't say much during our lunch hour; as ever, when his geophysics didn't pan out, he took it as a personal slight. Determined to redeem himself, he was keen to get on to

the site of the third circle. We left him to his personal quest watching the machine, as we helped the others in our earlier trenches.

The building in the first trench was intriguing. There was a small, square concrete floor, surrounded by what must have been a wall of heavy timbers like railway sleepers. There were also in the trench the remains of other buildings, which had obviously undergone heavy demolition. We came upon a sunken concrete trough, which looked as though it might have accommodated a piece of machinery. We were undoubtedly looking at more than one phase of the site's use. We kept coming across small plastic tags with numbers on them. We had learned from the farmer who owned the land that after the war the site, which he thought was a First World War anti-Zeppelin gun emplacement, had been turned into a pig farm. We concluded that each tag had once been attached to a pig's ear – which we guessed was what Banksie thought of his attempt to find the second circle. But then Olivia, who had been allotted the task of working out what was going on with the phantom circle, gave a shout. We ran over to her trench and what we saw made Banksie a very happy man. In the bottom of the trench was what looked like the top of a circular brick wall, though it had been bashed about quite a bit. Coming up from the area encircled by the bricks was an iron pipe. Olivia had found not only an old well but also Banksie's elusive circle. With his reputation intact Iain returned to his own trench.

It proved to be Banksie's afternoon, because he was the next to shout us over. The machine had uncovered the third circle. This was bigger than anything we'd seen thus far. Banksie obviously felt very pleased with himself as the machine removed bucket after bucket of soil from a massive concrete disc. There were no numbers on this one, but in the centre was a heavy circular iron mount with eight sawn-off bolts protruding from it. We knew from experience that we were looking at the mounting for a heavy gun. The farmer had been right – it was a gun emplacement. By now we had given up on the idea that it was an RDF station. Joy had come to visit us on the site and as soon as she stepped out of the car she knew that this was not the place she remembered visiting. The airfield was quite some distance away, and as Joy said, the chips would have been pretty cold by the time she had carried them all this way.

We knew now that we were dealing with a gun position, but what sort of gun was it? Was it a First World War anti-Zeppelin gun, as the farmer had told us, or did it relate to the Second World War? We suspected the latter, because as we understood it First World War anti-aircraft batteries were fairly mobile affairs, many of

them on trucks, and this was a huge purpose-built gun platform. According to our documents relating to the airfield a number of anti-aircraft gun batteries were located around the perimeter during the Second World War. Some of these had been manned by troops from the Glasgow Highlanders. There were eight light anti-aircraft Bofors guns, which were pretty mobile. There were also heavy anti-aircraft guns: a 3-inch-calibre Smith gun and four 4.5-inch guns, which would have required fairly substantial emplacements. Given the size of our gun mount and the platform in which it sat, there seemed little doubt that we had uncovered one of the 4.5-inch gun positions. We knew from Dave Davis that these things gave a heck of a kick when fired. If there was an air-raid while he and his mates were drinking in the Good Intent pub on the other side of the airfield they had to hold on to their drinks when one of the nearby anti-aircraft guns opened up – otherwise the concussion would knock them off the table.

Now we were all feeling fairly pleased with ourselves. We had started out to find an RDF station and ended up finding a lost anti-aircraft gun position. But it didn't finish there. Once we realized that the biggest concrete circle was a gun platform, we made an educated guess that the compass face might have been the base of a range finder used to sight the gun. The range finder would have provided the gunners with the height and bearing of incoming enemy bombers, possibly on their way to London or even RAF Hornchurch.

The Tett turrets

Flushed with our success up on the ridge, we returned to the airfield to try our luck once more. This time it was

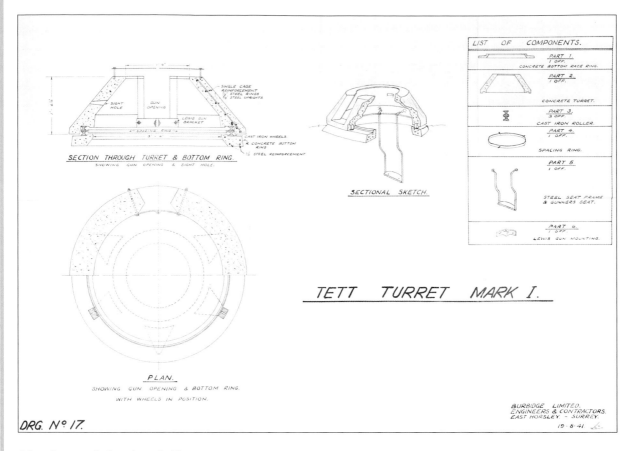

Manufacturer's drawing of a Tett turret

the turn of the Tett turrets to be subjected to our inquisition. The Tett turret is a very rare beast. The turrets were manufactured by a Surrey-based building company called Burbridge Ltd, to a design by Mr Tett, one of the company's directors. The original idea was simplicity itself. A concrete pipe, just over a metre in diameter, was sunk vertically in the ground and a steel-reinforced concrete turret was placed on the top. The turret had a slot in the side to accommodate a machine-gun and could be turned on rollers through 360 degrees. A machine-gunner, or perhaps a crew of two, would be positioned in the pipe, with the turret providing protection as he wreaked havoc with his machine-gun. The Tett turret was seen very much as a last-ditch defence, and designed to be positioned at crossroads or on the perimeter of airfields, as at Hornchurch.

The Tett turret was meant to be easy to assemble, lightweight and cheaper than the much larger pillboxes. However, when the design was submitted to the War Office it didn't go down too well. It was judged to be too cramped and not bulletproof against heavy fire; and because of its isolated nature it did not allow adequate command control. These are all fair points, but the thing that really struck us about them was this: if you go into it by climbing in through the top of the turret, how the heck did you get out without exposing yourself to enemy fire? We came to the rather depressing conclusion that if you were forced into a position where you had to use one of these things you would be fighting to the death, and retreat would not be an option – and such would have been the realities of the threatened German invasion in 1940.

The company went back to the drawing board and came up with a new version known as the Trench Tett. This went some way to dispel our criticism about access and more importantly retreat. The trench version was not positioned over a pipe but set on to a concrete slab, which allowed access from a tunnel or slit trench to the rear of the turret. From the presence of the concrete slabs it appeared that it was this later type of Tett that had been installed at Hornchurch. Although the Tett turret never went into full production, almost a hundred were built, but the company only ever sold thirty-one of them. According to the Defence of Britain Project, only five survived, two of which were at Hornchurch. So we were delighted to discover three more at Hornchurch, all partially buried or obscured by undergrowth.

We decided to investigate the two most obvious of the Tett turrets, sitting in open ground between the footpath and the edge of the airfield, where the land drops down to the marshes and the river. These turrets looked like Trench Tetts but there was no sign of the trenches to be seen. Here was another job for Banksie and his geophysics kit. Lo and behold, the results showed a many-angled dark line which might have been a zigzagged trench linking the turrets.

The turrets were full of rubble, soil and all sorts of junk and when it came to excavation, the first task was to empty out one. We were keen to climb inside and get a machine-gunner's eye view, but there was a lot of work to be done before that would be possible. The turret closest to the footpath was selected to be emptied – it seemed the best preserved of the two. Our

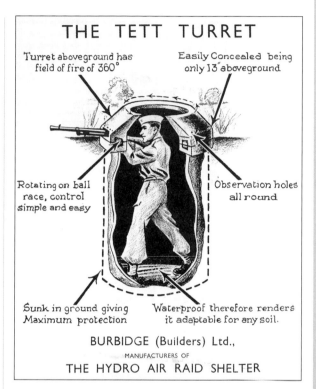

Advert for a Tett turret

first job was to remove the turret so that we could get access to the chamber below. We had seen a wartime photograph of men at the Burbridge builder's yard lifting one of the turrets on a long pole, so we tried to do the same thing, using a couple of lengths of scaffolding poles. Concrete scraped against metal and the poles began to bend under the strain, but as eight of us gave it our all the turret swung clear of its mount. Moving in a carefully rehearsed shuffle, we gradually lifted it away from the slab. It was a great relief to lower the heavy turret on to the grass, without a single crushed foot or twisted ankle between us. Banksie rolled up his sleeves and pulled the first lump of rubble out of the circular hole in the slab.

As he began to disappear down his newly created concrete burrow, we started work on the neighbouring Tett turret, which rested on a slightly smaller slab than that of its partner. Our intention here was not to empty the turret but to excavate the ground at the end of the slab in the hope of coming across the slit trench suggested by the geophysical survey. Once the turf was removed we were encouraged by the presence of gravelly soil in one half of the trench and much sandier soil in the other – signs perhaps that there was an archaeological feature here. Our suspicions were confirmed as we began to dig into the gravelly soil – this was definitely silt or backfill sitting in an artificial cut.

By now Banksie had disappeared entirely down his hole. The chamber under the rectangular slab was about a metre and a half deep, with brick walls rising up from a concrete floor. In among the rubble and rubbish Banksie was beginning to make some interesting finds. There were several small glass bottles, some of which were still sealed by a metal cap. Only one type of bottle comes in such small sizes, apart from those used to hold perfume. These were ampoules that had once held medicines and were part of a medical kit or hospital store. We guessed from the dirty brown residue in some of them that they might have held morphine, a pain-killing drug administered to the wounded or injured using a syringe. The airfield had its own infirmary where wounded pilots or ground crew received first-aid treatment, and the pilots would have carried their own first-aid kits in their planes. It came as a surprise to find these artefacts related to the wartime life of the airfield

Ampoules recovered from the Tett turret

here in the turret – we had expected it to be filled with nothing more than modern rubbish.

Our slit trench, for that is what it was, was also beginning to surpass expectations. Like the chamber, the trench was about a metre and a half deep, and to our delight we discovered that its sides were reinforced with corrugated iron, which during the war was known as wriggly-tin. Traces of wood survived on the floor of the trench, suggesting that it had been covered by duckboards. But perhaps most striking of all was the small pillar of sand which had a layer of fabric fibres running through it. They had once been sandbags and might have originally sat on the edge of the trench, giving it extra height. Further defensive measures were apparent in the form of lengths of rusty old barbed wire which had been thrown in with the soil used to fill in the trench after the war. Once we had emptied our short length of trench it looked amazing, almost like one of those reconstructions you see in a military museum. The chamber under the Tett turret was connected to the trench via a small concrete tunnel,

Workmen positioning a Tett turret at the factory

which like the trench was lined with corrugated iron. The tunnel, which was stepped up from the floor of the trench, remained full of earth and rubble but it was obvious that it would have been accessible only to men on their hands and knees. By allowing men to move freely into and out of the turret without exposing themselves to enemy fire, the trench clearly served an important purpose.

A very different story was revealing itself at the first turret. Iain had finished emptying the chamber, and in the process had created a mound of rubble and earth the size of a small car. Once it was empty we had expected to find an access hatch or tunnel in one of the underground walls, as there had been in the other turret. But there was no such thing. All the brick walls were solid, as was the concrete floor. Apart from the turret hole in the concrete slab that formed the roof, the chamber, which was about three metres long and just over a metre wide, was an entirely self-contained and sealed unit. The only way in and out was through the

turret, and climbing in and out would have been a very risky enterprise if attempted during enemy fire. Once in here you were not only stuck but also fixed in a permanent stoop. It was our idea of a nightmare. We reinstated the turret to get the full effect, which was horribly claustrophobic. What it must have been like

A brass fastening for a tourniquet

Caps from flares

The lens from a pilot's goggles

with the noise and smell of a machine-gun blasting away we couldn't even begin to imagine.

Our excavations had been a great success. We had discovered that one of the Tett turrets was connected to a slit trench, while for some reason the other sat in not so splendid isolation. It didn't take a rocket scientist to work out which turret would have made the most favourable defensive position. The self-contained chamber had proved itself to be something of a treasure chest – well, at least a medicine chest. In addition to the ampoules we found a small brass fitting, rather like a miniature anchor with the end of its two hooks tipped with small spheres. We hadn't a clue what this was until Andy Robertshaw arrived with a wartime first-aid kit and pulled out a length of rubber tubing with exactly the same fitting attached to one end. This was a tourniquet, which would have been tightly wrapped around a limb to stop the flow of blood from a wound. The small brass fitting was a fastening device, which would have

trapped and locked the rubber into place behind the small spheres. But not everything in the chamber had fallen from a medical kit. There were a couple of large brass caps, like the ends of shotgun cartridges, but about twice the size. These had come from flares, the type fired from a large pistol. They might have served a variety of functions, perhaps carried on aircraft and used on the airfield. Flares might have been fired to alert the squadron to a scramble, but they were more commonly used in emergencies. If, for instance, a pilot tried to land his plane without first putting down his undercarriage, a well-timed flare would alert him to his error.

These finds were fantastic, but we really couldn't believe our luck when Iain pulled out a rounded piece of glass framed in a brass mounting. We recognized it instantly. We'd found an eyepiece from a pilot's flying goggles. Of all the things we had hoped to find, this was undoubtedly near the top of the list. The glass was reinforced by a type of clear plastic which prevented the glass from shattering into the pilot's eye if the goggles broke. Our sense of achievement was topped off when Richard Smith, an expert on RAF Hornchurch and the battle of Britain, told us that these were type II goggles, which were standard RAF issue between 1938 and 1940 – which meant that they may well have been used by a Spitfire pilot during the battle. Imagine the sights seen through this little piece of glass!

The pillbox

One last part of the airfield's defences remained to be investigated. This had all the makings of a real mystery. Of the three surviving pillboxes, the one that sat very close to the ground unlike the others had no obvious entrance. If we stuck our heads through one of the gun slits or embrasures, however, we could see a trapdoor and the top of a fixed iron ladder leading from the floor of the pillbox, which was a metre or so below the ground outside. The shaft below the trapdoor was full to the brim with modern rubbish and water. It was obvious that if we could find a way in, through the trapdoor, it wasn't going to be a pleasant experience.

We had done some research on pillboxes and bunkers and had come across something called a battle headquarters. These were constructed on a number of airfields to provide underground control rooms. The idea was that from the shelter of one of these the station commander could direct the defence of an airfield in the face of ground attack. The only parts of the battle headquarters that were visible from the surface were a fortified observation post or pillbox and a concealed entrance. Beneath the pillbox, buried deep below the ground, were a pair of bunker-like rooms, accessed from the surface via a stairway. The only way to get into the

A pillbox

pillbox was to climb a set of ladders leading up from the room directly below.

When all our attempts to locate the concealed entrance drew a blank, we decided to try more dramatic means of entry. We guided the JCB into position outside the pillbox, just opposite the trapdoor, and began to dig. Bucket after bucket of claggy damp soil was removed. As the hole got deeper, it had to be made wider, and so it grew and grew. The first scrape of the bucket had uncovered a concrete shelf at ground level running around the entire pillbox, extending outwards for about

Braving the elements on the gun mount

a metre. This shelf proved to be the top of a wall of breeze blocks which supported the pillbox and sank down below the ground surface. The JCB bucket followed the wall downwards – first one metre, then another. Just as we were starting to think we'd bitten off more than we could chew, the wall gave way to a lintel and the top of an entrance. What a relief!

It wasn't the end of our worries, though. Water began to flood out of the entrance and into the bottom of our hole. The clay sides of the trench became even stickier and we had to cut them back at an angle to prevent them from collapsing. With Dave Sneddon's able assistance we dropped a pipe attached to a pump into the hole and began to suck out the water. Only when most of the water had been removed and we were

certain that the sides were safe did we dare enter the hole. It was obvious that even though we'd dug a hole about three metres deep we had only reached the upper part of the entrance. There was a narrow gap, which might have allowed us to squeeze through on our bellies, had it not been for the sodden, smelly rubbish which blocked the entrance and the shaft beyond. There was only one thing to be done. We donned waders and rubber gloves and began to clear out drink cans, plastic bags, bottles and other refuse. We'd come too far to give up now. We just gritted our teeth and got on with it.

After a couple of hours' work, which would surely qualify us to work with any refuse collection crew, we had moved enough trash to allow us through. Our Howard Carter moment had arrived. We placed wooden boards on top of the rubbish that remained; but these only went in so far – there was no way to avoid crawling over a horror show of waste for at least part of the way. In we went, belly down, like cave divers, kicking our way forward and reaching out for the ladder. Only a couple of rungs were clear of the rubbish, and so fortunately it wasn't much of a haul from the outside world up to the top of the shaft and through the trapdoor. We had made it. Adjusting our eyes to the half-light in the pillbox, we found ourselves standing in more rubbish, but nothing as unpleasant as what we had just crawled through.

Truth be told, the inside of the pillbox did not have much to tell us, except that the embrasures had once been sealed behind steel shutters. The real sense of satisfaction came from meeting a challenge. Archaeologically, our main aim had been to establish what sort of underground bunkers or rooms the pillbox was connected to. While digging the hole the JCB had pulled out twisted sheets of heavy corrugated iron, which could still in parts be seen lining the sides of the entrance hole. The pillbox did not appear to have been sitting above concrete bunkers, but it did appear to have been attached to a simpler tunnel or shelter lined with corrugated iron. The entrance to that still remained a mystery – it may have been some distance away from the pillbox. What was obvious was that the tunnel, which might have served as an air-raid shelter, had been destroyed not by bombing but by modern disturbance – possibly related to the quarrying. That was why the only structural evidence we came across were the twisted bits of iron that had previously been torn from their original positions. It was a little disappointing perhaps, but with our other triumphs behind us and our success in getting into the pillbox we didn't feel too downhearted.

Iain Banks excavates the E-pen

The fighter pen

With our understanding of the defences enhanced a thousandfold, it was time to look at the airfield itself, which would, we hoped, bring us even closer to the battle of Britain and the people who contributed so much to the RAF's victory. The airfield and the entire RAF station at Hornchurch was there for one purpose – to keep fighting aircraft in the air and to protect and service them when they were on the ground. The Luftwaffe did their best to destroy British aircraft while they were on the ground and at their most vulnerable. We have already seen how anti-aircraft defences around the airfield provided some resistance against enemy bomber raids, but inevitably German bombers got through and at Hornchurch a number of aircraft were destroyed on the ground. But this was usually when they were in the open, trying to take off. At most other times fighters were

In the ruins of an air-raid shelter with the E-pen

protected in pens, where they were serviced, refuelled and armed.

The fighter pens were also known as E-pens, because of their shape when viewed from the air. There was also a type known as a B-pen, so called because of its inwardly canted arms, which provided better protection than the straight arms of the E-pen. In both types banks of earth and concrete surrounded a rectangular area on three sides. The sheltered area was further divided into two bays by a central wall, usually formed from sandbags. Each bay could accommodate a single fighter. The fighter pen that survives at the northern end of the park, used today as a car park, is a good example. The concrete floor of the pen provided a firm base for the

planes to park on and drains around the outer edge allowed spilled fuel to be washed away. Metal rings fixed into the concrete surface provided attachment for the slings and ropes used to tie down the fighters during high winds or bombing raids. The fighter pens were also referred to as fighter dispersal pens because they were dispersed around the airfield and not grouped together, as such a concentration would have put large numbers of planes at risk from a cluster of bombs.

The rear bank of each fighter pen had an air-raid shelter inside it, which was entered via doorways at the back of each of the two bays, and usually another pair of doors on the other side of the bank. This shelter was for the use of ground crew and anyone else in the vicinity during an enemy raid. Dave Davis, our veteran ground crewman, told us that anyone caught outside a shelter during a raid would be disciplined. But, as he pointed out, this rule was commonly disobeyed, because if your plane was on a sortie and you were inside the shelter you couldn't see when it had returned, possibly in need of urgent assistance.

In 1940 there were twelve fighter dispersal pens (ten E-pens and two B-pens) at Hornchurch, which could accommodate twenty-four aircraft or two squadrons. Apart from the one that survives to provide protection to parked cars (today), all came to grief during quarrying operations. Or so it was thought – until the park's rangers pointed out to us a suspicious-looking bank. Covered with grass and small trees, the bank looked as though it was man-made, but there was nothing about it to suggest its origins as a fighter pen, as it appeared to be a single, curved mound rather than a bank with three straight arms. But we looked at wartime plans and aerial photographs of the airfield and the location of the bank appeared to correspond to the location of one of the dispersal pens.

As we were keen to find out how much of the airfield had survived, we decided to take a closer look at the bank and see if it was a lost dispersal pen. We took a bead on the middle of the bank and set our big yellow machine to work. At first we hit nothing but earth; then we hit rubble and stumps of twisted iron. There was definitely something substantial under the mound, but what it was we couldn't yet tell. After a couple of hours' hard work the mechanical digger had worked wonders. On one side of the bank a sloping concrete barrier had been revealed and, behind it, two low concrete walls. It was a fighter pen all right. We'd uncovered part of the

Mark V Spitfires in an E-pen

air-raid shelter, which without our interference would have been buried deep in the heart of the protective bank. But as with the tunnel connected to the pillbox someone had done their best to remove all trace of the feature. The JCB pulled out bits of heavy iron superstructure, which had been bent out of shape during an attempt at demolition. There was one particularly twisted set of iron girders that had once been a doorframe – and would have supported a heavy steel protective blast door. The concrete walls of the shelter bore the undulating impression left by corrugated iron, which had originally curved up from the floor and provided a vaulted roof, further protection being added by the earth heaped over it. The excavation trench carried right on through the bank and on the inside we had expected to uncover the concrete base on which the fighters stood, but as part of the demolition process this had been broken up and replaced by dumped ash and gravel.

Once again, we had proved that despite present appearances and past attempts to remove all trace of

0.303 cartridges with their cordite strips still in place, small reminders of the firing-range

the airfield, there were still exciting and important archaeological remains to be encountered at Hornchurch.

The firing range

Fighters such as the Spitfire, beautiful as they may have been, existed to perform one function – to shoot down enemy aircraft. To remain at the peak of their fighting fitness the planes were pampered and cared for by their ground crews. Engines were constantly serviced and overhauled, electrics checked and combat damage repaired. The guns also required attention and providing this was the task of the armourers, a specialist branch of the station's ground crew. As well as loading fresh ammunition, the armourers checked that guns were working to the peak of their efficiency – an ammunition jam during combat could be fatal. Guns also had to be set right in the wing, each of the Spitfire's eight machine-guns pointing slightly inwards so that the bullets converged on a small area at a set distance in front of the plane. The area of convergence had to be small enough to maximize the concentrated power of what were quite small-calibre bullets, but large enough to maximize the possibility of hitting the target. This process of setting the guns in the wing was known as 'harmonizing' and required the guns to be test fired. Firing took place on a specially built range, which was a feature of most fighter airfields. Planes were wheeled on to the range and their guns pointed towards the target. The rear of the plane was jacked up so that the guns were sighted parallel to the ground and the firing button pressed. After firing, the target was checked and the spread of bullet holes measured. If the spread was too loose or too tight, the guns were adjusted in the wing and fired again. During the battle of Britain, the standard distance at which the bullets came together in their harmonized concentration was 250 yards (228.6 metres) in front of the plane, but many pilots, through their own experience, found this to be too far and so had their guns set to a shorter range.

At Hornchurch, the firing range would have taken the form of a butt – a bank of sand heaped up against a wall – into which the bullets were fired. This was bulldozed away years ago. We knew from plans, however, where the firing range was located – it was on the edge of the airfield, not too far to the south of what is now the car park. This is now an open area of grass-covered ground through which the footpath passes. With nothing left of the upstanding features our only hope of finding some physical trace of the range was to use metal detectors to look for bullets fired on it. Olivia set out a series of survey grids and then set to work with Barry and Terry, a pair of local metal detectorists. As expected, most of what came to light was nothing but modern rubbish dropped by walkers – ring pulls from drink cans, coins, dog chains, foil sweet wrappers and anonymous bits of scrap metal. But among this chaff one or two little gems came to light.

After hours of fruitless effort Olivia and her detectorists were rewarded with their first real find: a 0.303-calibre cartridge, exactly the type of ammunition used in the Spitfire's machine-guns. Interestingly, the bullet had not been fired. The casing had been broken and the strips of cordite which by 1940 had long since replaced gunpowder as the propellant in bullets were still inside. If thrown on a fire today, these cordite strips would still burn furiously, even after being in the ground for sixty years. Before the day was over a second 0.303 cartridge case came to light. This time the bullet had been fired. Once the machine-gun in a Spitfire's wing had fired a bullet the brass cartridge was ejected through a hole in the bottom of the wing and the spent case fell to earth – even today cases are sometimes found where they landed – trapped in house gutters, for instance. Although we had only found two cartridge cases we felt lucky to have found anything, since not only was the range bulldozed away but brass cartridge cases were usually collected up after firing because they could be recycled. Just before the metal-detector survey came to an end we were treated to one more find – a brass service button from an RAF tunic.

Preserving the archaeological heritage of the Second World War

Many military and other sites relating to the Second World War such as RAF Hornchurch, which served their purpose during the war but then became redundant and surplus to requirements, have fallen victim to decay, demolition and post-war development. Airfields took up a lot of space, which in peacetime could be put to other uses, such as housing and industry. At Hornchurch it was the ground itself and its gravel deposits that prompted the removal of many of the buildings and structures related to the wartime airfield.

Airfields are of course only one part of a wide range of bases, defences and facilities constructed before and during the war, including anti-aircraft batteries, radar stations, command bunkers, air-raid shelters, munitions factories, naval installations, coastal defences, training camps, barracks and even prisoner-of-war camps. To gain some idea of the scale of construction one only needs to consider pillboxes, of which at least 20,000 were constructed during the war. In recent years it has been recognized that these sites represent an important part of our cultural and archaeological heritage, along with prehistoric monuments, castles, churches and other reminders of our shared past.

It would obviously, however, be impossible to

preserve all these sites, and many of them have long since disappeared anyway. But what we can do is be aware of them and make every possible attempt to make sure that we have an adequate record of all of them. Only when we have such data can planning authorities make informed decisions about what should be preserved and what can be sacrificed in order to make way for the new – decisions that may be based on the site's significance, its uniqueness, its levels of survival and its relationship to other surviving sites.

To this end English Heritage, Historic Scotland, CADW (which protects the built heritage of Wales) and other bodies such as the Council for British Archaeology and the Fortress Studies Group have implemented a number of initiatives to ensure that our wartime heritage is adequately recorded and its importance brought to the public's attention. English Heritage, for example, has begun a programme of recording wartime airfields. This is not a small task, as by the end of the Second World War 740 air bases of various types had been constructed in the British Isles and it is estimated that there are at least 250 different types of structures and buildings on British airfields – with probably just as many variations and sub-types. Where preservation is regarded as important, a site, or part of a site (a fighter pen, for instance), can be protected by law through scheduling or listing (the latter usually in the case of buildings still in use). The airfield at Biggin Hill, in Kent, which played a vital role during the battle of Britain, has been designated a conservation area, which is another way in which the future survival of sites can be ensured.

A recent example of a Second World War site that has been scheduled is the prisoner-of-war camp at Harperley in County Durham, which has 85 per cent of

Opposite and above **An RAF egg cup from the excavation of a rubbish dump at Hornchurch**

its original buildings still standing. Harperley is one of 1,500 POW camps used in Britain during the war, a hundred of which, including Harperley, were purpose-built.

The most intensive attempt to record Second World War sites to have been carried out in recent years is the Defence of Britain Project. The aim of the project, which ran from April 1995 to March 2002, was to locate and record Second World War anti-invasion defences. The survey was carried out by about 600 local volunteers, who brought to light nearly 20,000 sites.

Archaeological excavation also has an important role to play, and we are hopeful that at least some of the features we investigated at Hornchurch will be scheduled now that we have a good impression of the quality and levels of preservation on the site.

The ghost train – how the pilots described their bicycle convoys at Hornchurch

Conclusion

Many brave men and women served at RAF Hornchurch during the battle of Britain and in the subsequent years of the Second World War – people like our veterans, Joy, Dave and Peter. From talking to these three today it is obvious that they don't see themselves as heroes – they were doing their bit, just doing a job. That may be so, but if it hadn't been for their actions, and those of thousands of other WAAFs, ground crew, aircrew and pilots, the battle of Britain would undoubtedly have ended with the sound of jackboots goosestepping down British streets. All these people did their duty and we should never forget that, or the fact that many made the ultimate sacrifice while doing so. Neither should we forget the thousands of Luftwaffe pilots and aircrew who met their end far away from home, in the skies above a foreign country, doing what they believed to be their bit, their duty.

Just as we should remember the people who fought, so we should remember the places from which they fought. Veterans grow old and pass on but places last for ever. What better way to ensure that future generations learn from the lessons of the past than to ensure that at least some of these places retain some memory of their wartime experience? Hornchurch is one such place, which did its bit during those fateful four months of 1940. But over the years much has happened to change the place, to remove the physical traces of this wartime role. Once they had served their purpose, many buildings were demolished, and when the RAF sold the land much was destroyed by gravel extraction. The scars left by the quarrying and the rubbish dumping which followed were covered by landscaping operations that turned the place into a country park to be proud of but removed more reminders of the place's previous, less peaceful incarnation.

We hope that our archaeological investigation will go some way to ensure that these memories do not fade away entirely. The results surpassed our expectations on many levels: in both the quality and extent of buried structural remains – the gun emplacement, the Tett turret trenches, the pillbox complex and the fighter pen – and the outstanding nature of the artefacts recovered – the eyepiece from the goggles, medical equipment, flares, bullets and other objects. All these things took on a special meaning as the project was underway, as Britain was once again at war, this time with Iraq. It seemed strange to be excavating the remains of a war fought sixty years ago while listening on the radio to news of a war being fought today. We may learn important lessons about the value of human life from studying wars fought in the past, but sadly that doesn't make war a thing of the past; nor does it free us from the pain and anguish of wars fought in the present.

On our last day at Hornchurch, just after we had finished backfilling the trenches and were packing up the van, Olivia took a phone call from her family in America. There, at Hornchurch, she received the terrible news that her cousin Michael had been killed in the war

in Iraq. War had touched Hornchurch once more. Michael Kelly was a renowned American journalist covering the war for a well-known magazine and the *Washington Post*. He died close to Baghdad airport, when the Humvee jeep he was travelling in swerved off the road to avoid incoming fire. We were all stunned and our hearts went out to Olivia and her family. On one level it made what we do seem silly and small; but on another we realized that we had something in common with Michael and other war correspondents, in that we are interested in warfare, its impact and those people who take part in it, and we want to communicate our findings to other people. The difference is that we choose to report on wars long since finished; Michael reported on a war being fought now. Our job requires no courage, but his did, and it cost him his life.

DOVER 1940–44

DOVER

1940–44

IN MARCH 1990, A CANADIAN ASTROPHYSICIST CALLED GERALD BULL WAS SHOT DEAD OUTSIDE HIS APARTMENT. THE EVENTS LEADING UP TO HIS MURDER HAD ALL THE ELEMENTS OF A JAMES BOND STORY – SPIES, A ROGUE SCIENTIST, A CRUEL DICTATOR, ILLEGAL ARMS DEALS AND A DEADLY SECRET WEAPON. BUT THIS WAS NO FICTION.

It was Bull's professional interest in space technology that first brought him into contact with the world of big guns. In the early 1960s he headed an American- and Canadian-funded research project aimed at developing a gun-fired projectile which could deliver scientific instruments into the stratosphere and satellites into outer space. For one of his earliest prototypes he welded together two 16-inch guns from battleships, creating a barrel around thirty metres long. On one test firing in Arizona, in November 1966, the gun sent a lightweight projectile up to an incredible altitude of 120 miles. Over the years, Bull's interest in high-altitude research gradually led him to battlefield artillery, and he designed and built a number of long-range guns for purely military use, one of which, the GC-45, could fire a heavy shell twenty-five miles.

Opposite **Test-firing heavy guns**

Bull became a world-renowned artillery expert, and in his eagerness to share his knowledge he was willing to sell his wares to anyone who could afford them. In 1980 this commercial promiscuity landed him in hot water. He was sentenced to a year in prison for selling his inventions to South Africa after the US government had banned arms trade with that country. Soon after release from prison he got mixed up with the Iraqi government and its then relatively unknown defence minister, Saddam Hussein. It was a business partnership that would ultimately cost him his life. At the time, Iraq was embroiled in a bloody war with its neighbour Iran, in which Iraq used 200 of Bull's newest 155mm howitzers.

The Iraqi guns built by Bull grew in size and, under the umbrella of Project Babylon, a shadowy operation overseen by Saddam, peaked with one with a barrel 156 metres long, designed to rest against a carefully scarped hillside. This supergun was capable of firing a shell, possibly with a chemical or nuclear warhead, over a distance of up to 620 miles and was obviously a real cause for concern to potential targets within this range, including Israel. The gun was made up from bolt-together sections and required precision-machined parts, and the contract for

manufacturing these was given to a British company. In order to get round the embargo on arms trade with Iraq, the parts were described on the export licence as sections of oil pipe and a number of sections were successfully exported to Iraq; but in November 1990 the final batch was seized by British customs. By then Bull was dead, possibly, it was thought, at the hands of Israeli secret agents charged with preventing Iraq from benefiting further from Bull's expertise.

This was all high-tech, cloak-and-dagger stuff, but at heart the supergun is a fairly basic idea with a long history. Ever since artillery first became a viable weapon of war there has been a desire to build guns capable of delivering the heaviest payloads over ever-increasing distances. The massive medieval siege gun Mons Meg, for instance, which for ease of transport was made up from two bolt-together sections, bears a striking similarity to a section of one of Bull's superguns. Cast from iron in Burgundy, France, in the late fifteenth century it was capable of firing an eighteen-inch stone ball almost one and a half miles, which made it ideal for knocking holes in castle walls. It was used by the Scottish king James IV on the ill-fated campaign of 1513 which climaxed with his death at the battle of Flodden.

During the twentieth century Mons Meg's descendants came into their own, and with the world wars the superguns truly came of age. Heavy guns were fitted to battleships during the First World War and the Germans used Big Bertha, a huge railway gun, to fire shells at Paris from a position sixty miles away. In 1937 work began on a huge gun known as the Schwerer Gustav. The gun's barrel was a phenomenal thirty-two metres long and it could fire armour-piercing shells weighing over seven tons and about five metres long almost thirty miles. Hitler hoped to use his supergun to blast a hole in the Maginot Line, a chain of forts protecting the northern and eastern frontiers of France, but by 1939 the gun was still not ready and Hitler sidestepped the French defences, entering through Holland and Belgium. By 1942 two of the guns were finally ready for action, and were used with some success in the Russian campaign and in Poland, but the gun was too big to be practical, requiring a crew of 500 men. The Schwerer Gustav was the biggest gun ever to be used in combat.

Meanwhile, German big guns of more modest proportions were bombarding the southern coast of England around Dover from batteries in northern France. Hitler's scientists also developed a number of weapons capable of awesome feats of destruction. Among these were the infamous V1 flying bombs and V2 rockets, but it is less well known that

Opposite **Lindemann gun emplacement under construction in 1942**

Hitler's scientists developed a number of weapons capable of awesome feats of destruction

BACKGROUND

WITH THE EVACUATION OF THE REMNANTS OF THE BRITISH EXPEDITIONARY FORCE FROM THE BEACHES OF DUNKIRK IN MAY 1940, THE GERMAN ARMY MADE FRANCE THEIR OWN. ON THE OTHER SIDE OF THE CHANNEL THINGS LOOKED VERY BLEAK INDEED, AND ESPECIALLY SO FROM THE CLIFFTOPS OF SOUTH-EAST ENGLAND, JUST TWENTY-TWO MILES AWAY FROM THE FRENCH COAST. IT COULD BE ONLY A MATTER OF TIME BEFORE THE FULL MIGHT OF THE GERMAN FIGHTING MACHINE CAME STEAMING ACROSS THAT NARROW STRETCH OF WATER; INDEED THROUGHOUT LATE 1940 A CROSS-CHANNEL INVASION, CODENAMED OPERATION SEALION, WAS AT THE TOP OF HITLER'S AGENDA.

Opposite 'Against England' – German graffiti in one of the gun emplacements
Left A huge railway gun used by the Germans for their cross-Channel bombardment, covered by camouflage nets

As barges for carrying troops across the Channel were commandeered from all over Europe, the Luftwaffe took on the task of liquidating the RAF – air supremacy being an essential objective before any invasion took place. Through the summer of 1940 German bombers did their worst, first targeting convoys in the Channel and then dropping their deadly payloads on to land-based targets including RAF airfields (such as Hornchurch) and London.

The Germans also brought forward to the Pas-de-Calais five huge railway guns capable of firing shells up to thirty miles. These monster K-5 guns were sighted on the English coast and at regular intervals rained down huge steel shells packed with high explosives on to the port and town of Dover. Houses were destroyed, civilians killed and essential war work brought to a standstill as the bombardment forced people to take shelter underground. Dover was experiencing a unique type of warfare, the Kent coast being the only part of the British Isles to suffer German land-based artillery fire. It wasn't for nothing that this corner of England earned the *nom de guerre* Hell Fire Corner.

The shelling didn't stop with the railway guns. Hitler ordered the construction of a number of fixed artillery emplacements and once in position along the northern coast of France these guns added their murderous fire to the barrage. These new long-range batteries included the Friedrich August battery north of Boulogne (three 12-inch guns); Grosser Kurfürst battery north of Cap Gris-Nez (four 11-inch guns); Prinz Heinrich battery just outside Calais (two 8.5-inch guns); Oldenburg battery in Calais (two 8.5-inch guns); Lindemann battery between Calais

**Churchill and First Sea Lord Sir
Dudley Pound**

1940–44

and Cap Blanc-Nez (three 16-inch guns) and Siegfried battery, later renamed the Todt battery, outside Cap Gris-Nez (four 15-inch guns).

The British, down but definitely not out, were not going to take this pounding without fighting back. But the Dover area had little in the way of coastal artillery in place. Following a visit to a beleaguered Dover the concerned Prime Minister Winston Churchill requested 'Pray install a gun to shoot across the Channel', and work began on 24 June on the construction of a heavy-gun position at West Cliffe, near the village of St Margaret's at Cliffe, just to the east of Dover. The chosen site was on a golf course, perhaps a fitting location for a machine designed to drive a projectile as far as possible through the air. Golfers were still teeing off as newly laid rail tracks brought in three fifty-ton cranes to lift the great weights of metalwork. The mounting for the gun was delivered on 10 July and the barrel fitted by early August. The finished gun, the biggest permanently fixed British artillery piece outside Singapore, was nicknamed Winnie in honour of the Prime Minister.

The arrival of the gun was a closely kept secret, as a local shopkeeper found to his cost. Eager for a souvenir, the man took a photograph of part of the gun's mounting – and he was promptly arrested and had his camera confiscated. The arrival of the gun made St Margaret's at Cliffe an instant target for German bombs and so many of the village's residents were moved out of their homes and relocated at a safe distance.

Another gun of the same 14-inch calibre was to follow, located about a mile to the east of Winnie, on the other side of the village. Pooh, named after its pairing with Winnie, went into service in early February 1941. Both guns were operated by men from the Royal Marines Siege Regiment. On 21 August 1940, Winnie, with a maximum range of twenty-seven miles, became the first British gun to launch a shell on to mainland Europe from the other side of the Channel. The shell she sent was just shorter than a man and weighed 1,586 lb. On impact it sent out a deadly shower of razor-sharp slivers of steel – each capable of cutting a man in two or damaging equipment or buildings.

By the end of August 1940 the fight was no longer entirely one-sided and the heavyweights were ready to slug it out from both sides of the Channel.

The finished gun was nicknamed Winnie in honour of the Prime Minister

Our best attempt at bringing Winnie back to life

THE BATTLE

THE BATTLE OF THE BIG GUNS IN DOVER
AND FRANCE LASTED FROM 1940 TO 1944.
IN THE EARLY YEARS OF THAT PERIOD, IT
BECAME APPARENT THAT WINNIE AND
POOH WERE NO REAL MATCH FOR THE
STATE-OF-THE-ART GERMAN GUNS. THERE
COULD BE NO GETTING ROUND THE FACT
THAT THE PAIR WERE ALMOST HAS-BEENS
– FIRST WORLD WAR BATTLESHIP GUNS
BROUGHT OUT OF MOTHBALLS IN THE
COUNTRY'S HOUR OF NEED. ONE
PARTICULAR SHORTCOMING WAS THEIR
INABILITY TO HIT GERMAN SHIPS IN THE
CHANNEL – THEY WEREN'T FAST OR
ACCURATE ENOUGH TO HIT MOVING
TARGETS.

Opposite **AA guns firing at night**
Left **Churchill inspecting coastal defence stations**

Churchill became very concerned with the situation and ordered that more batteries be constructed. Accordingly, in 1942, Winnie and Pooh were augmented by batteries at Wanstone Farm (two 15-inch guns), Fan Bay (three 6-inch guns) and South Foreland (four 9.2-inch guns). Three 13.5-inch railway guns were also brought into action, their barrels stripped from an interned Vichy warship. These were known as Gladiator, Piecemaker and Sceneshifter. The latter was the first of these to be used and was hidden in Guston railway tunnel (about two and a half miles to the west of St Margaret's at Cliffe) from where it was pulled out to be fired.

The Wanstone battery was positioned to the south of Winnie, closer to the coast. Its two 15-inch guns, known as Jane and Clem (named after a popular female cartoon character in the *Daily Mirror* and either Clement Attlee or Clementine Churchill), were manned by crews drawn from the Royal Artillery's 540th Coastal Regiment. These guns, which had originally been destined for Singapore, played a very active role in maritime and counter-battery fire from the time of their emplacement in April and May 1942. By mid-1944 they had engaged enemy shipping on no fewer than fifty occasions and were credited with sinking twenty-five enemy vessels. Between them, Jane and Clem fired over 1,243 shells during the war, whereas Winnie, Pooh and the railway guns fired just 676 rounds.

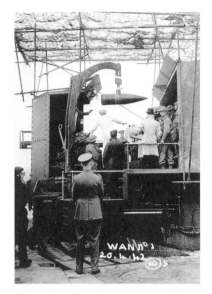

Above **Loading in progress at Jane**

Right **Heavy camouflage conceals Winnie**

Opposite **General Sir Frederick A. Pile inspects a Bofors gun**

All the Dover guns regularly came under fire from their German counterparts. War Despatch No. 5 (1 October 1942–28 March 1943), prepared by Lieutenant-Colonel H. D. Fellows, commanding officer of the Winnie battery, Royal Marines Siege Regiment describes one incident: 'The area was shelled on the nights of 9th and 10th Nov., a ready use magazine at No. 2 14" [Pooh] being hit, but the cordite was undamaged, and four rounds fell close to and around No. 1 14" [Winnie] main power house. Unfortunately a shell hit a slit trench at a neighbouring Bofors site killing 11 men.'

During this bombardment support facilities relating to both Winnie and Pooh were hit but the guns and their crews were unscathed. The tragic loss of eleven men from an anti-aircraft gun site serves as a reminder of the vital role played by these smaller guns and their crews. The first real threat to the Dover guns came not from the German guns but from air attack, against which anti-aircraft guns provided vital protection. A lowly Lewis gun drew first blood when it shot down a Messerschmitt 109 on 25 July 1940 while construction work on Winnie was still under way. According to the report by Winnie's battery commander this aircraft was the first of a 'bag' of six enemy planes downed between June 1940 and March 1941.

Both Winnie and Pooh were heavily camouflaged, using nets. The camouflaging was vital as, unlike their German counterparts, these guns were not protected by huge castle-like concrete casemates. The task was

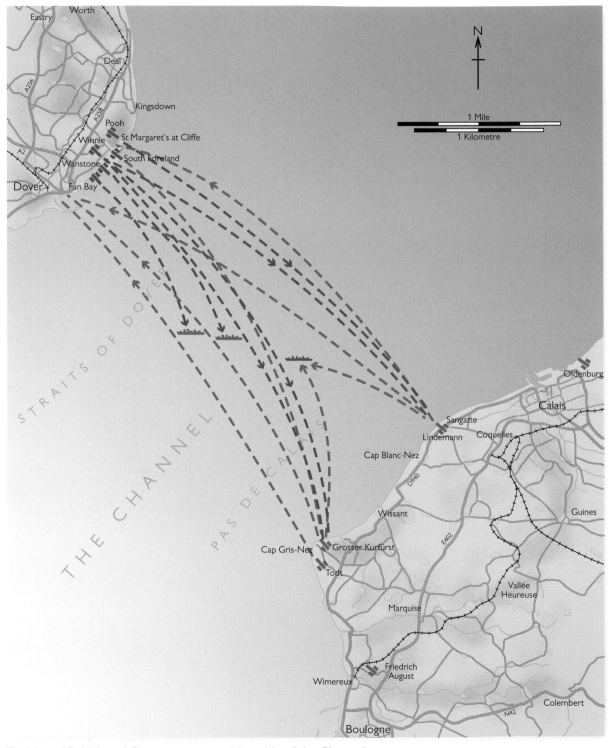

Position of British and German guns on either side of the Channel

carried out by a team of film set constructors under the direction of Sir Jasper Maskelyne, who learned the craft of concealment as a stage illusionist. As part of this effort to fool German aerial reconnaissance, dummy stand-ins for Winnie and Pooh were constructed some distance from the real positions, with telegraph poles doubling for the guns' barrels. In one of the lighter moments in the history of the big guns, the failure of this fakery became apparent when a German aircraft cheekily dropped a wooden bomb on the dummy Winnie position.

Jokes aside, though, the German bombardment was relentless. In September 1940 one Royal Marines gunner, a Sergeant Quarters Rating First Class called S. J. Flory, was on his way to his new posting at the Dover guns and witnessed what must have been a typical scene, which he describes in his memoirs:

> . . . our first introduction to Hell Fire Corner in the Dover area was when we arrived at Martin Mill Station in the evening of the 10th September. We were met by lorries to take us to our billets which was a convalescent home in St. Margaret's Bay called Porton House. On the journey from the Station to St. Margaret's Bay, there were sudden flashes and explosions mostly in the fields on both sides of the road en route. We were soon to find out that these were the guns from Cap Gris-Nez having a go.

Throughout the war, the German guns wreaked havoc in Dover harbour, and by September 1944, 2,284 German shells had landed on the port. The shelling was described in 1943 by the American novelist John Steinbeck, who visited Dover as a war correspondent. He described how a flash would be seen on a hillside in Calais and then, less than a minute later, there would be an explosion in Dover, with the sound of the blast echoing off the cliff walls. Twenty minutes later there would be another flash, followed by another explosion – and so it would go on, sometimes

By September 1944, 2,284 German shells had landed on the port

German big guns open fire on a convoy passing through the Straits of Dover

**Radar towers at Dover under
attack by German bombers**

all through the night. An hour after the last shell landed the all-clear was
sounded, but then the Germans might fire again, hoping to take people
unawares as they left the shelters. It must have been a nightmare.

By the time Steinbeck was writing the threat of German invasion had
long passed: with RAF victory in the battle of Britain (September 1940),
the entry into the war of Russia (June 1941) and the United States
(December 1942), and the Allied invasion of Italy in October of 1942 the
tide had turned and it was Hitler who was on the back foot. The heavily
fortified German big-gun positions were integrated into the Atlantic
Wall, a 1,242-mile-long network of coastal defences designed to hold
back a seaborne invasion. From as early as 1942 the German long-range
batteries began to conserve ammunition for the anticipated Allied
invasion. The situation had changed so dramatically that in July 1943
Winnie and Pooh were withdrawn from active service and put into 'Care
and Maintenance', which meant that even though they weren't in action
they were still looked after by 140 Royal Marines. The German shelling
continued, not as a softening-up exercise in advance of Operation
Sealion but to break down British morale by hitting land-based targets.
But as Steinbeck pointed out, the good people of Dover were made of
stronger stuff:

The German with his pageantry and his threats and plans, does not impress these people at all. The Dover man has taken perhaps a little more pounding than most, not in great blitzes, but in every-day bombing and shelling, and still he is not impressed. Jerry is like the weather to him. He complains about it and then promptly goes about what he was doing.

In reality, things weren't always so easily shrugged off, and there were complaints from some residents that they were being picked on by the Germans in retaliation for shots fired from the British guns, which had been positioned close by with no thought for the risks involved for local people. The evacuation of St Margaret's at Cliffe would suggest that this was not altogether true, and the complaints failed to take into account the fact that Dover came under fire from the German guns before the neighbouring batteries were constructed. Nonetheless, there was a feeling in some quarters that the big guns on both sides were engaged in a duel with no more of a military aim than to endanger the lives of local people and make their existence as difficult as possible.

But it wasn't just targets on land that suffered at the hands of the German guns. The guns on both sides served a vital tactical purpose in their maritime role of targeting shipping in the Channel, then and now one of the busiest sea lanes in the world. Dennis Colthorpe, who served on HMT *Reverberation*, an armed fishing vessel based in Dover, remembers how on 6 June 1944 when he was on escort duty in the Channel they had to make smoke to shield themselves from fire from the German batteries. Two ships were hit, one of them carrying 3,000 troops – most of whom were picked up out of the water. His own ship was hit by shrapnel but Dennis was unhurt, and later that day he got married in Dover.

D-DAY AND THE BEGINNING OF THE END

The Allied invasion of Europe on 6 June 1944, D-Day of Operation Overlord, is rightly regarded as a hugely successful mission, although, as the opening scenes of the film *Saving Private Ryan* remind us, not one without heavy cost. What tends to be forgotten, though, is that stubborn German defence of the coastal areas of northern France lasted until the end of September of 1944, causing the Allies to take much longer than originally planned to break out from the beachhead; and even after the invasion the German guns continued to pose a serious threat.

The job of taking the ground occupied by the German big guns fell to the Canadians, supported by the British cross-channel guns. The

Friedrich August battery was attacked by the 8th Canadian Infantry Brigade on 17 August 1944 and surrendered the next day. The Canadians lost 643 men – killed, wounded and MIA – in the storming of Boulogne, and captured about 9,500 Germans. The other batteries did not fall so quickly, with those at Cap Gris-Nez, including Todt, remaining in action, as did Lindemann, near Sangatte. Under orders to use up their huge stores of ammunition, the German guns destroyed 239 houses in the Dover area and damaged another 1,936 during the first three weeks of September.

With the evacuation of their non-essential personnel by boat from Boulogne on 1 September, the batteries became isolated pockets of resistance. To protect the flotilla carrying the evacuating troops from shelling, the German guns fired at the Dover batteries. Winnie and Pooh, which had been brought back into action in May, returned fire, followed swiftly by the guns of Wanstone and then South Foreland, firing on land-based targets for the first time.

This heavy engagement set the pattern for the days that followed. On 3 September, Lindemann and Todt shelled Dover. Todt quickly found itself under fire from the British guns, and returned counter-battery fire, causing numerous casualties at Wanstone. On 4 and 5 September Clem and Jane (Wanstone) took their revenge and hit Bruno at Lindemann, their crews claiming their first real kill in four years of combat (although a later inspection showed that while the Wanstone guns had knocked out Bruno's mechanics it was a German shell exploding in the barrel that actually knocked out the gun). Despite this success it was apparent that even after heavy shelling the German guns, in their heavy fortifications, survived, causing a real headache for the invading forces. Further ground assaults would be required to silence the big guns once and for all.

The 7th Canadian Infantry Brigade were charged with taking the Lindemann battery. Three infantry battalions (Royal Winnipeg Rifles, Regina Rifles and 1st Canadian Scottish) were supported by tanks of the 6th Armoured Regiment and guns of the 12th Field and 3rd Medium Regiments and the greater destructive power of the Dover guns. The operation began with counter-battery fire from the Dover guns just after 9.00 a.m. on 17 September, when Wanstone opened up on Lindemann, and Winnie and Pooh against the railway guns at Sangatte. Over two and half hours the Wanstone guns each fired sixty rounds, cooks and clerks having been drafted in to provide a constant supply of propellant. At 3.45 p.m. the guns were ordered back into action. Winnie and Pooh

Opposite **Dover under attack by Stukas**

One of the Lindemann guns (16-inch) after capture by the Canadians (note the heavy chain-mail for added protection)

joined against Lindemann but excessive barrel wear had become a serious problem and Clem's and Jane's shots began to fall short. Winnie and Pooh fired a total of 114 rounds and scored a number of hits. But at the end of the day, the bombardment, although phenomenal in scale, had little impact and the German guns were still fully operational. Containment was left to the 7th Recce Regiment, while the 7th Canadian Infantry Brigade moved on to assault Calais. The town was to fall on 1 October with the surrender of 7,500 Germans, at the cost of 300 Canadian troops.

By now the surviving German guns, including those at Lindemann, though contained were a thorn in the side of the Allied invasion force. On 20 September the American Army Air Corps dropped 5,600 HE bombs on the battery, creating a vast pock-marked wasteland – shell craters are still visible to this day. Unbelievably, even after suffering a number of direct hits, the guns remained operational. There was no other option but to send in ground troops. The guns' tenacity was surprising, because the gunners and the troops defending the batteries were far from first-grade, front-line troops, as for four years the batteries had been securely positioned behind the German front line. The big guns were also useless for close protection and most of them, with the notable exception of Grosser Kurfürst, were permanently fixed with their barrels pointing out across the Channel, which wasn't much help when their positions were assaulted from the rear. Defence against the coming ground attack fell to support troops in trenches and Tobruk turrets, a German type of pillbox.

On 25 September the 8th Canadian Infantry Brigade, consisting of the Queen's Own Regiment, the Regiment de Chaudière and the North Shore Regiment, began what had to be the final assault on the area at any cost. Tanks provided support fire, while flails cleared a path through minefields so that the infantry could get through the perimeter. It was hellish hard work. In addition to contending with the obstacles provided by bomb craters and minefields, the infantry came under fire from the Grosser Kurfürst guns firing inland – the only German guns capable of firing in all directions.

Flame-throwing Crocodiles (converted Churchill tanks armed with spigot mortars used to crack open concrete bunkers) and AVREs (Armoured Vehicle Royal Engineers) supporting the troops suffered heavy casualties from mines and anti-tank fire. As night fell only limited progress had been made and it looked as if the Canadians were in for a long hard fight. But the Germans had had enough, and the next morning the 285 defenders surrendered, many of them too drunk to walk, let alone fight.

The last dominoes to fall were the German batteries at Cap Gris-Nez, including Todt, which were subjected to artillery bombardment and then attacked by the 9th Brigade of the Canadian 3rd Division. After the Canadian Highland Light Infantry and the Nova Scotia Highlanders had begun to overrun the defensive positions – losing eight killed and 34 wounded, and taking 1,600 prisoners – the Todt garrison surrendered on 29 September.

The big guns had fallen silent for the last time.

The big guns had fallen silent for the last time

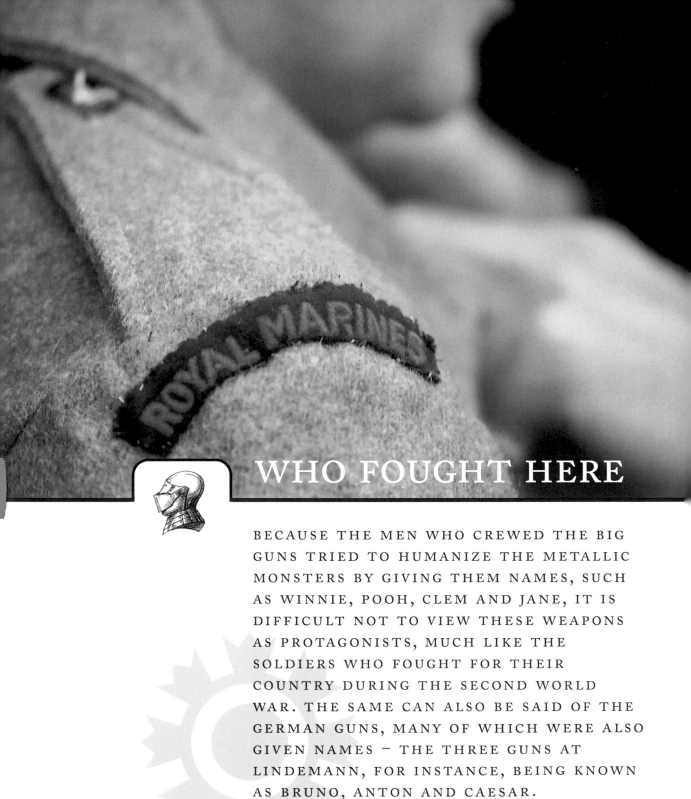

WHO FOUGHT HERE

BECAUSE THE MEN WHO CREWED THE BIG GUNS TRIED TO HUMANIZE THE METALLIC MONSTERS BY GIVING THEM NAMES, SUCH AS WINNIE, POOH, CLEM AND JANE, IT IS DIFFICULT NOT TO VIEW THESE WEAPONS AS PROTAGONISTS, MUCH LIKE THE SOLDIERS WHO FOUGHT FOR THEIR COUNTRY DURING THE SECOND WORLD WAR. THE SAME CAN ALSO BE SAID OF THE GERMAN GUNS, MANY OF WHICH WERE ALSO GIVEN NAMES – THE THREE GUNS AT LINDEMANN, FOR INSTANCE, BEING KNOWN AS BRUNO, ANTON AND CAESAR.

Neil working with the camouflage netting

At the outset of the war soldiers of the German army were much better equipped than the majority of their British counterparts, and so too were their guns. The German long-range guns in northern France were newly manufactured and specially designed for the task in hand. But as with so much else in the British defence, most of which was simply a reaction to German action, the first British guns made do with what happened to be at hand. This was especially true of Winnie and Pooh, which were old Mark VII naval guns that had been intended for use on First World War battleships.

To fire a big gun, a steel shell packed with high explosives is rammed into the breech end of the gun's barrel. Then a bag of explosive propellant (during the war this was cordite) is put in place behind the shell. The breech is closed and the propellant ignited, using an electronic charge or something akin to a shotgun cartridge. The explosion of the propellant pushes the shell up through the barrel and out of the muzzle. As the shell moves through the barrel it engages with the rifling – a series of grooves that spiral up through the inside of the barrel. A soft copper band fitted around the outside of the base of the shell squeezes itself, putty-like, into the grooves. With this tight fit the shell twists as it moves up through the barrel. This spinning motion is maintained as the shell flies through the air, keeping its flight straight, increasing its range and maximizing its accuracy.

One of the drawbacks of the British guns was a tendency for the barrels, and specifically the rifling grooves inside them, to wear out after

The men who crewed the big guns tried to humanize the metallic monsters by giving them names

THE AFTERMATH

ALTHOUGH DURING THE MONTHS
FOLLOWING D-DAY THE GERMAN
STRANGLEHOLD ON FRANCE WAS AT LAST
BROKEN, PARIS BEING LIBERATED SHORTLY
BEFORE THE GERMAN BIG GUNS
CAPITULATED IN SEPTEMBER, THE WAR
WAS FAR FROM OVER. THE GERMANS STILL
HAD A LOT OF FIGHT LEFT IN THEM AND
THE ALLIES WOULD SUFFER SETBACKS. JUST
AS THE LAST OF THE GERMAN BIG-GUN
BATTERIES WAS SURRENDERING, THE
ALLIES WERE PUTTING INTO ACTION A
PLAN TO INVADE THE GERMAN INDUSTRIAL
HEARTLAND OF THE RUHR THROUGH
HOLLAND AND IN ONE STROKE BRING THE
WAR TO A RAPID CONCLUSION.

Operation Market Garden was hugely audacious, involving one of the biggest airborne operations of the war. The idea was for paratroopers to capture a number of bridges across the rivers Maas, Waal and Neder Rijn, including the famous Arnhem bridge. The bridges were then to be held until relieved by an armoured flying column, clearing the way for a fast run into Germany. The mission was a disaster. At one point the Germans even liberated a copy of the Allies' detailed battle plans from the body of a dead officer. Great pockets of British, American and Polish troops became trapped behind enemy lines, and by 25 September 6,000 of them were left with no option but to surrender.

Reassured by their success in Holland in December 1944 the Germans mounted what was to prove their last offensive of the war. Their aim was to break through the thin American lines holding the Belgian Ardennes region, sweep through to Antwerp and in the process cut off the 21st Army Group and force the Allies into a negotiated peace. The German attack under the cover of foul winter weather took the Americans completely by surprise. But after initial rapid progress, in which American-held Bastogne was cut off, what has been described as Hitler's last gamble failed as his Panzers ran out of fuel and improved weather conditions allowed Allied aircraft into the air. Ground forces under Patton relieved Bastogne, and Field Marshal Montgomery organized a counter-offensive from the north. The Germans were driven back and by 1 February 1945 the Allied front was re-established. The cost on both sides was terrible – the retreating Germans left behind 90,000 dead and injured and 600 tanks, and the Allies lost 77,000 men, dead and injured, and 733 tanks.

After this battle, the battle of the Bulge, the end came quickly. With Germany's eastern front in tatters the Russians pressed westwards, taking Vienna in April. The British and Americans continued to move in from the west, with the Americans forcing a way across the Rhine at Remagen. The Ruhr and a huge part of the German army fell to the British and Canadians and by the end of April the Red army was fighting its way through the eastern suburbs of Berlin.

Winnie and Pooh, whose sole purpose had been to engage their German opposite numbers in counter-battery fire, obviously became redundant with the fall of the enemy batteries, their job well done. But for their crews there was still fighting to be done. The Royal Marines Siege Regiment crews were permanently stood down and many of the men were sent to the school of mines at Dalditch in Devon, where they learned how to clear mines from beaches in preparation for posting to

the **Dig**

When we go looking for the remains of battles fought hundreds of years ago – like Bannockburn or Edgehill – we're prepared for them to be hard to find. We don't expect such clashes, which lasted just a few hours – or a couple of days at most – to leave much in their wakes. We were pretty sure, though, that the Second World War would provide a different experience for us as battlefield archaeologists. Surely the traces of the greatest conflict ever to afflict the people of the world would be clearly visible fewer than sixty years after the fighting stopped?

Winnie

Winston Churchill's namesake was a breech-loading, 14-inch Mark VII gun. Barrel and breech mechanism together weighed almost eighty tons and the whole thing sat upon a massive mounting set into a deep gun pit. She was protected to the front by a steel barbette and camouflaged all around by a huge net of steel hawsers supported by steel poles. Railway tracks ran in front of and behind the gun – to bring in ammunition and other supplies – and other brick and concrete buildings were dotted around the immediate vicinity providing power, shells and explosives and everything else consumed by the monster. Just how hard could it be to find such a thing, built and used within the lifetimes of our own parents?

When we parked the van in the car park of a nearby caravan park and wandered down to look at the site, there was precious little to see. With our backs towards the Channel, we crested the ridge we knew Winnie had been located behind and walked down the slope towards the place where the wartime maps suggested the gun had once sat. We spotted a couple of brick-built sheds – ammunition stores – tucked into the ridge to our right, but other than that we were looking at a fairly

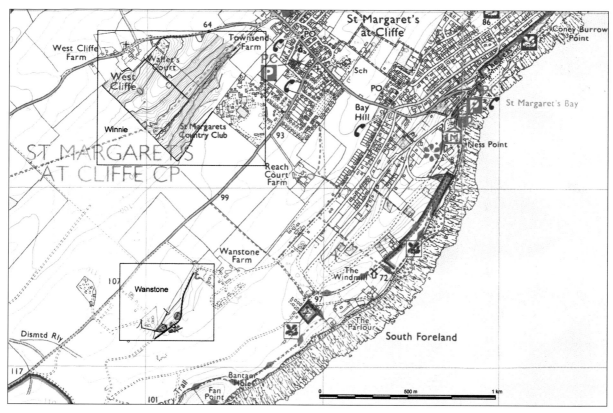

Map showing batteries – Winnie to the north and Wanstone to the south

featureless field. It is always salutary to see the apparent ease with which landscapes seem to swallow up all traces of actions of great moment and import.

During the war, this place had been alive with hundreds of personnel providing all the services required by the guns and a camp of Nissen huts had accommodated them – yet all that remained was the blast wall that had once offered some protection to those relatively flimsy structures. Nowadays, it seems to serve only as a back rub for the cattle that live in these fields, using the empty ammunition sheds for casual shelter. Somewhere close by was an underground hospital – the first of its kind in the Dover area. Built in 1942, in its final form it comprised two parallel tunnels, eighteen metres below ground, linked by three cross passages. Bomb- and shellproof, it was intended as a safe place in which to treat victims of bombardment

or, God forbid, invasion. Plans were in place to provide it with two weeks' worth of supplies in the event of such a catastrophe. The farmer, tired of losing beasts in it, had blocked up the last of the six entrances. Local kids had already destroyed the remains – iron beds, shelving and the like – by lighting fires in there. Evidence of all the activity on the site, above and below the surface, has largely disappeared from view – making it the preserve of people like us, battlefield archaeologists.

Reverting to the simple techniques we use when in search of any archaeological remains, we let our eyes take in the terrain and allow any surface anomalies to reveal themselves. Sure enough, we soon agreed that we could make out at least a couple of breaks of slope – large hummocks in the grass – that didn't look quite as God intended. Walking towards the most conspicuous of these, we noticed our first real clues: poking through

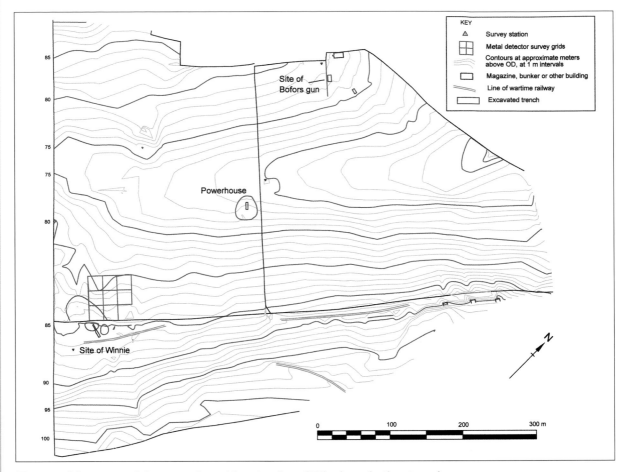

KEY
△ Survey station
Metal detector survey grids
Contours at approximate meters above OD, at 1 m intervals
Magazine, bunker or other building
Line of wartime railway
Excavated trench

Site of Bofors gun

Powerhouse

Site of Winnie

0   100   200   300 m

Topographic survey of the mound marking the site of Winnie and other trenches

back in to remove more of the heaviest rubble and then called on Helen and Dave, two of our doughty diggers, to reveal whatever remained of the structure. Like Winnie's trench, this too was soon going to get too deep for safety unless we took some precautions, so having donned protective headgear we set about shoring the trench sides to minimize the risk of cave-in. Health and Safety considerations satisfied, work got under way in earnest – and our team's labours were soon rewarded.

In addition to the stumps of a brick and concrete wall, here and there throughout the trench they unearthed lengths of heavy-gauge electrical cable and fittings. Our stump of wall was topped by what looked like a window sill – and ammunition stores or magazines

do not tend to have windows. With these clues, we turned once more to the aerial photos and documents relating to the site, and a convincing picture began to emerge. The surviving ammunition sheds up on the flank of the ridge above were alongside the line we knew to have been taken by the railway line that served Winnie with shells and cordite explosive. Their location made sense and seemed to make it less likely that the building revealed by our second trench had served the same purpose. Taking into account the heavy electrical cable and fittings, an alternative interpretation was presenting itself. Was it possible that we were excavating the remains of the beating heart of the camp that had served Winnie? One more look at the

A foxhole or rifle pit near the Bofors position – Winnie was just below the skyline at far right

documentary evidence and we were convinced – what we had uncovered was the engine room, home to the electricity generators that had provided the power to drive the guns and give life to the whole complex. The blast wall or bund on the aerial photographs fitted this hypothesis too. Were the generators to be destroyed by German guns or aircraft, Winnie would have been rendered as lifeless as if she herself had taken a direct hit and it made perfect sense that the building would have been protected by a substantial outer work capable of absorbing or deflecting blast.

Slowly but surely, Winnie and her associated complex of buildings were coming back to life.

The anti-aircraft gun

Winnie wasn't targeted only by the German heavy guns in occupied France. Her reputation was such that any passing German aircraft was likely to swoop down and take a pot-shot at her and at the team servicing her. So the whole area around the gun was provided with anti-aircraft guns of various types and sizes, positioned to make the place less appetizing to passing Junkers, Heinkels, ME 109s and the like. Our research had suggested to us that one such weapon – possibly a Bofors gun – had been located close by a farmhouse situated north-east of Winnie. It had been put in position as early as July 1940, to provide cover for the engineers and crew while Winnie was under construction. The farmer who works the land today had been a young man during the war. He was full of terrifying stories of near misses and attacks by enemy aircraft and he even had a couple of Bofors gun shell cartridges as ornaments in his home – souvenirs from the gun crew he and his family befriended. He directed us to the field where he recalled the anti-aircraft gun being positioned.

But a clean-up of the revealed surface gave us less than conclusive results. It was just possible to discern a series of regularly spaced, regularly shaped features. We couldn't rule out the possibility that these were the footings of a gun, perhaps a Bofors, but our findings were not quite strong enough for us to be certain. We hadn't conclusively pinned down the gun we were looking for, but our results had given us a fascinating insight into part of the network of defences that were in place to defend dear old Winnie.

Wanstone observation post

On almost any other part of the British mainland, there was at least some comfort to be had from the knowledge that there was someone else between you and the German foe squatting in France. But here on the south-east coast there was just a ribbon of grey water, beyond which the landmass of occupied France was often clearly visible. Put yourself in the shoes of the men and women who served at the big-gun sites and a sense of unease, of vulnerability, seems to soak in from the very ground. And if that sense of unease is palpable at the sites of Winnie, Pooh and Wanstone, where at least the terrain keeps the sea out of sight, down on the white cliffs it's almost overpowering. Here men occupied the Wanstone observation post, which served the guns by picking out enemy targets in the shipping lanes or on the French coast and keeping watch for any signs of the dreaded seaborne invasion. The crew would also feed back any sightings they had of enemy targets taking hits from British positions.

An aerial photograph gave us some idea of where the OP had been during the war, but today the site is lost somewhere within a ploughed field sloping gently down towards the cliffs. As we stood in that location for the first time, we imagined the plight of the folk who'd worked here. It's said that with a telescope, the men in the OP could read the time on the clock on the town hall in Calais. How close to the might of Nazi Germany would you have wanted to sit – especially during those months of the war when invasion seemed inevitable? Those crews were picking out targets that were within

On duty at one of Britain's coastal defence guns

A pillbox disguised as a beach-hut

range of the British guns. And they knew only too well that they themselves were easily within range of the German guns at Lindemann and Todt and Grosser Kurfürst. They could not have had much in the way of peace of mind.

The job of the OP was to operate a range-finder (a sophisticated piece of optical equipment) and relay information to the fire command posts, which in turn gave orders to the gun crews. Until the advent of wireless communications later in the war, German guns sometimes severed cables linking the various buildings. When this happened, runners had to be sent to find out what was going on. This sense of a life lived literally on the edge, on the sharp end of the war, added a special frisson to our search for that missing OP.

A walk over the ploughed field revealed a patch of ground that was conspicuously darker than the soil around it. It was about the size and shape of a badminton court and suggested to us we had found an area disturbed by human activity at some point in the past. This was enough of a lead and, accompanied by Banksie, we set off to carry out some speculative test-pit digging. This is a quick and simple technique – the

digging of little 'key-holes' to reveal glimpses of what lies beneath. We began work on one pit each and, as good luck led by informed intuition would have it, there in the bottom of one pit and sticking out of the section was a strip of corroded iron. We'd found a needle in a haystack. We called up the JCB to come in and open up a wider area and what came to light was almost beyond our ever-optimistic hopes.

As well as revealing the apparently structural iron, the lucky test-pit had given us a glimpse of the chalk layer lying beneath the plough soil. The machine exposed much more of that chalk and, to our amazement, showed that that surface had been worked on and modified before, a scoop having been removed to help create a semi-subterranean level. As we cleaned up behind the machine we could clearly see a 'step' down into the chalk and we began to get a sense of the tactic that had been employed: aware of the vulnerability of the location to enemy fire, the structure had been partially dug into the ground for shelter. Further back into the hill slope, our digging revealed the stump of a concrete wall, green paint still visible upon its inside face, irrefutable evidence of a building. Most

tellingly of all, there was also a heavy electrical cable – still overlaid with a terracotta warning slab marked 'danger' – running into the foundations of our structure. We had found our OP right enough. It appeared that it had been a semi-subterranean building, its foundations dug deeply into the chalk. The spoil from that excavation would have been heaped up around the sides of the OP to create a protective bund that would have also served to camouflage the structure from overflying aircraft. Although the building had been erased from view, the traces had survived.

Jane

Knowing that the guns at Wanstone Farm – Jane and Clem – had not been dismantled until 1957, we expected this site to be in rather better nick than Winnie

or Pooh, which had been taken apart much earlier. And we were ready to be impressed. The two 15-inch guns with barrels about sixteen metres long housed behind huge steel barbettes on bespoke concrete footings must once have been an awesome sight. We weren't to be disappointed.

The first things to see on arrival at the site of the Wanstone battery are the ammunition magazines. These concrete pyramids with their flattened roofs loom over the site with a gloomy presence. Other substantial buildings relating to the life of the gun battery also survive – hardly surprising given their brick and steel-reinforced concrete construction – though the more flimsy Nissen huts of the accommodation areas have gone. An anti-aircraft gun position is also intact. Jane and Clem were in front of all of this, towards the sea – and it was in search of any traces of this lethal double act that we had come.

Spearing into the sky from the partial cover of some bushes and scrubby trees were a pair of concrete pillars, or stanchions. From our research, we knew that these had once been part of the support framework for the heavy, steel camouflage netting that kept the big guns obscured from view. Using these as a marker, we pushed our way into the bushes – and promptly stumbled into a deep, concrete-lined depression. This massively built, waist-deep trench curved away from us on either side, apparently describing a huge semicircle. We had hit upon the footing for one of the guns; reference to the wartime plans told us it was that for Jane. All else was hidden from view by a mass of brambles, thorn bushes, stunted trees and other vegetation. As archaeologists, we're more used to digging in the soil, but from time to time we do have to attack overlying greenery before we

Preparing the gun mount for Jane

Jane takes up her position

can begin to see what we're doing. And so it was here. Calling in the rest of the team – Helen, Dave, Banksie and everyone else able to wield a shovel – we set to with a will.

As we hacked our way forward from the curving, concrete trench, we revealed a soil-and-rubble-filled depression. We could already see that the curved feature would once have helped guide Jane as she was rotated into position ready to lock on to a target and fire. Within the space described by the curve was the cavity for Jane's pivot point. The whole feature, from concrete curve to pivot point, seemed to be about eight metres across and to say that clearing it out looked like a back-breaking job is something of an understatement. A quick check with the RSPB had brought the news that this otherwise uninspiring clump of vegetation was a favourite haunt of rare marsh warblers, which meant we couldn't use our JCB here for fear of damaging their nesting habitat.

The necessary Herculean endeavours were led by Dave and Banksie. Bizarrely, they turned up some fragments of ancient pottery, mixed in with the bricks and steel and the rest of the detritus filling the well for Jane's mechanism. Final confirmation is still awaited, but initial examination persuaded us that the fragments were of a broken vessel last in use perhaps as much as 1,000 years ago. Its fabric and form suggested it was either Saxon, or perhaps even Iron Age in date. Clearly, Jane's builders had disturbed a much older settlement here at Wanstone Farm.

Finally, at a depth well over head height, we hit the base of Jane's footing. And what a sight it was. As we had thought, the curved concrete trench represented the arc traversed by part of the rear section of the gun. The barrel and breech were pivoted upon a point within the well so laboriously cleared out by Banksie and Dave – and the sheer scale of the construction left us humbled. Towards the front, two steel railway tracks cut

Jane being mounted into place, March 1942

Ready for action, April 1942

across our trench from east to west – part of the network that enabled ammunition to be moved from the magazines to the guns. They seemed hardly corroded – testament to the quality of their manufacture and, presumably, to a good coating of grease. In the bottom of the trench were the stumps of rivets and bolts so huge that they seemed to have been crafted not by men but by giants – rivet shafts as wide across as dinner plates, bolt heads the size of a boxer's fists. Clearly, though much effort had gone into removing the gun and her anchors, so massive were the fixings that they had proved immovable. It's hard to imagine that even dynamite could have shifted these things and no doubt they'll still be there in 1,000 years or more.

It's said that someone stationed here during the war painted a life-size version of Jane's comic strip namesake upon the outside of the barbette. But if her outer veneer was light-hearted, everything else about her was seriously heavyweight. Jane was no laughing matter.

The metal-detector survey

During the Second World War, you'd have been hard pushed to find any young lad who wasn't devoting at least part of his spare time to collecting shrapnel. All over mainland Britain, particularly in built-up areas, which tended to be the prime targets for German attacks, a hail of metal – bullets, bombs and shells, together with fragments from aircraft – was raining down, often day and night, providing rich pickings for little boys bent on gathering up as many different types of fragment as they could. (Strictly speaking, shrapnel refers to the metal balls contained within an explosive shell, which spray in all directions like a deadly hail. It is named after the British general Henry Shrapnel, 1761–1842, inventor of the shell.) We couldn't help but compare ourselves to those youngsters as we set about our metal-detector survey.

Our objective in searching for shrapnel was, however, rather more scientific than theirs. In order to

Metal-detecting behind Jane (hidden in trees). Most of the white flags mark German shrapnel

better understand the battle of the big guns and to appreciate what it must have been like to have been subjected to it, it was our intention to try to assess the nature, extent and intensity of the bombardment.

Using a 'total station' EDM, Olivia laid out the first of our survey grids, just down slope from Winnie. At least some of the German shells targeted on this gun had overflown their target. Olivia positioned a transect to enable our metal detectorists to pick up fragments of ordnance that had detonated to Winnie's rear. Metal detectorists are used to looking for precious metals, along with copper alloys, and are always mildly amused at having to reset their machines to look for iron and steel, which they might normally dismiss as worthless scrap.

Pretty soon, the telltale flags were decorating the grass, marking positive signals within the grids. The results, once the detectorists started digging them up, were just as we had hoped. Time and again, they called

us over to see shell fragments as well as spent and unfired 0.303 rounds. Time had failed to erase this most evocative of evidence of savage, long-distance fighting and it wasn't hard to get a sense of how Hell Fire Corner had earned its name.

Turning a shell fragment over in your hands is a singular experience. Six decades in the ground had done

Tunic button from a Royal Marine who manned Winnie

Shell fragment

Spent and unfired 0.303 rounds

little to blunt the cruel edges on these pieces of iron, steel and brass. Some of them weighed pounds, others just a few ounces, but any one of them was enough to end a life, or several lives, as it spun chaotically, white-hot, through flesh and bone. Some of the pieces were fragments of the drive band, the soft copper ring that forms the snug fit into the rifling in the gun barrel – which in turn imparts enough spin on the projectile to ensure its accuracy in flight. Had we had access to the German guns that fired them, we could have used ballistics examination of these bands to determine

which gun each of these shells had come from. Here then was real evidence of the deadly duel of the big guns.

The bullets told their own story: spent cartridges spoke of desperate attempts to bring down passing fighters and bombers with small arms fire; intact rounds suggested that they had been dropped from shaking hands in the heat of the moment.

There were more personal finds too – items that brought to mind ordinary men and women. It was a real thrill to find a tunic button from the uniform of one of

Unfired 0.303 bullets

Button from the tunic of a Royal Artilleryman

the Royal Marines who manned Winnie, the distinctive fouled-anchor decoration still clearly visible.

Wanstone battery

Jane and Clem – and the men who manned them – took quite a pounding from their German equivalents. We knew they'd endured a particularly tough time, for example, on 2 and 3 September 1944 when guns at the Todt battery notched up several direct hits; and things were bad enough to necessitate the construction of an accommodation block with room for over 100 people many metres below the surface to try to minimize the risk to the people based here. It was to Wanstone, then, that we next turned our metal-detecting intentions. This time we had Olivia put in survey grids both in front of and behind Jane's position, to enable us to assess the level of enemy ordnance falling short of and overshooting the target.

Once again, both areas were soon littered with signal flags. And if anything, the finds here were even more stomach-churning than those we'd unearthed at Winnie. We were working in the heart of the complex, which would have been, at the time, full of people going about their work, with the camp of Nissen huts close by, and it was chilling to find fragment after fragment of German shell.

As at every site, we plotted each individual find on the grid. Our results create the clearest picture ever attempted of the bombardment here.

It's one thing to read about Wanstone battery coming under attack from the German big guns; it's quite another, sixty-odd years later, to handle the very shell fragments that did all the damage.

And at Wanstone we found another button. This time, it was from the tunic of a Royal Artilleryman, bearing the motto 'Ubique' (intended to suggest that the Royal Artillery were to be found everywhere they were needed, but other soldiers teased them that it meant their rounds were likely to land everywhere except on target). Since Wanstone was manned by men

Magazines at the Wanstone AA battery – the gun would have been mounted in the centre

of the 540th Coastal Regiment RA (Royal Artillery), it couldn't have been better: it's people, not guns, who fight wars, and here was a remnant left behind by one of those souls.

Todt battery

We could hardly investigate the battle of the big guns without checking out the material on the French side of the Channel. With boyish excitement, we packed up our kit and shepherded our team of metal detectorists on to the ferry for some French leave.

The sheer scale of the German gun batteries in the Pas-de-Calais region of northern France beggars belief. Todt battery, close by the village of Audinghen, simply takes the breath away.

To get a sense of the look of the Todt guns from the rear – the way you'd have seen them if you'd approached them overland, as the Canadian infantry had to – think of a series of giant upturned mixing bowls, each three storeys high and with sides over three metres thick, squatting on the landscape like an overblown fungus. Viewed from the front, as they'd have appeared from the sea – into the aperture from which the mighty gun barrel protruded – each of these massive gun emplacements is large enough to be mistaken for some sort of amphitheatre. No matter how you try to describe them, these creations are simply outlandish and must be seen to be believed.

We wanted to see if we could pick up the remains of any British shells – from Winnie, Pooh, Jane or Clem – and any traces of the Canadian infantry's struggles to neutralize the German guns in the aftermath of the Normandy landings in 1944. Once again, Olivia laid out her grids – on the landward side of the emplacement, from which the Canadian attack would have come – and the metal detectorists got to work. And if we'd been impressed by how much Second World War material remained in the ground around Dover, the survival in the Pas-de-Calais was staggering. It was as though the shells had stopped raining down only the day before. Here among the trees that partially obscure the gun emplacements, it seemed that every other signal was a fragment of Allied artillery shell. None was large enough

Todt battery

Todt battery

to have come from Winnie or Jane, but all spoke of the advance of the Canadians, supported by smaller-calibre field guns and tanks.

The outer skin of the gun emplacement we were working behind (turret IV) was pocked with scars left by its attackers. In most cases they seemed to have caused just superficial damage, but the ground was peppered with the remains of the ordnance spent in the battle.

One find in particular pulled us up short and brought back to life the ferocity of the fight here: an almost intact armour-piercing shell – one of the hundreds or even thousands that were thrown at these massive structures. By a fluke of the way it had been damaged on impact it looked for all the world like a giant boxing glove – an iron fist indeed.

Near by, among the shell fragments, was the

Like an iron fist: an armour-piercing shell from Todt battery

occasional poignant find that speaks more of people than of weapons. Badly corroded, but still intact, the iron head of a shovel was recovered from just centimetres below the surface. A piece of kit familiar to any soldier, it would have been put to any number of everyday uses before it was lost or broken, or perhaps cast aside in haste as the place came under the final attack.

But it was the sheer volume of shell fragments that impressed us most here, revealing in graphic detail the struggle to liberate this corner of France.

A giant railway gun – now a rusting hulk

German observation post

From the cliffs to the west of Audinghen, not far from Todt, there is a clear view back towards the south coast of England. Here German conscripts, like the occupants of Wanstone observation post, were tasked with keeping watch, horribly exposed to enemy fire. We followed a well-worn coastal path from the main road out along the cliffs until we arrived outside a semi-subterranean, concrete bunker.

Its walls were daubed, inside and out, with the graffiti that is the lingua franca of bored kids everywhere. As we watched the pedestrians idling along the path between the bunker and the cliff edge, we wondered about our chances of finding much of interest. There would be ring pulls and loose change for sure, but what about the detritus of war?

We needn't have worried. Our metal detectorists were into the swing of things by now, enjoying the novelty of seeing rusted slivers of iron and steel greeted like the gold of kings; the finds at the Audinghen

A German bunker on the French coast

A Wehrmacht Eagle inside turret IV

observation post persuaded them once and for all that there really was something in this battlefield archaeology lark. Here on this clifftop they found the remains of a savage firefight. It was all laid out before us as though the crackle of machine-gun fire had only just faded. Shell fragment after jagged shell fragment testified to the relentless onslaught unleashed by the Canadians as they fought their way, metre by bloody metre, into this corner of France. We recovered the butt ends of shells, complete with drive bands – and also the nose cones, all of which would have turned into death-dealing shrapnel at the moment of detonation. And spent bullets and bullet clips – small rectangles of brass that had once held five rounds of ammunition ready to be loaded into a rifle – brought back echoes of the desperate defence put up by the Germans cornered in this bunker. We couldn't help but sympathize with the plight of those soldiers and think about the moment when they'd finally realized the game was up.

One or two of the signals caused us some hairy moments. Occasionally a detectorist revealed what looked like an intact and possibly unexploded piece of ordnance. It always brought a collective sigh of relief when a jagged edge was eventually found and it was established that the explosive charge had long since done its job.

There was also a find of a cartridge case from a French rifle round, which initially caused us some confusion. Towards the end of the war, however, the Germans were making use of every piece of weaponry and ammunition they could commandeer and a German defender here might well have been armed with a captured French weapon.

In all, our finds at the bunker painted a vivid picture. All that was missing was the smell of cordite and the smoke and din of battle. We had recovered more than enough material to bring a few frantic hours of the Second World War back to life.

Conclusion

The Second World War isn't remote to us as, say, the fourteenth-century wars of Scottish independence are, or the Monmouth Rebellion of 1685. The greatest conflict the world has yet seen touched the lives of our own parents and grandparents. Aircraft being spotted in 1940 by men and women in the Chain Home Radar stations on the east coast were making their way towards cities such as Manchester, home to young married couple Arnold and Peggy Pollard, or to Glasgow, where seven-year-olds Pat Oliver and Norma Neill (later Oliver) were sitting out air raids with their families in the closes of their tenement flats. Such connections

between our families and the events of the war are very moving for us.

When we go in search of guns like Winnie and Jane, or an observation post like that at Wanstone Farm, we feel a real sense of the importance of these places: battlefield archaeology is not only about the dim and distant past but can also give an insight into much more recent events that have shaped our own lives.

For these reasons, it was almost shocking to discover how little evidence of the Second World War remains. Winnie and Pooh – two huge guns that played such an important role in boosting morale in the early years, and were later key players in the events following D-Day – have gone, leaving scarcely a trace above ground. The camp is gone, the railway tracks are gone, the engine room has vanished, leaving traces that only archaeology can reveal. A single stretch of blast wall remains, alongside two ammunition stores now demoted to the role of cowsheds. Only with the help of a JCB were we able to locate the concrete footing for Winnie herself. The enigmatic defended trench we found while we looked for the elusive Bofors gun required every bit of the delicate treatment we would have deployed on a prehistoric site and was every bit as rewarding as a result. But again and again we were struck by the extent of the disappearance of important historical sites after fewer than sixty years.

Stripped of the overburden of rubble and scrubby vegetation, Jane's mounting had fared rather better. Surrounded by her towering magazines and other associated buildings, the gigantic footing that that 15-inch gun had once crouched upon was remarkably intact. We said to one another that the site should be cleaned up completely and displayed to the public as a reminder of the desperate fight that helped save the free world – and we meant it. Jane and Clem, shadows of their former selves though they are, still have the power to instil awe in today's generations. We were also thrilled that our efforts in that ploughed field just behind the white cliffs had put the Wanstone Observation Post back on to the map, for posterity.

But if the post-war years have seen many traces of the conflict disappear, our metal-detecting survey brought them back with a magician's flourish. If anything had the power to bring home the nature of the life-and-death struggle waged on our behalf, it was the bags full of shell fragments and spent bullets we recovered on both sides of the Channel, carrying the echoes of war back to our ears.

One lesson to be learned through battlefield archaeology (and there are many) is how quickly passing moments become buried history. The events of sixty years ago can be as hard to find as those of 600 years ago, or 6,000. Stage magician Sir Jasper Maskelyne was employed in 1940 to make the big guns invisible. The peacetime efforts to scrub as many traces as possible of the Second World War from the landscape have contributed to an even more amazing, and disturbing, disappearing act.

The Battlefields Today

Bannockburn

Ask any Scot what happened at Bannockburn and they'll likely tell you confidently it's the place from which the English were sent homewards, to think again. Ask them to direct you to the battlefield and things get a bit more uncertain. The best starting point for visitors is the Bannockburn Heritage Centre in the Whins of Milton, within Bannockburn itself, a suburb of Stirling. To approach from the north or south, take the M90. Follow signs for the A872 and then National Trust for Scotland signs will direct you. The centre is home to a splendid display about the battle, along with an audio-visual show that should be rousing for Scots, vaguely intimidating for English folk and thoroughly entertaining for everyone.

Up on the high ground to the rear of the centre is the inspirational statue of the Bruce, by Pilkington Jackson. Given the 360-degree panorama it enjoys, it's easy to see why this is said to be where the Bruce and his commanders made their camp. Turn to face in the same direction as the king and, looking roughly south, you'll see the modern road snaking towards you, roughly on the line of the Roman road along which the English king Edward II and his army advanced. Turn through approximately 180 degrees and you'll see Edward's intended destination, which the Bruce had come to defend: Stirling Castle, perched imperiously upon its crag of volcanic rock. To the right of the castle, and Stirling, the skyline is dominated by the Ochil Hills. The distinctively flat-topped mount towards the left-hand end of the ridge is the site of Dumyat, an Iron Age hillfort.

Looking towards the north and east, as you now are, you'll notice that the housing and other development peters out. The last terrace of higher ground you can

make out, in the direction of Dumyat, contains the Dryfield of Balquhidderock, one of the proposed scenes of the fighting on day two. Beyond that, the low-lying plain stretching towards the hills is the Carse of Stirling, flood plain of the river Forth. Hard to spot, but down there in front of you nonetheless, are the two streams that played a vital part in the battle's story: the Pelstream and the Bannock burn. Take directions from the helpful staff at the centre, and then it's a ten-minute car journey at most down on to the Carse. The low ground bisected by the A91 is the most likely scene of most of day two's activities. The most impressive

stretch of the Bannock burn in our opinion, and one of the sites we considered as contender to the title of the 'Great Ditch', is the mile or so between Beaton's Mill and Skeoch Mill. To reach this, again, take directions from the centre staff.

Edgehill

The action in this first battle of the English Civil War unfolded in the otherwise peaceful Warwickshire countryside north-west of Banbury. The M40 motorway will bring you from north or south to the general vicinity. The key locations are to be found to the north of the A422, the road linking Banbury with Stratford-upon-Avon. Edgehill itself, the dramatic escarpment that gave the battle its name, runs roughly south-west to north-east, between the A422 and the B4086. It was upon this ridge that King Charles and his royal army arrayed themselves before the fighting started, and down which they advanced, lowering their field guns on ropes. There is no overestimating the impressive, dominating feel of Edgehill itself. Put yourself in the shoes of the king or a soldier on that high ground before the fighting commenced, and it's easy to get a sense (however misplaced) of having the upper hand.

The Parliamentarian army awaited His Majesty's pleasure down on the level ground far below, beyond Radway. This is a strikingly pretty little place today, the quintessential English village. Find your way to the present-day parish church and inside, on the left under the bell tower, you'll find Kingsmill's statue, tucked in its niche. On the wall by the door are the two illustrations of the original Radway Church. The royal army advanced through the village, past the church and on to the plain beyond. Here things become a little tricky for today's visitor, since much of what was the battlefield is occupied by the Ministry of Defence base of DM Kineton, which is strictly off limits. Within the confines of the base are Graveground Coppice, a supposed mass grave, and possibly a second grave site known as Battleton Holt. Also on private land is the area we excavated in search of the ford across the river Dene, in the attractive village of Kineton; so too is the site of King's Leys Barn, though the fairly pronounced badger mound on top of it can be picked out from the top of Edgehill by those with sharp eyes and an OS map.

Despite the restricted access to the battlefield core, the area is worth a visit. The vista from Edgehill is breathtaking and, in the low-angled sunlight of evening or early morning, it's hard to miss the traces of ridge and furrow in the fields all around this part of Warwickshire. These marks of early agriculture, scoring the landscape like patches of corduroy, are among the finest examples in England. Stand on Edgehill and consider the highly mobile battle that took place below you, and you'll have sense enough of those momentous events.

Sedgemoor

There's a somnolent air in the little villages around the site of Sedgemoor battlefield; there seems little sign of urgent activity and the quiet is palpable. Changed days then – since this part of the south-west of England was home to a veritable hotbed of rebellion in centuries past.

Take the M5 towards Bridgwater and then the A372 to the village of Westonzoyland. Here Feversham's government forces encamped before the battle and here was the destination of Monmouth's doughty rebels when he marched them out of Bridgwater on that fateful night. Stand with your back to the Sedgemoor Inn and look at the houses directly opposite. Behind these are the paddocks within which Feversham and his top brass made their lodgings in the then manor house of Weston Court.

For a look at features related to the fighting, make your way to Bussex Farm, on the northern fringe of the village. Obviously the farmland is privately owned and must be treated as such, but there's a track from close

by the farmhouse leading past Monument Field on the left and Mortimer's Field on the right. Monument Field has a granite stone memorial with a bronze plaque. It is in this field that strong local tradition places at least one mass grave of the rebels. Mortimer's Field bears the unmistakable line of the Bussex Rhine. This drainage ditch, which had such an impact on the progress of the battle, survives as a wide meander that still retains standing water, if the rain's been heavy enough.

It is in the fields around here, and off to the north and west beyond Monument Field towards the village of Chedzoy, that the fighting raged. Given the peaceful air about the place today, it's hard to imagine it as the scene of such horror. Only the claustrophobic atmosphere created by hedges and modern drainage ditches provides a sense of fading menace.

Bridgwater too is worth a visit – if only for the Admiral Blake Museum, on Bridge Street, which displays relics of the battle.

Killiecrankie

Scotland's scenery doesn't get any better than at the Pass of Killiecrankie. And if the place itself wasn't enough of a draw, it was of course the scene of a battle featuring drama, derring-do and the death of the charismatic Bonnie Dundee.

Take the A9 towards Pitlochry. Just to the north of the town, the road bisects the battlefield itself and on the western side of the road, there's a National Trust for Scotland visitors' centre, dedicated to the battle and to the natural history of the surrounding Pass of Killiecrankie. Signs from here lead you on foot towards

the river Garry cascading dramatically through its rock-cut gorge. You'll be directed to the Soldier's Leap, where a government soldier, hotly pursued by Jacobites, is said to have leapt the gorge.

The slopes above and to the north-east of the A9, further north from the visitors' centre, were the scenes of the fighting. It was upon one of the distinctive terraces below nearby Ben Vrackie that Bonnie Dundee's Jacobites were arrayed. Down towards the vicinity of Urrard House they charged and clashed with Mackay's

forces. Urrard House is a private home, but it has within its grounds the grave mound and monument raised to the fallen of the battle. Elsewhere hereabouts, also on private land, are the remains of buildings likely to have been used for cover during the fighting.

Hornchurch

While Hornchurch was once a sleepy Essex village, separated from London by miles of countryside, now it's swallowed up by the city's sprawl. Take the A13 east towards the likes of Dagenham and Romford, then pick up the signs for Hornchurch, towards the north, and follow the signs

for Hornchurch Country Park. You'll know you're getting close to the site of RAF Hornchurch when street names such as Bouchier Walk and Lock Close start to trigger memories of heroes.

After a spell of being denuded by gravel extraction, the remains of the famous airfield are now preserved within the very attractive bounds of Hornchurch Country Park. There's a car park just about where Suttons Lane turns into Airfield Way, and from here it's just a matter of following the paths through the park. The airfield's defences – Tett turrets, pillboxes, Spitfire E-pens and the like – are scattered all around. It's a pleasant place to spend time – the most common fliers nowadays being of the feathered variety, for the ponds and pools that fill the former gravel pits attract all manner of birdlife.

The Good Intent – a favourite pub with battle of Britain flyers and still serving pints and pub grub – is on the Southend Road, instantly recognizable by its sign featuring a diving Spitfire.

Dover

The sites of the British guns are worth a visit just for the opportunity to take in the magnificent spectacle of the world-famous white cliffs of Dover. From Dover, head out of town uphill, past the castle, and take the A258 towards St Margaret's at Cliffe. Although Winnie, Pooh, Jane and Clem are located on private farmland, all the sites are accessible via the public footpaths behind the white cliffs. Winnie was located close by the village of West Cliffe, and a footpath here will take you on a line between the surviving blast wall that once protected the camp of Nissen huts and the remaining ammunition

sheds. The entrances to the underground hospital are here, too, though now filled in. Past the sheds, the ground slopes steeply down to the right (north). It was within these fields that Winnie and her associated complex of buildings, anti-aircraft guns and defended positions were located, though there is little to see on the surface now.

Jane and Clem are to be found on land belonging to Wanstone Farm, further to the west. From St Margaret's caravan park, head west and look for the sign, on the left, for Wanstone Farm. The track will take you past the former Block House, on the left. Take the next right and follow the track for just shy of half a mile until you reach a little car park beside the pyramid-like

ammunition magazines and other buildings related to the Wanstone battery. The locations of Jane and Clem are in the scrub directly in front of the car park, towards the sea.

The coastal path out of St Margaret's at Cliffe will lead you along the top of the white cliffs. Keep a careful eye out on either side of the path and you'll spot pillboxes, shelters and sundry other remains of the defences along this part of Kent.

A visit to the German guns, in the Pas-de-Calais region of northern France, is also a must for anyone seeking to appreciate the nature of the cross-channel battle. From Calais, take the A16 south to junction 7. Turn off here towards the villages of Wissant and Audinghen. The area here is littered with remains of the Second World War and the massive gun emplacements of the Todt battery are still intact. The Todt Museum, inside one of the emplacements, in the village of Harzingelle, near Audinghen, is home to a fascinating collection of wartime memorabilia. Ask in here for directions to the other emplacements which are close by.

ACKNOWLEDGEMENTS

Our second campaign of battlefield investigations would not have been possible without the dedication, enthusiasm and support of a small army of people. The team of professional archaeologists from Glasgow University and the production crew from Optomen Television gelled as a tight unit, sharing triumphs and disappointments alike. We had some fantastic fun together, sharing some truly unique experiences. It seems hard to believe that over the last twelve months we have carried out six full-scale projects – an effort that has taken a huge amount of organization, stamina and at times nothing less than sheer grit and determination.

Our adventures have taken us the length and breadth of the country and on our travels we have been assisted by local archaeological groups and metal-detector clubs. To all these volunteers we express our gratitude. We would like to thank all the landowners who kindly gave permission for our work to take place. Thanks to everyone listed below (to anyone we may have accidentally left out our sincerest apologies – you know who you are).

ARCHAEOLOGISTS

Dr Iain Banks, an old friend and accomplice, for doing such a great job keeping everything together; our fantastic team of field archaeologists – Paul Duffy, better known under his stage name of Paulo Dufé, Helen MacQuarrie, who brought glamour into every trench she inhabited, Dave Sneddon, a new arrival who instantly became part of the family; the surveyors who kept everything in its place and did such a wonderful job of overseeing metal-detector operations – John Arthur, who recently became a father, and Dr Olivia Lelong, who brought a new type of grace to the tripod; Andy Robertshaw for his expertise, constant good humour and never-ending supply of costumes; all in the Glasgow University

Archaeological Research Division (GUARD) office for their support and assistance – Jen Cochrane, Chris Connor, Ross McGrehan and Mel Richmond – and the University of Glasgow and the Archaeology Department for providing office space; Natasha Ferguson for giving up so much of her own time to clean and catalogue metal-detector finds; Angela Boyle, osteologist at the Oxford Archaeological Unit for being on standby (maybe next time?); the brilliant team of JCB operators – Hayden, Peter and Co.; Minerals International for the use of their splendid sovereign detectors, and particularly Desmond Dunne of the Brandon office.

OPTOMEN TELEVISION

Pat Llewellyn, executive producer and the visionary who made it all happen (don't let this woman take you out to lunch – next thing you know you'll find yourself presenting a TV series!); Paul 'Ratso' Ratcliffe, series producer and director, a fashion icon even when waddling around with his waterproof trousers rolled halfway down his legs – '"Once More" Paul!'; Jennie Macdiarmid, assistant producer and researcher, who by the time we got round to Killiecrankie couldn't resist the temptation any longer and took up the trowel; Sasha 'Cool Beans' Mantel, researcher and a man who really needs to take some tips from Paul on how to revise his wardrobe – think Ali G crossed with Del Boy Trotter; Richard Hill, our cameraman, with whom we shared many a knowing look with the one eye that wasn't permanently wedged into the slowly disintegrating viewfinder (sorry we couldn't get a photo of your beloved red passion wagon in the book); Rex Phillips,

sound recordist, whose resemblance to Paul Newman and constant readjustment of microphones with chilled paws earned him the moniker 'Cold Hand Luke'; Patrick Acum, assistant cameraman, whose ribald stories got more and more outrageous as the shoot progressed; Richard Herd, who could get anything, any time – if you had to do some hard time in a prison camp, he'd be the man you'd want as a friend (glad to have you as one anyway, Rich); Joe Cooper, general good egg and assistant cameraman, whose showbiz lifestyle is the envy of all; Carolyn Stopp, who was a cheerful ray of sunshine even in horizontal rain; Jeremy Cracknell, who with boundless energy ran a very efficient tuck shop out of the side of his white van, which he guarded like a rabid bulldog; Rosie Allsop, production manager, who managed the impossible and kept us all on the financial straight and narrow (now where did we put our receipts?); Dominic Ozanne, who's coming into the river with us next time; the team in the edit suite who do such a great job putting the programmes together: Philippa Daniel, Daniel de Waal, Ray King, Chris Phinikas, Martin Roche, Paul Plowman.

BANNOCKBURN

Lorna Main and Stirling Council, Fiona Watson, Jennifer Miller, Elspeth King, Derek Alexander, Robin Turner and the National Trust for Scotland, Alo Parfitt, Noel Fojut and Historic Scotland, Mrs Johnston at West Plean, Mr Muirhead, Donald Findlay, Judith Fairley, Elizabeth Jeffery, Stephen Digney, Alastair McKenzie, Graham Bryson, Mounted Division of Strathclyde Police, Stewart Burthwick, Joe Cooper (JCB Driver), James Miller, David Deans, David Hartwell, John Barron, Michael Burke, Kenneth Shirra, Nicholas Mulholland, Hugh McIndoe, All from the Antonine Metal Detectors Club.

SEDGEMOOR

Barry Sagar, Mr and Mrs R. Roberts, Robert Dunning, Robin Clifton, Mr and Mrs Norman Fry, Bob Croft and Somerset County Council, Richard Brunning, Chris Webster, Rob Iles, David Dawson, Steven Minnitt, Mr Perry, Mr Fisher, Mr and Mrs Winn, Mr Lewis, Tony Bradford, Mr Baker, Mr L. G. Heal, Mr and Mrs Triggol, Audrey Fry, Mr and Mrs Gillard, D.

Jenkins, G. A. Fry, Francis Farr-Cox, Peter Higton, Hayden Bale, Brian Steers, Dave Woodhouse, Tony Jefferies, Jon Pettet, David Gadd, Mal Guy, Jerry Morris, Dave Holder, Patricia Creed, Bill Stebbing, Gillian Townshend, Pat Buck.

KILLIECRANKIE

David, Victoria and Mark Cairns at Urrard House, all at Blair Castle, Polly Freeman, Libby Macrae, Jim Forbes, David Stevenson, Lieutenant-Colonel Alisdair Johnson, Peter Jarvis, Martin Hinchcliffe and the National Army Museum, Sandy Lyons, Jackie Liehne,

Jim McCreadie, Gerald McAleer, John Ward, Ian Kibble, Ben Block, Ian Marshall and the Association for Certificated Field Archaeologists, Dennis Topen, Gerry Herns, Bruce Henry, Stephen Clancy, Catherine Smith, Michael Block.

EDGEHILL

Jonathan Parkhouse and Warwickshire County Council, John White, John Lilwell, John Boswell, Anthony Forsythe, Mrs Roots, Revd Christopher Lamb, Colonel Ingle, Sergeant Major Klaus and the guys on the range at DM Kineton, Mrs Bryant, Mr and Mrs Butler, Mr and Mrs Holland, Mr and Mrs Robinson, John Chandler, Stephanie Ratkai, Peter Edwards, Peter Randerson, Kineton Scouts, Brownies and Cubs, Nora Carlin, Martin Peglar and the Royal Armouries, Nick Berry, John Holland, George Smith, Pat Smith, Glenn Fleuchar, Peter Spackman, Clive Heritage, Susan James, Ron Pinnock, Carole Walton, Stuart Robbins, Dick Burge, Richard Prew, Dr Paul Stamper at English Heritage.

HORNCHURCH

Alan Cooper, John and Mick – the fantastic Countryside Service Rangers at Hornchurch, Peter Brown, Dave Davis, Joy Caldwell, Dave Vicerey-Weekes at Bexley Archaeological Group, Andy Brown, Sandra Russel, Kim Sangster, Claire Gillett, Pat Devauk, Ann Al-Jalili, Colin Harwood, James Elliott, Barbara Elliott, Beryl Rose, Pip Pulfer, Trevor Waite, Keith Schnaar, Sheila Schnaar, Steven Griffin, Angela Griffin, Elizabeth Smyth, David Lawrence, Adele Melvin, Sian Turner, Nick Truckle at English Heritage, Havering Council, Ken Willcox, Richard

Smith, Squadron Leader Paul 'Major' Day, Colin Wheeler, Janice Guyton, Rene Harwood, Sian Turner, Barry Molon, Terry Wiston, Peter Higton, Hayden Bale, Craig Slanel.

DOVER

Major Ben Archer, David Davis, Duncan Pennock, Chris Wren, Colin Downer, Maurice Worsley, Joe Daly, Adele Melvin, David Lawrence, Ann Al-Jalili, Pip Pulfer, Pat and Peter Godden, Stan Blacker, Robin Dowdeswell, John Williams and Kent County Council, Denis Hickson, Mrs E. Bushell, Mrs Humphrey Smith, Bob Dare, Philip Harland, the National Trust, Win Wakefield, Andrew Richardson, Mark Parrington, St Margaret's Holiday Park.

Thanks to our friends at Michael Joseph/Penguin: Chantal Gibbs, Lindsey Jordan, Keith Taylor, Catherine Lay, John Hamilton, Anne Askwith, Elisabeth Merriman, Kate Raffan, Nikki Pullen, Chris Callard, Clare Pollock, Stef Hinrichs, Kate Brunt, Cath Rowse, Tom Weldon and Louise Moore.

Also thanks to Craig Burgess for page make-up and design, and Mark Read for his real talent for a picture and his good company over the entire period of *Two Men in a Trench*.

And not forgetting: Trevor Austin (part of the National Council for Metal Detecting), National Council for Metal Detecting, Phil Pepper at JCB, Flame Torbay Costume Hire.

FURTHER READING

GENERAL

Fiorato, V., Boylston, A., and Knusel, C. (eds.), *Blood Red Roses: The Archaeology of a Mass Grave from the Battle of Towton, AD 1461*, Oxbow Books, Oxford, 2001

Freeman, P.W.M., and Pollard, A. (eds.), *Fields of Conflict: Progress and Prospect in Battlefield Archaeology*, BAR International Series, 958, Archaeopress, Oxford, 2001

Harrison, I., *British Battles: Amazing Views from www.getmapping.com*, HarperCollins, London, 2002

Keegan, J., *The Face of Battle: A Study of Agincourt, Waterloo and the Somme*, Jonathan Cape, London, 1976

Kinross, J., *Discovering Battlefields of England and Scotland*, Shire, Princes Risborough, 1998

Newark, T., *War in Britain*, English Heritage/HarperCollins, London, 2000

Pollard, T., and Oliver, N., *Two Men in a Trench: Battlefield Archaeology – the Key to Unlocking the Past*, Michael Joseph, London, 2002

Seymour, W., *Battles in Britain, 1066–1746*, Wordsworth Editions, Ware, 1997

Smurthwaite, D., *The Complete Guide to the Battlefields of Britain*, Penguin, London, 1984

Young, P., and Adair, J., *Hastings to Culloden: Battles of Britain* (3rd edn), Sutton, Stroud, 1996

BANNOCKBURN

Miller, T., *The Site of the Battle of Bannockburn*, Historical Association Leaflet 85, 1931

Morris, J. E., *Bannockburn*, Cambridge, 1914

Nusbacher, A., *The Battle of Bannockburn*, Tempus, Stroud, 2000

Reese, P., *Bannockburn*, Canongate, Edinburgh, 2000

Scott, R. McN., *Robert the Bruce, King of the Scots*, Canongate, Edinburgh, 1982

Scott, W.W.C., *Bannockburn Revealed*, Elenkus, Rothesay, 2000

Traquair, P., *Freedom's Sword: Scotland's Wars of Independence*, HarperCollins, London, 1998

Watson, F., *Scotland, a History 8000 BC–AD 2000*, Tempus, Stroud, 2001

EDGEHILL

Kineton and District Local History Group, *Kineton: The Village and its History*, Kineton Local History Group, Kineton 1999

Peachey, S., *The Edgehill Campaign and the Letters of Nehemiah Wharton*, Partizan Press, Essex, 1989

Roberts, K., and Tincey, J., *Edgehill 1642: First Battle of the English Civil War*, Osprey Military Campaign Series, Oxford, 2001

Tenant, P., *Edgehill and Beyond: The People's War in the South, 1642–1645*, Sutton, Stroud, 1992

Young, P., *Edgehill 1642*, Windrush Press, Moreton-in-Marsh, 1995

Young, P., and Holmes, R., *The English Civil War*, Wordsworth Editions, Ware, 2000 (first published 1974)

SEDGEMOOR

Chandler, D.G., *Sedgemoor 1685: From Monmouth's Invasion to the Bloody Assizes*, Spellmount, Staplehurst, 1985

Earle, P., *Monmouth's Rebels*, Weidenfeld & Nicolson, London, 1977

Little, B.D.G., *The Monmouth Episode*, W. Laurie, London, 1956

Roots, I. (ed.), *The Monmouth Rising*, Devon Books, Exeter, 1986

Stradling, W., *A Description of the Priory of Chilton-Super-Polden and its Contents*, George Awbery, Bridgwater, 1839

Whiles, J., *Sedgemoor 1685*, Picton Publishing, Chippenham, 1975 (2nd edn 1985)

Wigfield, W.M., *The Monmouth Rebels 1685*, Somerset County Records Society, Somerset, 1985

KILLIECRANKIE

Barratt, J., 'Rorke's Drift in Tartan', *Military Illustrated*, no. 153, February 2001, pp. 33–39

Duke of Atholl, *Chronicles of the Atholl and Tullibardine Families*, Edinburgh, 1908

Elliot-Wright, P.J.C., 'Birth of the Thin Red Line – English Firing Tactics, 1660–1708', *Military Illustrated*, no. 80, January 1995, pp. 20–25

Fforde, C., *A Summer in Lochaber: The Jacobite Rising of 1689*, House of Lochar, Colonsay, 2002

Mackay, H., *Memoirs of the War carried on in Scotland and Ireland 1689 to 1691*, Bannatyne Club, Edinburgh, 1933

Macknight, J. (ed.), *Memoirs of Sir Ewen Cameron of Lochiel, by his grandson, Drummond of Balhaldie*, Maitland Club, Glasgow, 1842

Reid, S., *Highland Clansmen 1689–1746*, Osprey Warrior Series, Oxford, 1997

Reid, S., 'The Highland Charge: Bravehearts or Scarecrows?', *Military Illustrated*, no. 103, December 1996, pp. 16–20

Scott, A.M., *Bonnie Dundee*, John Donald, Edinburgh, 1989

Stevenson, D., 'Scotland's Leather Guns', *History Scotland*, November/December 2002

Terry C.S., *John Graham of Claverhouse*, Constable, London, 1905

HORNCHURCH

Hanning, P., *The Spitfire Log*, Souvenir Press, London, 1985

Lake, J., *Twentieth Century Military Sites*, English Heritage, London, 2000

Price, A., *Battle of Britain Day, 15th September 1940*, Greenhill Books, London, 1990

Smith, R.C., *Hornchurch Scramble*, Grub Street, London, 2000

Wood, D., and Dempster, D., *A Summer for Heroes*, Airlife, Shrewsbury, 1990

DOVER

Brown, I., Burridge, D., et al., *20th Century Defences in Britain: An Introductory Guide*, Council for British Archaeology, York, 1996 (reprinted 2000)

Ladd, J.D., *By Sea, By Land: The Royal Marines 1919–1997*, HarperCollins, London, 1998

Reed, J., 'Cross-Channel Guns', *After the Battle 29*, Battle of Britain Prints, Stratford, 1980

Saunders, A., *Hitler's Atlantic Wall*, Sutton, Stroud, 2001

Sources

Anon., 'Detailed Narrative of Actions in which the Royal Marine Siege Battery was Engaged – September 1st–September 20th, 1944'

Anon., 'The Guns of Wanstone Farm'

Collyer, D.G., 'When the Marines Manned the Guns'

Fellows, H.D., 'Secret War Despatch Nos. 1–5, 1941–43'

Perret, T., 'Sir Muirhead Bone, Permanent Artist . . . Temporary Royal Marine'

PICTURE CREDITS

BANNOCKBURN 1314

p.14: *Battle of Bannockburn* by Brian Palmer, Cranston
Fine Arts; p.16: *The Field of Bannockburn* by Samuel
Bough, Agnew & Sons, London/Bridgeman Art Library;
p.17: Edward I, © The British Library; p.18: John Balliol,
King of Scotland, © The British Library; p.21: *King Robert
I of Scotland*, engraved by E. Harding, Private
Collection/Bridgeman Art Library; p.22: *The Death of
John Comyn, the Younger* by Felix Philippoteaux, Private
Collection/Bridgeman Art Library; p.27: *Aylmer de
Valence, Earl of Pembroke*, engraved by W. Maddocks,
from *Ancient Armour* by Samuel Rush Meyrick, Private
Collection/Bridgeman Art Library; p.19: *Bruce and de
Bohun* by John McKirdy Duncan, Smith Art Gallery and
Museum, Stirling, Scotland/Bridgeman Art Library; p.30:
The Battle of Bannockburn in 1312 by the English School,
Private Collection/Bridgeman Art Library; p.33: *Battle of
Bannockburn 1314* from the Holkham Bible Picture Book,
The Art Archive/British Library/British Library; p.36*:
Statue of King Robert the Bruce* by the English School,

Private Collection/Bridgeman Art Library; p.44: *After the
Battle (R. Bruce)* by Sir William Allen, Cranston Fine Arts;
p.45: Declaration of Arbroath, by kind permission of the
Keeper of the Records of Scotland; p.46: *Treatise of Walter
de Milemete*, The Governing Body of Christ Church,
Oxford; p.64: *Dr Willard Libby with sandal*, © Hulton
Getty; p.65 *Dr Willard Libby in UCLA Lab*, © Hulton Getty.

EDGEHILL 1642

p.72: *Sir William Waller* by Cornelius Johnson (or
Jonson), by courtesy of the National Portrait Gallery,
London; p.74: *A Cavalry Engagement of the Civil War* by
John Frederick Herring the Younger, Fine Art
Photographic Library; p.71: *Charles I* by Sir Anthony van
Dyck, Burghley House, Stamford, Lincolnshire/Bridgeman
Art Library; p.78: Earl of Essex, Mansell/Timepix; p.79:
Charles I raises his standard at Nottingham, engraved by
J. T. Williams after original art by G. Cattermole, Mary
Evans Picture Library; p.83: *Oliver Cromwell* by Samuel
Copper, Private Collection/Bridgeman Art Library; p.84:

Prince Rupert, Count Palatine, attributed to Gerard Honthorst, by courtesy of the National Portrait Gallery; p.85: *Dragoons* from Johann Jacobi von Walhausen's *Kriegkunst zu Pferde*; p.89: *The Battle of Edgehill, 23rd October 1642* by Michael van der Gucht, Private Collection/Bridgeman Art Library; p.90: *Sir Thomas Fairfax* / HUTCM,79 by unknown artist, Cromwell Museum, Huntingdon; p.94: *Training instructions* from Johann Jacobi von Walhausen's *Kriegkunst zu Fuss* (Oppenheim, 1616); p.96: *The Country's Complaint* by the English School, Private Collection/Bridgeman Art Library; p.100: *Attack of Baggage Train at Edgehill* by Richard Beavis, The Art Archive/Private Collection; p.102: *Prince Rupert, his Last Charge at Edgehill* by Stanley Berkeley, Sotheby's/AKG images; p.104: *The Country's Complaint* by the English School, Private Collection/Bridgeman Art Library.

SEDGEMOOR 1685

p.130: *James, Duke of Monmouth and Buccleuch (1649-85) in Garter robes* by Sir Peter Lely, Philip Mould, Historical Portraits Ltd, London, UK/Bridgeman Art Library; p.131: *Sodalis (*also known as *Saudadoes/Soldada)* by Van De Velde, © National Maritime Museum, London; p.132: *James II* by Sir Godfrey Kneller, by courtesy of the National Portrait Gallery; p.134: *Reception of Monmouth by the Ladies of Taunton* by the English School, Private Collection/Bridgeman Art Library; p.136: *A Battle Scene* by Jan Wyck, Victoria Art Gallery, Bath and North East Somerset Council/Bridgeman Art Library; p.141: *John Churchill, 1st Duke of Marlborough* by John Closterman, by courtesy of the National Portrait Gallery; p.142: *The Defeat of the Rebels at the Battle of Sedgemoor. 6th July 1685* by the English School, Private Collection/Bridgeman Art Library; p.143: *The Morning of Sedgemoor* by Edgar Bundy, © Tate, London, 2003; p.146: *The Life Guards* from John Ogilby's *Coronation of Charles II*; p.148: *English Pikemen of 1689* from Robert Morden's *Discipline of War, 1689*, by courtesy of the Director, National Army Museum, London; p.150: *Duke of Monmouth pleading for his life before James II* by John Pettie, South African National Gallery, Cape Town, South Africa/Bridgeman Art Library; p.151: Playing cards depicting the aftermath of Monmouth's Rebellion by the English School, Private Collection/Bridgeman Art Library.

KILLIECRANKIE 1689

p.180: *John Claverhouse* by unknown artist, by courtesy of the Scottish National Portrait Gallery; p.181: *Dundee is killed* by Stanley Berkeley in *British Battles*, Mary Evans Picture Library; p.182: *Site of Dundee's death*, engraving by W. H. Bartlett, Mary Evans Picture Library; p.184: *William III* by unknown artist, by courtesy of the National Portrait Gallery; p.186: *View of Dunkeld* by John Slezer in *Theatrum Scotiae*, © Trustees of the National Library of Scotland; p.188: *Battle of the Boyne* by Jam Wyck, The Art Archive / National Army Museum London; p.189: *Sir Ewan Cameron of Lochiel* by unknown artist, by courtesy of the Scottish National Portrait Gallery; p.190: *Battle of Killiecrankie* by Alan Herriot, Cranston Fine Arts; p.195: *Battle of Drumclog* by courtesy of the Director, National Army Museum, London; p.197: *Charge of the Macdonalds* by Harrington Mann, University of Aberdeen; p.199: *Dundee leads a charge* by Noel Paton in *Lays of the Scottish cavaliers*, Mary Evans Picture Library; p.201, *Jacobite Rising* by unknown artist in *Cassell's History of England*, Mary Evans Picture Library; p.202: *Jacobites carry Dundee* by Noel Paton in *Lays of the Scottish Cavaliers*, Mary Evans Picture Library; p.206: *Dundee and his wife*, etching by Charles Kirkpatrick Sharpe (1869), Mary Evans Picture Library; p.213: *Lochiel's charge* by unknown artist, University of Aberdeen; p.215: *Shield*, University of Aberdeen.

HORNCHURCH 1940

p.244: *A successful Messerschmitt*, Associated Press; p.246: *RAF pilots stand on plane for photo*, Imperial War Museum/HU70350; p.248: *Churchill watches 'Stirling'*, Associated Press; p.249: *Messerschmitt 100 at end of combat*, Associated Press; p.251: *Flight takes off*, Imperial War Museum/CH5761; p.252: *View from German bomb-aimers*, © popperfoto.com; p.253: *RAF pilots at aerodrome in France*, TRH Pictures; p.255: *Plan drawing of German Do 217E2*, Imperial War Museum/CH10386; p.257: *Watch towers*, Imperial War Museum/CH5764; p.258: *Me 110 on bomb run over England*, Associated Press; p.258: *Junkers (7) begins recovery from attack*, TRH Pictures; p.259: *A. C. Deere with friend*, Imperial War Museum/CH.9455; p.261: *Spitfire destroyed*, Imperial War Museum/HU70347; p.23: *German plane destroyed*, Public Record Office; p.262: *Battle of Britain* by Paul Nash, Imperial War Museum/P26/7; p.264: *Spitfire with mechanic in cockpit*, Imperial War Museum/HU70346; p.266: *View from a German plane*, TRH Pictures; p.268: *Plan drawing of Me 109F*, Imperial War Museum/CH10388; p.269: *Adolf Galland*: TRH Pictures; p.270: *Two German pilots stand for a photo*, TRH Pictures; p.271: *Captain Bader climbs into cockpit*, © popperfoto.com; p.272: *A Nazi pilot*, © popperfoto.com; p.273: *A.C. Deere by Orde*, TRH Pictures; p.274: *German pilots get ready*, TRH Pictures; p.276: *Ground crew have photo taken*, Imperial War Museum/HU70351; p.278: *Pilots playing cards*, Imperial War Museum/CH5750; p.279: *Ground crew fixing plane*, Imperial War Museum/16; p.280: *Spitfire is re-armed*, Imperial War Museum/CH1458; p.281: *WAAF making repairs to plane*, Associated Press; p.282: *WAAF Air Transport Auxiliary*, TRH Pictures; p.283: *New deliveries for Luftwaffe*, TRH Pictures; p.284: *Crashed plane*, Public Record Office; p.285: *Bystanders look at crashed plane*, Public Record Office; p.294: *Tett turret plan*, Public Record Office; p.295: *Tett turret drawing*, Public Record Office; p.297: *Workmen positioning Tett turret*, Public Record Office; p.308: *The ghost train*, Imperial War Museum/CH5747.

DOVER 1940–44

p.312: *Test-firing somewhere on the South Coast*, © popperfoto.com; p.314: *Nazi gun emplacement*, Associated Press; p.316: *Gun firing*, Dover Museum; p.319: *Railroad gun is channel menace*, Associated Press; p.320: *Churchill with First Sea Lord*, TRH Pictures; p.322: *AA guns firing at night*, © popperfoto.com; p.323: *Churchill visits north-east England*, TRH Pictures; p.324: *Loading in progress*, Dover Museum; p.324: *Heavy camouflage conceals AA guns*, Dover Museum; p.324: *Brig.-General Sir Frederick A. Pile*, © popperfoto.com; p.327: *German big guns fire on convoy*, TRH Pictures; p.328: *Radar towers at Dover being shelled*, Associated Press; p.330: *Nazi raid over Dover*, Associated Press; p.332: *Canadian Infantry captures 14"* guns: TRH Pictures; p.339: *Demonstration in use of petrol bombs*, © popperfoto.com; p.354: *Guns look out from coast*, TRH Pictures; p.354: *War fortifications*, TRH Pictures; p.357: *Huge gun mount*, Dover Museum; p.357: *A gun mount for Jane*, Dover Museum; p.358: *Jane being mounted into place*, Dover Museum; p.358: *Jane is ready for action*, Dover Museum.

Every effort has been made to contact the copyright holders. We apologize for any unintentional omission and would be please to insert the appropriate acknowledgements in any subsequent edition.